D1103817

# ANXIETY
## IS NOT
# DEPRESSION

Cliff Wise

authorHOUSE®

*AuthorHouse™*
*1663 Liberty Drive*
*Bloomington, IN 47403*
*www.authorhouse.com*
*Phone: 1 (800) 839-8640*

*Cover design by performingpixel.com*

*The drawing on the cover is a self-portrait by the author while in tenth grade in 1962. Color enhancement by John Cavaleri.*

*Published by AuthorHouse 04/06/2017*

*ISBN: 978-1-5246-8655-0 (sc)*
*ISBN: 978-1-5246-8656-7 (hc)*
*ISBN: 978-1-5246-8654-3 (e)*

*Library of Congress Control Number: 2017905196*

*Print information available on the last page.*

To my wife, Marilyn, for her understanding and
encouragement in all aspects of life
She is everything I would like to be.

# Contents

# Acknowledgments

I would like to thank my brother Bob for his help in editing. I have learned a lot from him in the past and marvel at his sense of humor and understanding of people. He is a very interesting guy.

Thanks also to James Carville. Two of his books, *We're Right and They're Wrong* and *Stickin': The Case for Loyalty*, are intimate insights to his world and the forces that make up who he is. They are also informative and funny. His straightforward and honest writing style gave me a mental framework of how to approach this very personal and terrifying subject.

My cat Fernando sits every day between my legs as I type, sleeps, and looks up for the occasional scratch. Fernando has since passed over to cat heaven.

# Disclaimer

The methods and tools described in this book have been acquired over my lifetime in different and sometimes unusual ways. I have tried them all, and they work to varying degrees. I have also experimented with other methods that are not included because they did not provide the positive results I needed or any outcomes at all. I was often not aware that I was experimenting with skills that would help me fight anxiety, as I was not cognizant that anxiety was a problem I had until I was in my forties and spending a lot of time and money with psychologists, referred to as "shrinks" in this book.

Methods acquired in these instances were part of a general learning experience. I am not a doctor, and I have no medical training. I am not a psychologist or psychiatrist, but I have briefly studied psychology in college and considered majoring in the subject. The purpose of this book is to describe to myself and other interested parties what I have learned. I do not recommend to anyone that he or she try any of these methods to fight anxiety or for any other reason without professional supervision. These methods have worked for me to varying degrees and should have value for others, but I feel that consultation with properly trained personnel and supervision is essential before trying any of these methods, even if they seem simple and innocuous on the surface.

It has taken me sixty-two years to gather the information found in this book, and most of the methods I use have been acquired and incorporated into my being over long periods of time. Experimenting with them after only reading this book could be disastrous. I have also used many methods in combination, which may have different results for other people than the results I experienced. Everyone is different and will have varying experiences using these methods. I am writing this book to help people gain insight into a problem, not to harm them. Please consult with a professional.

# Introduction

This is a story of a journey, in part an account of my efforts to fight anxiety. I have included my life experiences for several reasons as they should provide relevant background to the development of my disorder, but more importantly I am hoping that someone out there will realize that part of his or her problem is similar to my own. Discovering similarities in others may be the why we are attracted to others. Hopefully by seeing yourself in me, you will learn about why you do or do not do certain things. The first part of resolving a problem is to realize that it exists.

I will make an attempt to follow a chronological path in describing various methods I have learned or developed to combat anxiety. This will be complicated because many of the methods are not independent but are intertwined in much the same way that thoughts are. I am not an expert in learning processes other than my own. I am not an educator, a psychologist, or psychiatrist. I make reference to methods other than the one I am describing if I feel they are interrelated. If I have an aha moment later in life, I may swing forward in time to describe it, if it relates to what I am describing. I try to keep this movement around in my life to a minimum for the sake of space and time. I also write in a general flow. I am trying to avoid a "how to do it" type of dialogue or bulleted list of methods. Some of my content may be straight babble, but hey, it's my book.

I have a perception of the way I developed my methods. I can't judge how close this perception is to reality. Some were developed when I was very young and may sound silly to an adult. They actually were a part of my life and, more often than not, were reactions to situations rather than any kind of positive thought process on my part. If my behavior resulted in a method that I could use to combat anxiety, then I include it as a method.

At an early age, I was forced to learn how to solve my own problems. The main benefit of this is that I developed an open mind. I have developed the ability to incorporate a good idea into my way of doing things without a lot of habit building and anguish. If I find a good idea, I try it out immediately and often adopt it as soon as possible as part of my way of doing things.

Most of the methods will have information about the origin, as I understand it, and where or from whom I learned the method or got the idea. I may add anecdotes that I think are important or interesting. This is not a scholarly work. The scientific method is completely thrown out the window on this one. I have included descriptions of some of the physical and mental processes I have experienced. Some of these will be ideas from my standpoint based on what I have learned and tried. My assumptions may be incorrect from a medical standpoint. I include a list of methods and where they can be found in the appendix.

I have tried to give credit where it is due. I have included real individuals in my examples and have tried to respect their privacy by changing their names. Published authors and personal heroes keep their real names. Some will be offended; others will be relieved. If someone gets bent out of shape about my use of a method that he or she developed or were in one of his or her books or if I misrepresent his or her idea, please don't sue me or accuse me of plagiarism. Just let me know, and I will correct it and give you credit. The purpose of this book is to describe and define my own journey. I have tried so many things and read so many books and articles that I can't possibly remember the sources. Out of this mélange came the methods I use to solve my own problems.

I will be writing most of this out of my head. I don't want it to become a research project. I think that would bog down the spontaneity of the book. The Germans have a word that covers this type of thought, *weltanschauing*. The closest words in English are "worldview," but they don't mean the same thing. The German mind actually looks out at the world from a spot inside their consciousness. This book is my *weltanschauing* on anxiety. Robert Reisch, former secretary of labor, wrote a book, *Locked in the Cabinet*, in which he made a similar claim of writing from his point of view and recollection, and he was severely criticized for lack of accuracy. It was still a great book and well worth reading. I got the idea from him, and if I am criticized, I will be in good company.

For the last twelve years, I have been taking medication for my anxiety. I have tried several types of drugs and settled on one that works for me. The medication has enabled me to view my disorder from an entirely different and fresh perspective, from the outside. I believe it enabled me to write this book. Anxiety did not allow me to finish very many projects in the past.

I do not think it is appropriate or useful for me or for you at this point to disclose which drug I am taking. I would have to consult with professionals to make sure that there would be benefits to the public before disclosing the name, so don't ask. If this book becomes popular, I will do that, and then look for me on TV, hawking some drug or other. I will ask for a lot of money to do this, but I will be sincere.

I sincerely believe, if I had access to some or all of the methods described in this book at an earlier age or at least the ability to realize that anxiety was the cause of a lot of my problems, then I would not need to be taking medication now. I hope to be free of them at some time in the future, and I am working toward that goal. I feel that patterns of behavior and their accompanying chemical reactions in the body are constantly changing. This is a reaction to the progression of age and to what we are doing in our lives. If I had been able to make changes earlier in life by using methods I learned later on, I feel I could have lowered my anxiety to a normal level.

Most people who know me think I am a very mellow dude, like really laid back. They think that nothing bothers me. If they read this book and then found out that I wrote it, they will freak out. I don't know where this comes from. I think that maybe it is a façade that I learned to keep my parents on an even keel. If I had problems, they immediately went into overdrive, which just exacerbated the whole problem. I learned to project the idea that I had no problems. I would wait until later to vent my frustration on some inanimate object. I carried this over into my intimate relationships. I once had an argument with my wife, stormed out of the house, and grabbed my chainsaw. And by nightfall, I had cut down and stacked thirteen locust trees that I hated. People who are intimate with me have no delusions about how mellow I am. They know there is a deep well of turmoil.

They say that everyone has one book in him or her. I wish mine were about something else like travel or sailing. Anxiety has been a major bore in my life and kept me from a lot of peace of mind and enjoyment. I have had a good life but one that anxiety controlled. I surely would have had a different life without the anxiety. I am philosophical about this to the extent that I believe I will reach the same point in the end and learn that the anxiety merely dictated the path. I will expand on this later. I hope that information about my ordeal will benefit those with the same problems.

When I was writing this and told various individuals I was writing a book on anxiety, some would say, "I would like to see that. I have a [cousin, friend, uncle, whatever] who is depressed, and that might be useful to them."

Some people glom anxiety, depression, and even stress into one thing in their mind. My opinion is that they are three separate things. They all can have an effect on the others, like throwing a bit of gasoline on a fire, but in my personality, they are separate and distinct.

# Panic Attacks—A Good Place to Start

I had my first panic attack when I was about six. I had been visiting my grandparents in North Attleboro, Massachusetts, with my parents. It was time to go home. I didn't want to leave because I was having a good time. North Attleboro was a fun place to be and different from the routines of home in Larchmont, New York. I think I made a problem for my parents about leaving. This prompted an acrimonious debate and eventual high-volume argument about leaving. Our family was dysfunctional, and arguments were not rare. I felt sorry that I could not express my opinion without causing so much trouble. I remember having that thought a lot back then.

I went outside to get away. There was a large, concrete pad behind the house where I used to play, and on the pad was a large push broom with very stiff bristles. I liked the *ssssst* sound the broom made against the concrete and how the bristles flicked the dirt and pebbles out in front. I even liked the cloud of dust that would form around the broom. It was made of little dust bubbles, beings whose lives were momentary. You could smell the dirt.

I could hear the arguing in the background. I was perfectly set up to bust my panic attack cherry. The broom suddenly slowed down. *Sssssssssssssssssssst. Sssssssssssssssssssst.* I lost control of it. My hands were still on the handle, but I could not stop it. It went back and forth as if under its own power. There were hands pushing on both of my temples, squeezing my head, trying to crush it, but I could not turn to see who it was. My breath was suspended, like I had the wind punched out of me, and there was a hollow vacuum in the pit of my stomach. A darkness began to take over, not unlike a solar eclipse. I could only see what was directly in front of me. Everything sounded so far away. I felt cold. Still the broom went *sssssssssssssssssssst, sssssssssssssssssssst*. I was trapped.

After a seeming eternity, the light returned, and I could breathe again. I turned to face my attacker and found that I was alone. This is when the real terror set in. I dropped the broom and ran inside toward the warm familiarity of the argument I had sought to escape. I did not have the concept of dying at that age, but it was my first experience of not being me. It was the first bump on a long and winding road.

The second major panic attack came at about age forty-two. I had just returned from a business trip to Spain. Things were not going well with the company I worked for, and I was not getting any support from others in the office. I had just written a memo to the owner of the company, recapping the situation and asking to be reimbursed for my expenses. I had reverted to writing memos to ask for anything personal because I was incapable of asking for something for myself. I could ask for anything for someone else, but not for myself.

After delivering the memo, I went upstairs to my office and had trouble breathing. I thought I was dying. My vision tunneled and darkened. My temples pressed in against my brain. I lunged at the phone to call my fiancée to say good-bye. She was at lunch, but her secretary promised to tell her that I loved her. I didn't have much time. I called my shrink.

She said, "Welcome to the other 80 percent of the population. You're having a panic attack."

There was a lot of time spent between these two attacks trying to avoid having another one, even to the extent of trying to duplicate the attack with the broom. At that time, I wanted to learn as much about them as possible to make sure I could control them. There was also something fascinating about experiencing something other than day-to-day reality. It's the dark side, I suppose. I was playing with fire.

I know now that a lot of people have these kinds of attacks on a regular basis. My mother did. She used to have to pull the car over to the side of the road to have them. I didn't know about this until recently. She took tranquilizers when I was in my teens, so I will refrain from getting into the environment versus genetics argument. I don't have a feeling about the connection between my disorder and hers. It is probably a bit of both.

Some would say, since I did not have major panic attacks on a regular basis, my anxiety problem is somehow diminished, somehow less than theirs is. I disagree. I feel the severity of the disorder should be determined by how dominant the disorder is in the individual's life. In my case, it was totally dominant. There is no doubt there are people who have severe anxiety attacks who, because of their physical and mental makeups, are able to lead normal lives. I was able to prevent major attacks by employing defense methods.

One of these was the classic "going home and rolling up in a ball in the corner." I actually used to get in a fetal position on my bed and shut down. I did not sleep or spend a lot of time thinking about anything. I tried to get everything slowed down and under control.

The stage was set. I had some sort of genetic makeup that was starting to intrude on reality. I had experienced a full-blown anxiety attack. I needed relief from my environment. I was being pulled in a lot of directions. Without realizing it was happening, I developed my first coping method.

# METHOD—Gazing

I got the definition of gazing from one of Carlos Casteneda's books, but I was doing it on a regular basis as a child. I was surprised that anyone else on the planet was doing it when I read that book. I still do it from time to time but now more for fun than anything. It can also produce eye strain and a headache.

In this technique, you allow your eyes to drift or relax out of focus. You will be looking at something, but your focus will not be on the object. As a result, that object seems to split in two, and the images overlap. On the computer keyboard, the G and H would be superimposed on each other, as would all other adjoining keys. But the G would also appear to be in its original place. The F and G keys would seem to be adjacent or superimposed, depending on where you looked. This has some effect on depth of field, and the area around the F and G seems to lose its attachment to the real world.

This is particularly effective when gazing at something natural that does not have sharply defined edges, like rocks. I would use gazing when looking into the water. I could squat for a long time when I was a child. I spent my summers on Cape Cod and had an unusual freedom from adults for long stretches of time. They were watching but from a distance. We lived near a protected bay, and the water was usually calm and warm. I would squat at the water's edge and gaze into the miasma of life, the hermit crabs, and minnows at my feet. I would sometimes do this for hours, only becoming aware of the passage of time when the tide would rise around me and rock me off my feet. I did this to get away. I don't remember having any thoughts. I just watched. I guess I was meditating. I feel sorry for children who are boxed in by their parents, especially at the beach. Every time the child makes a move for the water, he or she is corralled back onto the beach. I never had to learn to swim. I just enter the water and become a part of it.

There is an adult version of gazing. I discovered it during my frequent jaunts into the woods and parks near where I lived. When you are walking in the woods, you are the only thing that is moving except things the wind is moving. If you stop to rest or spend some extra time in a particularly beautiful place and keep quiet, then soon you are the thing that is stopped, and everything else begins to move. There is an incredible amount of life in most places. When a relatively large animal like you comes blasting onto the scene, all the other forms of life pause to see what you are. If you stop moving and talking, these other beings, most of which have a short attention span, begin to go about their usual business. You have become part of the scenery. I find the transformation to have a calming effect. If another hiker or, even worse, a mountain biker comes clattering into view, you can see this process repeat itself.

I drive a lot. If I am on a parkway or freeway and there is little traffic, I can relax my eyes for a second, and it seems like I am stationary and the scenery is moving past me like a movie. This continues after I refocus my eyes. What is probably happening is that the act of relaxing your focus gives a temporary alternate perspective to the reality around you. It relaxes me. I don't recommend trying this while driving though.

# METHOD—Following Ants

As a child, another great escape was ants. They fascinated me. I have probably been bitten and stung by more kinds of ants than anyone in Larchmont, New York. This method involves following an ant until it returns to its nest and then finding another one to follow. Your world somehow transforms into theirs. You can feed them and set up great lines of ants. You watch wars and kidnappings, herding of aphids, great building projects, murder, hunting and gathering, and courting. Sex takes place underground, I presume.

When I was forty and still enjoying this relaxing pastime, I watched an entire war in the lobby of the Eko Holiday Inn in Lagos, Nigeria, a conflict that no one else saw. The war took place below a lamp in the lobby. The cement table that the lamp was on was cracked, and ants had built hives inside. One type of ants was in its flying cycle, something they do to form new colonies. All ants fly at one stage of their lives. These flying ants have been fattened up by special keepers and guided up through the tunnels for their only flight, to find a mate and start a new colony. They looked soft and pampered. Another, smaller, and more aggressive type of ant was attacking and capturing the flying ants before they could take off and dragging them into their nest, no doubt to some horrible death or enslavement. They were darker and had large jaws for piercing and snipping. Ferocious, they would swarm over their larger prey, eventually gaining an advantage of numbers over size. I thought of early man hunting the powerful mastodon.

Shifting your focus to a smaller—yet no less dynamic world than the macro one we live in—is a way of getting out of your environment. I would guess that this is what avid bird-watchers, fishermen, and hunters do, but ants are cheaper, and you don't have to go very far to find them.

As an aside, I learned in Africa that ants and termites usually fly shortly after a rainstorm. This is when the ground is soft, and they can more easily burrow into the ground to form a new nest. I forgot this once back in the United States and, shortly after a rainstorm, drove over to the national seashore nearby at Sandy Hook at the southern point of New York harbor.

The ants were everywhere. We had to leave. I felt sorry for the parents who had driven all the way down from New York to give their kids a day on the beach, only to be pestered and driven off by millions of flying ants.

When I see ants in the yard flying up from the ground, I get them to climb on my finger, and I propel them into the air. I call this ant launching. The neighbors probably think I am some sort of nut, except for the ones who know me and know I am a nut. When you are lonely as a kid, you have to entertain yourself. This was in the pre-computer days.

I was enrolled in preschool. I don't know if it was kindergarten because I didn't last very long at the Catholic school where I was first enrolled. I was there long enough to completely reject the socialization process and have some interesting experiences, however. My brother and I have differing views of hell on earth. His is working in a steel mill. Mine is being in a confined space with several ruler-toting nuns. That they have an attitude, and a mission is a given. The mission is to get you ready for marine boot camp at Parris Island.

At the usual age, I wound up going to a real public school kindergarten. I wasn't very social. I guess I had spent too much time by myself. My brother is four years older than I am and went to Catholic school. Four years was a great gap at that age. In that first school, we had to enter from the back of the school to our little classroom, and I could never get the door open. I was late a few times because of that door. I felt trapped outside, which is different from being trapped inside.

This is the first time that I noticed the shallow breathing reaction that comes with anxiety problems. Shortly after the shallow breathing would come the adrenaline and the extra strength that would get the door to open. I was usually out of breath by the time I got into the class.

We did dumb things in that school. I didn't understand that we were being socialized. Everything seemed like an imposition. The nuns in their black and white habits were trying to turn me into a robot. We had cookies and milk, and then it was naptime. I could never nap. I don't think that I ever napped until after I wound up in the army, and then napping became a product of complete and utter boredom. My Irish grandmother told me that nuns sold their hair to give money to the church.

During one nap, I decided to find out. I slid over the floor on my back to where the nun was sleeping in a rigid wooden chair and ever so carefully lifted her habit that was hanging over the back of the chair. I found short hair!

The next thing I knew, she was straddled over my prone body. A small fist appeared beside her ear, which grew at an alarming rate until it punched my lights out. The other time I got punched out was just after we were warned not to touch the nativity scene. The nun left the room, and naturally I picked up the infant Jesus to take a look. One girl in the class was a bully. She was larger than most of the boys and very strong. I guess I was a challenge to her dominance. She approached me in a scolding aggressive posture, slapped my hand, and repeated what the nun had said.

The infant Jesus tumbled through the air in slow motion with my grasping hand hopelessly trying to break the warp barrier, catch it, and retrieve my future. The infant exploded in a perfect star upon impact with the linoleum. This time the nun worked on the soft tissue of my midsection, I guess so she would not leave any marks. The first time you have your breath knocked out, you really think you are going to die.

Public school was a relief after Catholic day school. I had a few friends in grammar school, crushes on cute girls, and great male teachers, and all in all, I thought it was a pleasant time. I fell in love with my first-grade teacher. She had just graduated from college and was a radiant blonde with the most pleasant features and demeanor. Something was special there. If every class had been like hers, school would have been heaven. In subsequent grades, I spent a lot of time in the principal's office, detained for disrupting class or some other boredom-related offense. Our principal was the very description of stern. She is the first woman I ever saw in a formal suit. She was tall, and the suit hung from her square shoulders, straight down to her hem without a wrinkle. She never said anything but had this stare that could melt steel at fifty yards.

We took batteries of tests, and the results showed I was going to be the valedictorian of my senior high class. So I was given differential treatment. The principal and several of the teachers wanted to skip me two grades, but my parents wanted me to have a normal upbringing with my own age group. Little did any of us know that I would not even graduate from high school with my class. I wasn't last, but I was not even there for graduation.

There was no challenge for me in grammar school so I was bored most of the time and didn't acquire any good learning habits, at least not for the stuff you needed to get good grades. I always got straight As with the usual comment of "daydreams" or "does not pay attention." Boredom creates conflict, which fueled the development of my anxiety.

My parents spent a lot of time traveling on business and left us home with my grandmother, leading to more conflict. I was the tallest kid until sixth grade, maybe even including the faculty, which an embarrassment. I adopted the habit of walking bent over to avoid the stares from the other kids. The only time I was completely free from anxiety was when we were doing arts and crafts. It was also the only thing that I enjoyed both in school and at home.

# METHOD—Drawing

For me, drawing was an escape. Drawing is, by nature, a solitary endeavor. It is usually quiet, and people respect the fact that you need to concentrate to get it done. The annoying doting parent will suddenly stop bothering the kid when he or she picks up a crayon. I got good at drawing because I wanted to be left alone. I don't think that many people are born artists. If you do anything for ten thousand hours, you are going to be good at it. Anyone can learn to draw. You can take courses and learn the technique, or you can buy materials and just do it. Art is the most subjective thing going, so you can draw socially acceptable or unacceptable things. Some will like and hate both. The important thing is that people leave you alone when you are doing it. You move into what my brother calls "the zone." They can all see that you are in there. The zone is where time stops and the anxiety can't penetrate.

My wife has noted that I have developed an ability to get in the zone in ways other than drawing. An example would be drumming, and I can do it equally as well in public as at home. She claims she can see a change on someone's face when he or she goes into the zone. Children seem to have a closer connection to the part of art where you are applying paint or crayons to paper than adults do. I feel that this is because the process of becoming an adult is about the process of learning a lot of definitions and concepts that kids can't grasp. This is why so-called "refrigerator art" is so brilliant. It is unencumbered by all of this adult noise about what should be what. I knew a grammar school teacher who had framed her student's art (with permission from the students and parents) and decorated her apartment with it. It was the greatest private art collection I have ever seen.

When you start to draw, just let it go. If you try to duplicate the outside world without a lot of training, you will be disappointed. One technique I found helpful in dealing with the duplication of reality thing was drawing without looking at what you are drawing. We started with bicycles. You would look at the actual bicycle but not the paper. The results were just astounding. The bicycles had more character than we could ever have drawn by trying to duplicate them.

Drawing, as with most methods, is about the method and not the materials. I find that, if I go out and buy several materials before starting anything (with the exception of woodworking), I am building certain anxiety level into the method. My expectations are elevated, and for me, anxiety and expectations are siblings from hell. Get a pencil and a piece of typing paper, and get on with it. If you don't like the results, see if you can make two points with a turnaround jump shot into the wastebasket. Pencil drawing is legitimate. It will last hundreds of years.

# METHOD—Learn What
# Frustration Tolerance Means

I am not trying to blame anyone for how I did or did not learn things, the missed opportunities, or any of that important stuff. But I must say the way you first do things is usually the way that someone else has demonstrated how to do them. This doesn't necessarily have to be in a learning situation but can be the simple "monkey see; monkey do." The people I observed doing things I wanted to do had very high frustration tolerances. They would continue pushing forward until the task was finished, no matter what. I learned this term from Dr. Norman, one of my shrinks and a former professor at Harvard. People with a high frustration tolerance can put up with a lot and do not quit easily. Those with a low frustration tolerance fly off the handle easily when faced with adversity. You know who you are.

Most of the people in my family have what is commonly referred to as "short fuses," which is nothing more or less than a low frustration tolerance. The bad part about being short fuse-oriented is that it is easy to learn and becomes a habit. This is not a parent-bashing book, but that is where I got my training. It is a common occurrence in our family to have regular outbursts of frustration, intolerance, or anger. It can happen with one person or more than one, a chain reaction. It usually consists of yelling at the top of one's lungs and is sometimes accompanied by the destruction of the inanimate object that caused the frustration. The more expensive the item, the less likely it will be destroyed. All of the Danish porcelain somehow survived years of outbursts, which led me to believe that some value system is lurking below the surface.

The yelling got to me. I would react by pulling the covers up over my head. Even if I weren't in bed, I would do it mentally. I had this set of internal covers that I could pull up at any time. I still have this reaction whenever I hear anyone yelling. Physically speaking, I get this blinding injection of adrenaline and accompanying anxiety.

This happened so often that the reaction began moving over into other parts of my life, outside of my parents and grandparents. Others in a similar situation would get these small injections of adrenaline, but mine always seemed to be a flood. I had no control over it. I became addicted to it. There was a time in my life when I was growing independent of my family but before I was living with any woman when my daily routine was a series of blasts of adrenaline interspersed with periods of coasting, like a car with a big engine but only a first gear.

For example, I would get up in the morning, take a shower, and start getting dressed. All of this was in slow motion. The clock was going at its usual pace, but I wasn't. And it would get to the point where I would be late. I would then explode at something stupid, like trying to get my tie at the right length. The adrenaline would hit the system, and I would shift into high gear. I would be dressed and ready in a flash. I actually felt better when this happened. When I tried to explain this to the people I wound up living with, especially women, they just didn't understand what I was talking about. I described it as "getting myself going." I didn't see anything wrong with it and found it hard to believe that it would upset others.

As I began to realize that this behavior was causing others harm, I knew I had to change. First, I had to admit that this was an uncompromisingly stupid and antisocial habit. I then talked to therapists and tried relaxation techniques. I encouraged criticism from those close to me. I never completely cleared this from my behavior patterns until I started my medication. I consider this to be a real addiction. Giving up smoking is a piece of cake in comparison.

My first insight into frustration tolerance came at about age twelve, a big year. I gained a lot of insight in my twelfth year. I intended to build something and tried to saw through a piece of wood with a handsaw. I tightened the wood into a rusty old vise in the garage. The saw was dull and flip-flopped if you didn't saw in a perfect straight line. My arm quickly tired, and I gave up. Soon thereafter I was in a furniture repair shop, and I saw a kid about my age saw through a similar piece of wood. He just kept sawing until it was done. I was astounded. I went right home, put the wood in the vise, and sawed right through it. What a feeling of accomplishment!

My frustration tolerance got so low at one point that I would explode when my shoes came untied. Hey, let's make that a method.

# METHOD—Think about a Basic Change You Can Make to Eliminate an Anxiety

As a case in point, I never learned how to tie my shoes properly. I guess that this is because my mother never learned how to either. The way I tie them causes them to become untied easily, usually when I was tromping down a crowded sidewalk on 42$^{nd}$ Street in New York City in a snowstorm with shopping bags and a briefcase that was always poised to fall off my shoulder. This used to drive me absolutely bughouse. I try not to wear shoes whenever possible, but I have to wear them most of the time. As a child, I always wore tie shoes because that was bought for me. I remember these hideously klutzy shoes that I had to wear to make my feet grow properly. I think they were called "Stride-Right." They really worked well, but it was like wearing a pair of Western saddles on your feet. When I began buying my own shoes, I tried penny loafers because that was in style. What a revelation! Shoes you could actually put on and forget about for a whole day!

Without even a conscious effort, I began switching all of my shoes to loafers, boat shoes, sandals, and clogs. Boat shoes have ties, but they are leather and come untied only about every six months. When I was in the business world, I wore tassel loafers from Brooks Brothers. These are acceptable anywhere. I do wear sneakers to play tennis and work out because I'm too cheap to buy the fancy sneakers with the Velcro closures.

I have these great wooden clogs that I bought in Holland for about ten bucks. They have leather tops but huge wood bottoms that go all around your heel. You can walk in four inches of mud and not even get wet. The Dutch call them *klompers* because that is what they sound like. Klomp, klomp, klomp. The Dutch don't invent new words for everything like we do. I never would have bought anything like *klompers* if all of my shoes were tie shoes, and I would still be spending at least twenty minutes a day tying my shoes.

It is amazing all of the cool stuff you can find if you just change one small thing like eliminating most shoelaces from your personal world. I did it, and what's more amazing is how doing so gives you a feeling of power, freedom, and control over your life.

Now we are getting into my life in junior high school. I never studied in grammar school or junior high. I used to read the encyclopedia rather than textbooks. World Book could have used me for advertising, had they known. Textbooks were boring and only about the same dumb subject. This was back when a computer the size of a notebook today took up five floors of an office building and had a three-shift staff of eight changing burnt-out tubes to keep it running. You might guess that I had attention deficit disorder, but you would have to factor in the fact that I could also follow an ant across the yard for two hours. I began to get into trouble with grades in junior high when studying was required to keep up with what was going on.

Some wise guy educator decided that you could keep everyone on the same page by creating problems that everyone had to figure out. If you didn't figure out the problems or do the problems and find out what the answer was, then you were the class dunce. I just thought that the system was transparent and shallow. My problem was that I had no interest and, as a result, no studying skills. I guess that's the reason why the teachers wanted me to skip grades in grammar school, so I would be challenged. I started failing everything. I went from straight As without studying to straight Fs without studying. It was more than a challenge. It wasn't the kind of thing where you sit in a room with a book and later come out with some knowledge. You had to have a method of remembering what they wanted you to remember, studying skills. I had been reading interesting stuff in the encyclopedia and remembered it because I liked it. Here I was faced with learning stuff that was boring because the educators realized it would be important to students later in life. Encyclopedia stuff was never on the tests.

# METHOD—Evaluate Threats as Though They Were Offers

My grades got so bad that, in ninth grade, they even threatened to put me in "119," the classroom where they put all of what they call today "special Ed" kids. They put them in there and kept them in there. There was none of this moving from class to class like the other students. I thought this threat was so unfair, thoughtless, and egregious that I accepted it. I thought, *Great! Now I won't have any assignments, and I can continue doing what I want, reading the encyclopedia and National Geographic.*

I was going to marry a Nubian princess and live in the desert south of Egypt anyhow. My acceptance of 119 was not received well. Parents, deans, teachers, and I were all hauled in. Everyone tried to figure out what my problem was. There were some tense moments because I was not cooperating in the process. I really had no idea what was going on except that I felt screwed up. Screwed up was a term used in the 1950s and 1960s to describe general inabilities to behave like everyone expected you to. Now they have terms like Attention Deficit Disorder (ADD), and Attention Deficit Hyperactive Disorder (ADHD). Everyone had been so busy telling me how intelligent I was and expecting so much that all was not keeping an eye on me. I was on unsupervised autopilot. Not good unless you are being raised by wolves. The system caught up to me, and I was totally unprepared. I could not fit into their definition of right and wrong. The system was set up to deal with success, not failure. I was already lost.

I soon became rebellious, which was easy because, as a child, I was already independent from being left alone. My parents traveled to Europe on business for long stretches, and I summered on Cape Cod where there were two simple rules, breakfast at eight thirty and dinner at five thirty. I lived with my paternal grandmother, who was a peach and a good friend. There were no shoes. I wore a bathing suit. I carried around a towel and a hoe, which I used to fight the tide with every day. And I had the two rules.

I started spending full summers on Cape Cod from about age ten on. This lack of supervision, which I dearly loved, added to my sense of independence. Eventually the rebelliousness got me into more trouble, and I was again a regular in the school office. If I knew I were going to get kicked out of class for not having completed an assignment, I would just go straight to the office. Preempting the teacher kicking me out of class by going straight to the office almost caused me to get suspended. I had preempted their punishment process.

Nothing seemed to be going right. I was getting into the period in life where all things become interconnected. Everything had a cause and effect. Somehow, I got to senior high school even though I was having major anxiety problems throughout this time. I also managed to avoid spending any time in 119, proof it was a hollow threat. They probably realized I would recruit and train the Special Ed kids into an elite unit and break out of there.

There was a lot of time spent curled up in that ball and many sleepless nights. My developing body chemistry was changing about the same time that it was becoming fixed. The fixed part was the dependence on great rushes of adrenaline and other chemicals I was becoming addicted to, even though they were terrifying. Most boys my age were going through puberty. I had the same hormones trying to break through, but the fear and fright chemicals were almost acting as blockers. I don't feel that I ever truly completed the puberty thing. Something is missing. I thought the failure of my body to fully make the transition was a punishment. I was getting locked into some strange ebbs and tides in my body. I knew something was out of whack, but I could not figure it out. At the time, I probably thought that everyone was going through the same thing, that it was actually normal.

# METHOD—Learn to Manage Success Rather Than Failure

Let me interject something here. I learned this about myself in a neuro-linguistic programming (NLP) seminar when I was fifty-seven years old. This is something to keep in mind as the story unfolds. I was having trouble with authority. You can deal with authority in three ways, three paths, if you like. You can accede to it and do what they want, in which case they will take credit for any success you have. You can go against it or make it work against itself, in which case they will reject responsibility for any failure you have. Or you can agree to what the authority demands and do what you want, in other words, live a lie.

My way turned out to be the second way. My parents were ignoring me for the most part because they weren't around. The only way I could get any attention was by getting low grades in school and getting in minor or borderline real trouble. I got a lot of attention this way. At the same time, I was withholding the part where they all could take credit for my success. I was flunking out. This was my only power. The long-term result was that I went to a second-rate college and had to work like hell to catch up with my peers later on in life.

In the long run, I can't decide if it would have been better if I were a perfect student, went to a great college, and worked on Wall Street. There is no way to know that. As the Greeks say, you judge a man at his end. The facts are, if you take the first path, you are learning how to manage success. If you take the second path, you are learning how to manage failure. The third path is negative as well. Following the second or third paths results in screwing yourself in the long run. It's your choice entirely. It is hard to turn any path around later on in life. I'm still working on it.

Now let's return to 1959, a long, long time ago. I mentioned that I was not very social. This now progressed to asocial. This is different from antisocial. Girls had entered into the equation, and every encounter became an adrenaline-soaked close encounter with an anxiety attack. I enjoyed being around females and had some close relationships, but I was too shy for dates. I still don't understand three social things, at least from my perspective. These are dating, dancing, and marriage. I would guess that my self-esteem was already heading down that slippery slope when I reached the dating age. I thought that the idea of asking someone to spend time with you was just absurd. Some girl would come up to you in the cafeteria and say, "So-and-so has a crush on you." I would feel this wave of heat go up my spine, and my lunch tray would start to shake. I mean, what was I supposed to do?

Once in ninth grade during the first day of class, a female friend of mine grabbed me and dragged me out into the hall just before homeroom began. Someone wanted to meet me. She introduced me to the most beautiful Latino girl I have ever seen. I was speechless. We just stood there until the teachers came out and got us. I never asked her out or carried her books home. I just smiled at her. What an idiot I felt like.

I have read that shyness is an inherited trait. I can't really evaluate that, but I don't disagree with it. I have always been shy. In third grade, I developed a tremendous crush on one striking blonde classmate. She radiated. She was so friendly and pleasant that she made me feel calm. She declared that I was her boyfriend. I made the mistake of telling my mother about my newfound love. This was a big mistake.

My parents used to tease me by mentioning her name. I would blush and suffered an embarrassment akin to real pain. I would often run out of the room. They continued this torture well into my teens. I never understood why they found so much amusement in this. I don't know what effect, if any, this had on later developments or anxiety, but I can tell you that shyness is real and anyone who tortures his or her kids because they are shy will spend his or her first day in hell with me at the controls. The pitch will be hot and the pikes sharp.

I asked out four women in my entire life. For the first one, my brother had to write a script for me to use. I actually had sweat dripping from my forehead on the phone by the time I got up the courage to call her. She accepted but got a better offer the next day for the same dance and cancelled.

The second was a good friend, Sue. We spent a lot of time together just hanging around and talking. She and her parents were calm. I would walk home after an afternoon of that calmness, and the further I got away from her and the closer I got to my home, the more anxious I would get. I was invited to a debutante cotillion at Westchester Country Club, the center of Catholic country club power, probably in the whole metropolitan area. The cotillion is this huge choreographed formal dance designed to present the young debutantes to society. They used to print photos of the group in the *New York Times* and other newspapers.

I needed a date. When it came time to actually ask her out on a date, rather than just hang out with her, I was faced with the worst of my fears, that being a no. As I began my stuttering and stammering, for some reason I began to back up across her lawn, finally falling backward over a hedge. She managed to say yes even though she was splitting a gut laughing at me. Sue moved to India with her family, but we have made contact again through email.

The third was for my senior prom. I had been busted for painting graffiti on the school parking lot. A friend who had joined the air force had brought home an orange Day-Glo sticker that was used to mark nuclear weapons. This was before Day-Glo was available to the public. You could see it from a mile away. The only word on it was "dangerous."

I immediately put it on the bumper of my car and picked up a nickname. I was caught painting "dangerous" in the spot where I parked my car every day. My starter did not work so I had to park the car on a hill wherever I went so I could roll down the hill and jump-start the car. My parking space was the only suitable one for this in the school lot. I had to get up early to get this space.

I'll return to the story. When the cops showed up, I dashed to the edge of the parking lot and slid down a thirty-foot embankment to the running track that separated the junior and senior high schools. Halfway across the infield of the track, I could see an area shaded by the junior high building. I took off for that at adrenaline high speed, zigging back and forth in case the cops opened fire. (What an imagination!) Just before I reached the safety of the shadows, I heard someone yelling.

A split second later, the cop I had just flattened and I were tumbling head over heels in the dust. When I realized it was a cop, I said, "I'm sorry, officer."

He asked, "Didn't you hear me yelling? I couldn't figure out which way you were going, and I was just trying to get out of your way."

Here we are, having this conversation on the ground. Those of us who were busted that night, about twenty of us, had the choice of going to commencement, which I wasn't going to anyway because I was not going to graduate, or the prom. I asked this cute Italian-Irish girl to the prom, my third date. When I arrived to pick her up, all of the Italian and Irish cops who had busted me were there, along with the superintendent of grounds for the school. They were all her uncles. Of course, as soon as we got in the car, the spaghetti strap holding up the top of her gown broke, and we had to return to the house to sew it back on and endure another round of jokes at my expense. Finally, the fourth woman I asked out, about twenty-five years later, is my wife.

I did have other relationships with women, but they just happened with no asking them out on dates. This led to some fairly odd relationships because, like so many other things, if you don't take the initiative, if you don't decide what you want and go after it, you have to deal with what comes along.

Dancing without alcohol is still something I don't get. I went to dancing school, but I was always the last one to ask someone to dance, which of course all the males had to do. I was usually the last, so I got to dance with the same girl a lot. I guess this was as much adolescent insecurity as anxiety. Dancing must have been invented to preserve society. Several thousand years ago, the tribal leaders realized the population was declining. They invented dancing to get people close enough to each other where the hormones would take over. This led to propagation. It became a part of our ritualized society. It makes sense to me. One of my favorite bumper stickers reads, "Alcohol for hundreds of years convincing white men that they can dance." Or something like that.

Marriage, the third thing I don't understand, is like dancing, so antiquated that I figure something else should have replaced it by now, although I don't have any suggestions. I saw an interesting bumper sticker the other day. It read, "Why do I have to get married? I didn't do anything."

Beautiful women still intimidate me, although they are attracted to me for some reason. I went in to meet Sophia Loren once in New York. She was at a book signing. I was sick at home and got up, put on a tie, and took in the train just for this. I bought her book and stood in line, the only fortyish guy in the store. I was going to ask her to have tea with me later in the afternoon. If she said no, then she would join the short list of women

I had asked out. I approached the table and did the best Ralph Kramden impersonation ever done. Ham-a-da ham-a-da ham-a-da ham-a-da. She stopped, looked at me, and gave me the biggest and longest smile I have ever had. What a gift.

Around age sixteen, I started experiencing migraine headaches. There are two types of migraines, the painful type I would get on occasion and the "painless" kind I would get frequently. Both are associated with a dilation or widening of the arteries in the cerebrum in the brain. The painful kind is debilitating. My head hurt so much that I had to keep walking. I could not sit down or lie on the bed. They would last for five hours or so. They usually occur at night. After pacing for hours, I could finally lie down on the bed and sleep, although it was more like passing out. The next day I feel that someone had rewound all of my experiences of the last few weeks and erased them. Slowly I would make connections like phone numbers and people's names. By the next evening, I had reconstructed most of the previous weeks' activities, but it was less than a real memory. My family doctor diagnosed these headaches, but apparently not much was known about them, and the only treatment available was aspirin. He was unable to diagnose the painless migraines. I could only tell people that they were sometimes set off by flickering florescent lights and I had flashing wormlike things blocking my vision. My vision itself was cut down severely with no perceptible peripheral vision. I know that strobe lights can trigger an epileptic seizure so there may be a connection. The migraines would happen just before school tests on a regular basis. I could not really see the test for a good part of the hour, which made it difficult to score the test. After my full eyesight returned, I felt slightly faint, and my skin was cold. I felt like lying down. I was accused of not studying, which was true, but, more importantly, of faking the attacks, which was untrue. That was disconcerting. I was not being dishonest about it. I scoured my mind to find any way that I had created this condition. It seemed like the migraines were a weekly occurrence. I can remember handing in tests with no answers scored or with answers scored at random.

One time this led to serious trouble for me and major criticism from the administration of the school, the faculty, and my parents. It seems that the state of New York was trying to market its standardized testing system, the Regents' Exams, to other states. I took an Algebra Regents' Exam for the second time, answered the first four questions, and then waited out the mandatory two-hour period before I could leave. The first four questions are usually very easy in order to relax the person taking the exam. They are the mathematical equivalent of "Is a frog's ass watertight?" I got an eight on the exam.

The following week, I was hauled into the principal's office to meet with a representative of the board of regents from Albany, the algebra teacher, and my parents. A meeting in the principal's office is reserved for capital punishment cases. It seems I had skewed the results of the test, and they had to include this in their marketing report. In any kind of an academic report like this, they have to report three different kinds of test averages, the mean or mathematical average, the mode where most of the scores fall, and the median, the number in between the highest and lowest score. Prior to me taking the exam, the median average was in between forty-five and one hundred or around seventy-two. After my two-hour nap, it had dropped to about fifty-four.

They were really angry. Did I know what this could mean to the state of New York? I answered honestly that, if they were going to use the scores for marketing, they should have informed us beforehand. That got a big rise out of them. Jail was even mentioned, but I knew that was a hollow threat, like 119, although the regents' representative would have loved to have dropped me off at Sing-Sing on the way home, dead from strangulation. Sing-Sing is a maximum security prison on the Hudson River. I think they have "Old Sparky" there – the electric chair.

It went on and on with me being the culprit. I guess I was put on some kind of a hit list after that. Everyone seemed to have my number. Fortunately, I had the acceptance method. I just answered the threats of suspension and spending hours after school with an "okay" or "go ahead." I wish I had the foresight to add, "Make my day." There was no sense in fighting this particular tide. There is no doubt that anxiety was causing the migraines.

Other troublemakers were in the school. They were heroes among a certain group of students, mainly the ones I hung around with. It is the sort of adulation that a hockey player gets for spending long stretches in the penalty box. I figured they were causing trouble to draw attention to themselves. They seemed to like the attention. I didn't like any. I wanted to be left alone. There is some difference there, for what it is worth. I was not treated like a hero because the troublemakers felt I didn't have any control over what I was doing. I probably expressed my feelings about that and lost all possibility of hero status among the underachievers. If spending time in the school office is equivalent to the hockey penalty box, then I was the superhero.

About the same time, I started getting into troughs of depression and experiencing debilitating back spasms that would occasionally keep me in bed for a few days. The depressions were interesting. It is sort of a natural progression with the downside being sort of like a standard deviation curve, "bell-shaped," with another standard curve on the upside. It was like a controlled roller coaster ride.

It worked with such regularity that I could almost plot mentally where I was. It became a part of my life. It is a well-known phenomenon that people who experience extraordinary events often think they are normal, that everyone else has the same problem but they just keep it to themselves.

The classic example is childhood sexual abuse. My depression cycles are certainly not on that level, but it is really strange that I accepted depression as a normal part of my life. It even seems strange to me to say this, but I almost enjoyed the depressions. It was a relief of some sort. I had developed very acute observational powers. I had observed many people to see if they had the same cycles as I did. It is easy to see that all people have cycles, but it is amazing in retrospect that I thought I could discern the complicated cycles of depression in almost all people.

It was more than fooling myself. It was looking through a distorted lens that enabled me to say to myself that it was all right. There never was any doubt in my mind that I was screwed up, but it was okay because almost everyone else was too. When I finally realized many years later that I was using this lens as a crutch, I was very disappointed in myself. I thought the one thing I could count on back then was myself. I thought I could trust myself, but I was wrong. This was in the early sixties before terms like "dysfunctional "became popular. It turns out that a great number of the population is screwed up. I don't care that I was right. I cared because I thought I could trust myself, and I was wrong. I really was like everyone else, something I never really wanted to be.

# METHOD—Playing Music

Somewhere around my fifteenth birthday, I bought a guitar from Mrs. Cohn over at the New Rochelle House of Music. The song "The Day the Music Died" was written about her, or so I have heard. Don McLean was a guitar teacher in her store. I took a few lessons but was more interested in playing than learning scales, so I quit that. For some reason, it is impossible for me to remember songs, so after forty years of playing, I still don't know one, not even any of the twenty-five or so I have written. They all just sort of fade away. I think that a lot of this has to do with a lack of finger memory. There is a missing link between the brain and the fingers. I just deal with sounds and chords.

The important thing about playing music is that it can take you into the zone. You know how you go over a tune in your head all day after you hear it and you just can't get it out? Well, if you play an instrument, the tune that remains in your head is something that comes from your own creativity. It keeps the anxiety down for quite a while. I have had similar experiences with hand drumming and singing. I have read that hand drumming is used as therapy for people with Alzheimer's disease. It must reattach a connection that was lost. Because Alzheimer's involves the death of brain cells, perhaps the drumming establishes alternate routes in the brain.

If I were a good musician, that is all I would do, be an itinerant musician. The people I have the most respect for are musicians and authors. I was in a rock and roll band for a while in high school, and I still think of those good times. My parents let us twang away in the basement for hours on end. For me, playing is different for me than just listening to music. I became very involved in listening to music with Buddy Holly and the Big Bopper and through the British invasion. I used the Beatles *Rubber Soul* to mend a broken heart, the first girlfriend I really got involved with. I later used heavy rock and roll, like Led Zeppelin and the Who to instigate mood swings. These were like mini-elations and depressions, sort of like a break from the tedium of the groaning depression roller coaster.

I don't include listening music as a method probably because of the misuse of it, although it might work for others. Just listening is too passive to have a great effect on serious anxiety. It would be like trying to meditate on April 14 if your income tax forms were not finished yet.

The one exception to this is to listen to music that is intended to relax you. I play it after I work out or do a round of yoga. I use a recording of Tibetan meditation bells. These bells make vibrations that can be felt in the body. Most New Age music falls into the category that would be useful for this purpose. After a full round of yoga, I put on the music very quietly. I then assume the Yogic corpse pose lying on my back with legs spread slightly apart and arms slightly away from the body. I touch my forefingers to my thumbs and touch the tongue lightly to the roof of the mouth to complete the energy flow in my body. I take twenty-five deep-controlled Yogic breaths and then release my breathing to its normal rhythm. This packs your blood with oxygen and allows deep relaxation. It is a good time to meditate.

If I don't have the time for a full round of yoga, which takes about an hour, or if I just want to fully relax my spine, I put on the music and then stretch my back using several exercises that my movement teacher, Mr. Flay, taught me.

Lying on your back, you draw the right knee to your chest while extending the other straight out. You then switch legs and pull your left knee toward your chest while extending your right leg straight out. You repeat this exercise six times. After this, you inhale and pull your knees to your forehead for six reps and then inhale and hold your shins or ankles and push against your hands with your legs. Also do this for six reps. If you have someone to assist you or a low piece of furniture as a substitute, you have the person hold your ankles from below while you inhale and push down. Do this for six reps.

When you finish these exercises, you pull your knees once more to your chest and slowly lower your legs to the floor. While you are doing this, you concentrate on keeping the lower lumbar part of your spine flat and on the floor. If you are successful, your lower spine will be absolutely flat on the floor. I then assume the corpse pose as per above and practice breathing and meditation.

Note: This is the only exercise I use or know of where you inhale and press or contract your muscles against your breath. This is named the

Valsalva maneuver, which causes an increase in abdominal and blood pressure. It is not a great idea, especially for older adults or anyone with a hernia. I asked Mr. Flay about this, and he said the breath helps to push against the spine from within and flatten it. Another exception may be Pilates, but I don't know enough about that yet to comment.

The first time I learned this from Mr. Flay, we had been at an art exhibit in a cathedral, St. John the Divine, in Upper Manhattan, New York. The floors were solid stone blocks. This type of floor causes my back to tighten up, and the tightness, if let go long enough, would lead to debilitating spasms. We returned to his apartment/studio, and he announced that he was going to fix me up. It would usually take me at least a night of rest to relax my back after a bout with the stone floors. The whole exercise session described above takes about six minutes and lying in the corpse pose for about ten additional minutes. I got up expecting some relief but was amazed that the tightness was completely gone. This little routine has saved me several times. I have done it during long flights and even once in a park in London. I had been down in the South End, I believe, watching all the freaks with Day-Glo Mohawks, and my back started tightening up. After sixteen minutes on the grass doing these exercises, I was ready for the next ten rounds. I probably had a few grass stains, but that would be a mark of honor in that crowd.

Lately I have added one additional exercise to this, the so-called "old man's stretch." While I am lying on my back, I have my knees bent and my feet flat on the floor. My hands are clasped behind my neck, and my elbows are touching the floor. I lift one leg and drape it across the other knee, sort of like crossing your legs if you were sitting. I put my calf right on my other kneecap. I then use the weight of the upper leg to pull over the other leg. The object is to touch the (now) lower knee to the floor. This is one of the best exercises to stretch the lower spine. I do six reps. I taught this to a good friend, Bud, and he has been doing it religiously for ten years with great results.

I'll return to playing music. Today's *New York Times*, January 9, 2001, had an article on the front page entitled, "The Dawn of Music for Man and Beast." I will quote the first and third paragraphs.

> Researchers have concluded that the love of music is not
> only a universal feature of the human species, found in
> every society known to anthropology, but is also deeply
> embedded in multiple structures of the human brain
> and is far more ancient than previously suspected … The
> researchers have published evidence that music making is
> at once a primordial human enterprise and an art form for
> birds, whales and others in the animal kingdom.

Music making, as mentioned, gives me an entirely different feeling than just listening to it. When something comes from within (and it will), you are making contact with the very basic core of your being. Playing an instrument, even badly, can be a mystical experience and will put you in contact with a creative place where anxiety does not exist. As with any method, a simple beginning will ease frustration and increase enjoyment. You can start with a penny whistle or a recorder. They are like flutes that you play from one end. Harmonicas are okay, but the holes are hard to find. They all aid in breathing. Most music stores carry hand drums. I started my guitar lessons with a lousy guitar that I was renting. The neck was too fat, and the strings were too hard to press down. I could only play for ten minutes or so before my fingers started to hurt. Guess what? I didn't practice that much.

If you decide to buy an instrument, get a good one. If you can't afford what you want, get another cheaper type of instrument of good quality. You then put a dollar in a jar someplace to start saving up for that instrument you want. That is what I did, and I found (or was found by) an old Martin guitar that is older than I am. An instrument of great quality will almost teach you how to play. If you have finger memory problems, like I do, try a harpsichord. Hang around in music stores or instrument music stores. I have found that salespeople in music stores generally leave you alone unless you ask a question. Then they become very animated and helpful. They love to talk about their favorite things, music and instruments. They usually have quiet rooms where you can try out instruments in semi-privacy.

If you get an instrument, try to leave it out at home where you can see it. The key to getting good at anything is doing it frequently, even if for only a few minutes at a time.

# METHOD—Be Invisible (Not Recommended)

Seeking invisibility, I found it was easy to slip into and out of situations without being noticed. It was similar to not getting wet by running through the raindrops. It takes practice but can be done. In high school, I didn't get involved in any formal activities, except a brief attempt at football. I kept my mouth shut in class and spent a lot of time under my car. The administration kept trying to put me in advanced classes for the intelligent and achieving few, and I kept dropping out of them for ones that didn't require studying, for example, from physics to physical science. I took plane geometry two and a half times and then dropped it. The background noise at this time was a constant low-grade war with my parents and the school administration.

When I was a half credit behind in my senior year, I wound up doing a postgraduate year to get my diploma, working in McDonald's in the afternoon. I kept such a low profile that some people didn't even know I was there, and those who did, quickly forgot me and a lot of other invisibles. That is the way I wanted it then. With the exception of some people I met and four teachers—two English teachers, an industrial design teacher, and an art teacher—I consider my four years at the sixth-ranked public high school in the country to have been a total waste of time. It was not all their fault, but nonetheless, a TWT.

The main reason for not using this method is that it takes you out of the loop. It takes you out of the society loop but, more importantly, out of your own loop. You lower the anxiety of interacting with others by not participating, but you don't gain the experience of doing something. You can become invisible to yourself. It is almost a non-method, and it doesn't lead to anything except more invisibility. For me, it was boring and, in retrospect, counterproductive.

# METHOD—Suicide (Definitely Not Recommended)

I have a few words about suicide. Some would say that I was chickening out by not including this as a method. Dr. Lilly, one of my heroes mentioned elsewhere in this book, brought to my attention that the court of law was the real reality in societal life. When you are in court, you are dealing with a strict set of rules, and nobody in his or her right mind would want to be there. Suicide is beyond reality. It doesn't do anything for the person committing it. As a former colleague of mine, Tom Hale, put it, referring to still another colleague of mine who had just blasted out his brains during a stroll on the beach one morning, "It's a short-term solution to a long-term problem."

I thought about suicide seriously. I was afraid that, if I tried that, I would blow it, but I gave it some serious thought. I was afraid that I would be the one person in a billion who would survive an eighteen-story swan dive and just wind up mangled rather than fully dead. When I was about eighteen, I finally decided not to. The reason, a conscious decision, was that I was curious about the outcome of my life, my raison d'être. Later when I was about thirty and working in New York and into reading a lot of philosophy, I was on the subway and reading a book by Albert Camus, *The Myth of Sisyphus, Essay Absurdity and Suicide*. I remember my astonishment when he declared, "There is only one really serious philosophical problem, and that is suicide." There is, of course, more to it than that one quote, but I interpreted his thoughts to mean that there is only one decision you have to make in life, whether or not to commit suicide. Once you made the decision, you either killed yourself or got on with your life. I felt semivindicated by reading that. It seemed like a valid thought.

I don't disagree with aspects of suicide, especially the euthanasia angle, but I now realize that a lot of it is tied to depression, which is not necessarily a permanent condition. If you could interview people who had committed suicide, I'll bet that most of them didn't really consider the aftermath, what they leave behind, the people who carry the hurt to their graves. A lot of the hurt is guilt. You always hear people saying, "I wish I had known that she was in such a bad place. I should have known. I should have been there for her." Well, it is really hard to be there for a suicidal depressed person. It is not like taking the car keys away from a drunken friend, a temporary intercession. It is so hard because we don't have the tools. Suicide and depression are the province of professionals, and if you intercede, you feel like you are turning in your buddy. There is also the denial. I said a few times in anger that I was going to kill myself. I was never taken seriously. That was when I was really thinking about it.

Don't commit suicide. If you do, you won't accomplish anything useful. Everyone, even your dog, will feel bad. Don't do it. Spend the effort convincing someone that you have a problem. Keep saying it until he or she gets it. The natural reaction, even from family or loved ones, is going to be denial. You may need to shout really loud to get them to pay attention to you. Several people who attempt suicide and fail, the ones who can be interviewed after they recover, never really intended to kill themselves. They just wanted someone to pay attention to them, to take them seriously. Who knows how many people attempt suicide in this way and miscalculate the means and really die? This is a terrible tragedy for everyone, including society. You can get treatment that will show results relatively quickly, and you can get over your problems and be a happy person. Thoughts of showing them or getting back at people by taking your life can be dealt with in other ways.

I had a Greek friend who told me that there was an expression in the Greek language that could be expressed in English as, "The best way to punish someone is with your own success." Think about that. If you really want to get back at someone, make a success out of yourself. And then, if you really want to stick it to him or her, offer to share your success with him or her.

Unfortunately, a stigma is still attached to mental disorders, such as depression. I find it interesting that my local phone book does not list anything under "suicide," "suicide prevention," or "depression." You would think, with five listings for "animal carcass removal," there would be some listing in the phone book that relates to suicide prevention. The phone book does have a listing for emergency numbers on the first inside page. The applicable listing, "psychiatric crisis intervention line," is somewhat obscure.

I called the local help line listed there, and I was informed that these twenty-four-hour services are run by hospitals in our area, and our local group would be helpful to the person considering suicide. Another avenue would be the police. The only difference would be that the police might not be as good at assessing the situation and might just send over a car to pick you up to take you for help. The good thing about the police is that, when it comes to trouble, they are easy to convince. They take everything seriously. The short form is that organizations that can help should be easier to find.

# METHOD—Always Have a Lottery Ticket in Your Pocket; Nobody Ever Commits Suicide with a Lottery Ticket in His or Her Pocket

Now that I look back at it, I wish I had made more out of high school. There were many good opportunities. I had really wanted to be an architect. We had a career day at school one day, and I rushed in to get a good seat to find out what I was going to be doing for the rest of my life. He started off by saying that architecture was 90 percent mathematics. I had no math skills. This was before calculators. The school also had good language courses. I could have avoided thousands of hours studying languages later if I had taken advantage of them. I had a big problem with studying, in part because of my lack of challenge in the earlier years, in part because I was trying to get my parents to pay attention to me, and in part because the anxiety didn't allow me to finish anything.

I had somehow developed a bad thought process habit, which didn't allow me to concentrate on any thought for an extended period of time. I could concentrate on things, but not thoughts. I could spend hours building a World War II airplane model or drawing but not think about anything for more than a few minutes. Any thought I had would eventually turn to violence. I would think about a date with a girl I had a crush on, and it would end up in a car crash. I would think about skiing and then a skiing accident. I would break my leg and have the bone sticking out. I would think about sailing, and everyone would drown in a squall. It was a hideous thing.

As a result, I had to do things rather than think about them. I picked up a lot of skills and interests because of this. This problem I had with all thoughts turning to violence is now gone due to the medication I am on. The only way I could stop it back then was by getting drunk. One of my shrinks categorized this behavior as anesthetizing myself. True, it works great. This was back in the time that there was little penalty for driving drunk, so every Friday and Saturday, I was out at the bars. I was tall enough to get served with fake IDs and started serious weekend binging when I was sixteen. Summers at Cape Cod were surprisingly alcohol free. The greatest thing about alcohol is that it lowers your inhibitions. I don't know of any other drug, legal or not, that will do this, and I have tried a lot of them. This allowed me to talk to girls without freaking out and have a lot of fun with my friends without being my usual uptight, anxious self. After I became self-sufficient, I used alcohol as a method to control mood swings. I guess, if you evaluated me according to Alcoholics Anonymous standards, I would be an alcoholic since age sixteen.

The major problem with self-medicating with alcohol is that you eventually are not going to know anyone who does not drink. If you don't get addicted to the drug, you get addicted to the lifestyle. This is in addition to all of the diseases you will contract and all of the brain cells you kill along the way. I have since learned that there are methods that will replace self-medicating with alcohol, and in the interest of not getting slammed for recommending alcohol consumption to troubled people, I will not list it as a method, even though it may have saved my life.

If you are having a problem with alcohol or your parents or grandparents were alcoholics, you should read *The Adult Children of Alcoholics Syndrome* by Wayne Kritsberg. Alcoholism is such a pervasive disease that the effects are felt for generations after the actual alcoholic has done the damage to himself or herself and his or her family. I had alcoholics on both sides of my family. My grandparents, with the exception of my maternal grandmother, all had personal drinking problems, and they all behaved like alcoholics because of the effects that alcoholics had on them. My parents were involved in a very heavy drinking business crowd in New York City, and they had to entertain three or four nights a week. Despite their alcohol-infused lifestyle, they didn't actually have to be alcoholics to act like alcoholics. Alcoholics trained them. They, in turn, trained me. I harbor the alcoholic traits of my grandparents and probably their predecessors, and I would have even if I had never had a drink. It is an insidious disease that has implications that reach far beyond the individual.

The strange thing about the psychiatric community and alcohol is that half of the shrinks I have met don't think it is a problem in itself, at least not with me. I have been through many evaluations. One was by a psychiatrist, a medical doctor. I told her that I thought I realized I was using alcohol for self-medication and wanted to stop. I had read about a few drugs that would lower the desire for alcohol and "mood elevators," the term in use back then, could replace the alcohol. She told me that I had to stop drinking for six months before she would prescribe any drugs.

I replied, "If I can stop drinking for six months without any anxiety side effects, then why do I need you?"

Self-medication with alcohol is definitely not the way to go.

# METHOD—Find a Legal Violent Activity That Will Dissipate Your Anxiety through Physical Force

I started working when I was fifteen, the age you had to be to caddy at the local golf clubs. Caddying was one of the few jobs open to fifteen-year-olds. I learned a lot about golf, and some of the members would ask for me as a caddy because I would give those lessons around the golf course and I was a clean-cut kid. I even caddied for the club pro when he was giving lessons. It was good exercise. I was not very good at team sports, but I was very good at some individual sports such as trap shooting, ice skating, downhill skiing, water skiing, and swimming. I used golf as a release. There was a driving range a few miles from where I lived.

When the anxiety got to be too much, when I felt like a balloon ready to explode, I would drive up there, buy a large bucket of balls, pick up a driver, and beat the crap out of those balls. From caddying for the pro, I knew how to stand and swing. Sometimes I would simply flabbergast the other adult golfers. They would see this 175-pound, curly-haired kid standing six-foot-two drive up, grab a basket of balls and a lousy driver out of the barrel, and blast balls 275 yards out past the lights, one after the other. Then he'd get in his Hillman Minx with no muffler and leave a big patch of rubber on his way out of the parking lot. It used to kill them.

It got expensive to do this, so I eventually developed a method of attaching a golf ball to a fishing line. I had to duck a lot, but I could get the same effect of blasting the balls and deflating that anxiety balloon, and I could do this in the backyard.

Later I started hitting tennis balls against the garage until my parents put an end to because I was going to break something. (It would really drive them nuts.) I migrated to a bridge overpass and drove all the neighbors nuts down there. I hit the ball hard. I actually became a fairly good tennis player after a while by doing this, but I never got serious about tennis because I don't like to win. I hate to get awards, whether they are handshakes or silver cups. I guess it's because I lose my invisibility. I have quizzed good golfers and tennis players that I have met over the years about what they really enjoy about the game, and a lot of them have said, "Hitting the ball."

For ten years or so later on, in my thirties, I substituted splitting wood with a mall to fight my anxiety buildups. I (or rather Tony, my outside, Vibram sole boot-wearing, chainsaw-wielding alter ego) would get permission to cut down dead trees on private property with his chainsaw. I would cut them into eighteen-inch pieces and split them. It was a real Zen thing. You had to think of the mall as being through the wood before it even hit the wood. It was great stuff. I did about five cords or so a year. That is a pile of wood twenty feet long, four feet high, and four feet wide. I am a real fireplace fire nut, so this provided me with free firewood.

Many of the psychologists I have worked with ascribe to the theory that you have to let out your building anxiety a little at a time to avoid the ultimate explosion. I agree with this, but I could never find a reasonable way to do this and did not involve violent activity like hitting golf balls or tennis. The shrinks did not have any good methods for me to try. It is agreed that suppressing the building pressure will just lead to a larger explosion. I wish I could comment on social activity like dancing or sex to dissipate anxiety, but I am too shy to have learned much about those activities. For me, a combination of controlled violence and a gradual replacement of that with some of the other methods like yoga and Tai Chi, which take a long time to learn, works best. I'll have more on these later.

My postgraduate year in high school was okay. I had a lot of time to look around at art schools. Even with my lousy grades, I was tacitly accepted at some pretty good schools. Several schools like Carnegie Tech and the University of Georgia had reserved some slots for academic underachievers like me who had promise in the art field. The Art Center School in L.A. was interested. This is where most of the automobile designers come from. As mentioned, I had a good portfolio due to the efforts of a few good teachers and my escapist stuff at home. One of my teachers actually had a small exhibition of our artwork in the Modern Museum of Art in New York. (Woof! Talk about bragging rights!) I had the clipping from the *New York Times* with a mention of this "impossible flying machine" I had constructed. I drew cars, houses, and nudes from my imagination. I was drawing the perfect life. The college professors who looked at my portfolio reacted like they had never seen a nude before, but they were impressed.

One of my cars produced in industrial design class with one of my four favorite teachers even drew the attention of the president of Fiat in Italy. It's a long story.

So, I could have gone to art school anywhere in the United States or Italy. I decided not to go to any of them. What was I going to do with a master of fine arts degree in five years? The only explanation I have for that was that I was terrified that I would not be able to do anything for that long. I went to liberal arts college in Iowa and took five years to squeak out of that one.

So here I am—a nineteen-year-old virgin with no academic skills, a great general knowledge, good life learning skills, low self-esteem, abandonment issues, high anxiety, and a medicinal weekend addiction to alcohol. I had blown the opportunity to commit suicide and go to art school, and I'm in Iowa. I had managed to keep a sense of humor. I thank people like Bill Cosby, Johnny Carson, and Steve Allen for that, along with a friend in high school, Bill Budnoy, whose parents had actually been in vaudeville. I still use some of those lines that Bill's father taught him and he, in turn, gave to me.

I blew another good opportunity during my high school years. I drove up to White Plains one day to check out a karate school. I talked at length with the master of the dojo. He spoke of discipline, self-esteem, training, clear thinking, and the like. I would have signed up if the application didn't contain an idiotic promise that you would study karate for the rest of your life. I was naïve. I have since learned that karate and other martial arts instill very positive beliefs and good habits in practitioners. I wish I had done that at that time. I'll have more on these later.

# METHOD—Self-Help Books

In high school and college, I began reading many self-help books. I read all of the Dale Carnegie books, *How to Win Friends and Influence People*, and all of that. I must have read twenty-five self-help books. I have to be careful about what I say about self-help books because this book could be construed as one, although I feel it is a bit more personal. I don't remember anyone bringing his or her own life experiences to the table so the reader can see a reason for his or her recommendations.

I can only recommend a few books in this category, which I do elsewhere in this book, because most deal with themes. Some of the authors are brilliant people and excellent writers, but they still deal with themes. By that, I mean that the idea of what the book was about preceded the writing of the book. They got an idea of what they wanted to write about and used their intelligence to fill in the blanks. The books I recommend are written, like this one, by people who, like Einstein, are shaving one morning and … Boom! The theory of relativity appears. (No comparison between Einstein and me is intended.) These people write books that look at things in a completely new way, not just from a different angle. They are not how-to-do-it books. I'm not putting down self-help books. I just don't remember any of them.

# METHOD—Lose the Excuses;
# Take the Responsibility

The first shrink I went to see was during college. They had a counseling center there. I was having a few problems and, with the encouragement of my girlfriend, decided to talk to someone about them. The psychologist was very perceptive. He short-circuited my list of problems and asked me why I was always making excuses about everything. I denied it. He repeated a few excuses I had made. With a little coaching, I realized I made excuses about everything. There was always a reason why anything did or didn't happen. My excuse making had something to do with responsibility and my desire to avoid it. Somehow I walked out of his office and never made another excuse. It was a tremendous relief and a newfound freedom.

The only reason I went to college was to avoid the draft. By the time I finished high school, 1,500 Americans had already been killed in Viet Nam. I was pretty anxious about getting killed in a war. Parsons College was actually a good place for me. Southeastern Iowa is very isolated for a kid from the New York suburbs. The main wildlife in Iowa is flies, houseflies to be exact. You get to see flies do everything: defend turf, mate, eat, jockey for position on the ceiling over the cafeteria line, and so forth. One even landed on my cake at dinner, flipped over, gave two kicks, and croaked. It didn't say much for the cake. When I get to be God, houseflies are the first to go and then mosquitoes, horseflies, coat hangers, and ironing boards, all in that order.

Parsons had a trimester system so the school was open all year. If you had below a 2.5 grade point average out of a possible 4.0, you had to go to school all year. I established a 2.0 right away and wound up going for two and a half years straight. I actually had to get kicked out to get a semester off. I had been studying Spanish so I went to Puerto Rico and worked in construction. The lectures at Parsons were all taught by PhDs, which was rare even in good schools, and they were not allowed to publish, so you could actually talk to them in their offices. They were top-notch professors.

The school also had an additional hour of discussion classes for each hour of lecture taught by teachers with master's degrees. If you had below a C grade in any course, you had to go to tutoring, which was taught one-on-one by someone with a bachelor's degree. They literally crammed the stuff down your throat, which was great for me. I didn't join anything and steered myself away from fraternities. It was too visible. I managed to find a girlfriend even though there were six males to every one female. She was the nicest person I had ever met. She was very supportive and nurturing. She was smart and had good studying skills. We used to have dates in the library where we would study. She taught me how to memorize things like Spanish dialogues. I was learning to learn at nineteen.

By this time, I had developed a bad habit of attacking and destroying inanimate objects when I got mad. It was nothing new really, but it was becoming a habit. The balloon would fill to a certain point ... Bang! I would explode. I came very close to hurting myself badly a few times, and I destroyed some things that I was fond of, like my guitar, but - somehow - I felt better, if deflated and better can exist as synonyms.

I started seeing a shrink at the counseling center at school once a week. This was the same shrink who weaned me off making excuses. The regular visits opened up a can of worms that I didn't want to see. I was sort of saved from confronting my negative behavior through therapy in a way by a chance encounter with a trustee of Wagner College in New York City. They had a junior year abroad program in Bregenz, Austria. He pulled some strings for me, and I was accepted. I exercised my abandonment issues by abandoning my girlfriend who had helped me so much, something I was to repeat many times. I have tried to find her several times to apologize, but to no avail.

I imagined I was going to figuratively take off a huge overcoat when I boarded that ship to Europe and leave all of my problems behind. Right ...

# METHOD—Run Away from Yourself (Not Recommended)

Running away from yourself works but only postpones the inevitable. It doesn't fix anything. It is like blowing the money you had saved to pay your taxes on drugs, but only worse. The year in Austria was so great that I spent the next ten years trying to duplicate it. I learned German, made great friends, skied fifty days that year in the most beautiful mountains, the Austrian Alps, hitchhiked all over the place, and traveled all over Europe by train after school was over. My parents were inveterate (business) travelers. As a child, I had traveled around the East Coast with them, mostly visiting family between Maryland and Massachusetts and skiing in Vermont and Canada. I had traveled to Europe once alone at age twelve when my mother was in danger of dying in a Norwegian hospital. She lived. I used to go into New York alone on the train at age eleven or twelve to visit friends. I couldn't tie a tie yet, so I would slip it over my head, keeping the knot tied for the next day. By the time I got to Austria, I had made trips around the United States, visiting friends in other colleges. I had lived in Puerto Rico. I loved going to new places.

# METHOD—Push Through a Displaced Anxiety to Get to What You Want

In Austria, I traveled every weekend and tried to get to as many new destinations as possible. I would begin planning on Monday for the next weekend. I remember that a pressure would build up during the week about where I was going to go. By Friday, I would have a real fear of going. Of course, I would go anyway. I would worry (angst) about where I was going to stay, the weather, money, or just everything. When I got there, I just went into arrival mode, which I was good at because I had done so much traveling in the past. The anxiety pressure disappeared, and I did what I had to do.

I remember opening the window of my hotel room in Munich the first time I was there, lighting a cigarette, and wondering why I had been so uptight about going there. I was just elated to be there in the world's biggest party city in the month of October. Oktoberfest is a monthlong festival of beer drinking and all sorts of related fetes of general good-natured depravity. This anxiety I had about traveling was what I call a displaced anxiety. It was an anxiety about something I loved to do. It was like the approach-avoidance dilemma that lab rats often face when they have to step on an electric grid to get food. By pushing through the anxiety, I got to Munich, and I did have a ball. This travel anxiety is something I still experience, but I have learned that the reward is worth the pain.

# METHOD—Always Remember Who You Are; Stay within Your Bounds

I also met a woman in Austria who would not have looked twice at me at home if I had been driving a Ferrari convertible with hundred-dollar bills hanging out of my mouth. She was a very pretty debutante from New Jersey and a lot of fun. Her mother was even prettier and a member of the Junior League. During the sixties, this was about as far away from a card-carrying communist as you could get. I had avoided "these-kind-of-people" while in the USA like the plague, and here I was with one.

I learned many years later that, when you are in a foreign culture, you are bound to get thrown into a group of strangers and wind up in a relationship with someone you would not even have the opportunity to make an acquaintance with at home. All of your barriers that you have carefully constructed get removed. If you are silly enough to try to bring this relationship back home, all of the barriers reappear, and you are stuck big time.

I remember standing on the deck of the freighter I sailed home on in Marseilles, France, our last port of call before heading for New York. I was looking in the general direction of Austria and had the strangest thought that I would never see that woman I had met in Austria again. I was right. I still married the lookalike who waited for me in the States. It lasted five years. It was the highest anxiety I had ever experienced. I think I know how Lyle Lovett felt when he married Julia Roberts.

The only thing that makes games playable are rules. You could not play a game if you could change the rules during the game. The analogy here is to stay in bounds. If you get an opportunity that is out of (your) bounds, it has a built-in anxiety producer if it does not work out. People who have anxiety problems don't fail at something and then say to themselves, "Oh, well, I guess that didn't work out."

There is a lot more gnashing of teeth and pulling of hair with us. My brother used to admonish me to choose friends who were complementary to me. I didn't know what he was talking about. I didn't choose anyone. I always thought it was coincidence. If someone were nice enough to pay attention to me, then he or she deserved my attention and respect. After the first marriage, I had a better understanding of what he was talking about. I hear she is happy now, and I am thrilled. We learned from each other what we didn't want. It was a starter marriage.

I have mentioned abandonment a few times without any explanation. It is like chicken pox. If you get it, you know that, if you live long enough, you are going to have shingles, a very painful nerve, and a skin disorder that usually appears on the lower back. They are the same disease at different stages. Once you get abandoned, you are going to have to deal with it later in your life. You are going to either abandon other people, or you are going to pick people who are going to abandon you. Either way, you are going to get blindsided by it. There is no way that you are going to learn by yourself how to deal with it or to see it as a cause when it happens. This is what makes it so insidious. People who are physically or sexually abused when they are young are more likely to be abusers when they grow up. It is a cycle.

Abandonment is like that. I have a close friend, Jaid, who has that attitude that you should at some time in your life forget about what happened to you in your youth and get on with your life. He uses as an example a woman whom he had great interest in. She had major abandonment issues. She expressed this to him in an incomplete fashion. She told him that her issues stemmed from the (one) time that her mother left her on her twenty-first birthday to travel to Paris with her lover. I can guarantee that was not the first time she had been abandoned, although it might have been the first time that she realized that she had been abandoned many times before. Divorce and death can be forms of abandonment. It is a complex topic.

We have many abandonment issues in my family. My particular one was that my parents kept coming back. I have to put it that way to keep my friend Jaid in line. They traveled a lot on business to Europe and South America right after the Second World War. This was back in the times when, if you were late for a transatlantic flight, they would hold the plane for you. Because of the nature of the business and the distances, they would stay away for three to four months at a time. They stayed in the best hotels and hung around with the power crowd of that time. I was left with my brother and my Irish grandmother. Four months is a long time in the development of an eight- or nine-year-old. A lot happens. A lot of development takes place.

Well, they would come back and expect me to be the same person. They would treat me the same as when they left and impose the same rules. (Yes, they were control freaks.) I would rebel, and a conventional war would take place for the next few weeks. Then either I would go to Cape Cod, or they would pack up for Buenos Aires or Hamburg. This went on for about five years.

Finally, one day I had had it. We were going somewhere, and I was dressed, jacket and tie. They were trying to prep me for the social encounter to come and were laying down the ground rules for my behavior that day.

I stopped in front of the house and said, "Look, if you are going to go off to Europe for four months at a time, stay in your fancy hotels, and hang around with Count this and Duke that, then don't think that you can come back here and boss me around!"

If they had been wearing false teeth, shattered porcelain would have covered the front walk. I was even amazed at what I had said. After the smoke had cleared, I think we had some sort of an understanding.

The whole point is that, if they had left and stayed away, I would have had abandonment issues. Because they kept coming back, I had major ones. I fight with it every day. I have to restrain myself from cutting and running. Having a place to go or not has little to do with it. There is no logic involved.

I have just a little piece of advice when dealing with parents. This is from a shrink. You can change the way that your parents deal with you, but you can never change the way they deal with each other. They are joined at the forehead.

I was only abandoned once by anyone other than my parents, the second girl I ever asked out. She moved to India with her family. Her father was an expert on the Indian filmmaking community, and he was on a sabbatical. Our relationship was just beginning to grow. The reason that I mention this is not that this caused any anguish at the time, even though the loss of a good friend saddened me, but it didn't cause any anguish. I was so inured to the abandonment thing that I just packed up and went to Cape Cod for the summer. I wondered a lot about what feelings, if any, I really had. I still do.

# METHOD—Stop Second-Guessing Yourself

I should have entitled this method "Try to learn how to stop second-guessing yourself" because this is so hard to do if you are anxious. I used to second-guess myself all of the time. What was worse was that all someone had to do to get me going was to suggest to me that I should second-guess myself. I would be sitting in the driveway with the car loaded for a weekend of skiing, the key in the ignition, and my hand on it, ready to start the car, and someone would ask, "Are you sure we have everything?"

I think you know what I am talking about. I would have to go through a mental list of everything needed and then locate everything in the car mentally before turning that key. I would then steam at a low boil for the next two hours.

I had some interesting things happen when I was in a second-guessing state. The day that my student group left Europe for home, we were all in London. We all had schedules. The group was going to catch a train that would take them to Southampton to board an ocean liner for New York. I was leaving from the same station, Charing Cross, to take a train to Dover to catch a ferry to Belgium. I was on my way to Switzerland and Italy with a Eurail pass in my wallet. (Almost free rail travel for students). With that, I could go anywhere in Europe. I was booked on the last train that would connect with a ferry in Dover. All of the students boarded the train for Southampton, including my fiancée-to-be, and departed. I had a few hours to kill before my train left. I checked my suitcase and went for a walk in the neighborhood of the station.

I had a (then) major dilemma on my mind. A very sexy woman had made an offer that I could stay with her in London for a few days. That would have been spectacular. I was tempted to break some rules and have some fun. I definitely had the devil on one shoulder and the angel on the other whispering in my ears. This was before cell phones, and people looked askance at you having a conversation with yourself.

On the other hand, I wanted to get to Switzerland and visit some friends and then get to Italy where it was warm. London always seems cold. It makes me think of a quote by Samuel Clemens, "The coldest winter I ever spent was summer on Puget Sound." He could have said that about London.

I was chewing on this dilemma for about two hours. Stay and play; leave and warm up. I returned to the station well in advance of the train's scheduled departure and retrieved my suitcase. I looked at the different tracks stretching like fingers out into the rain and noted where each one was going, still distracted by my dilemma. To my horror, the train for Dover was leaving in about one minute, and they were shutting the gate. I tore over there and asked and then begged with the uniformed official who was poised to lock the gate to let me in.

"I'm quite sorry, sir, but it is beyond the scope of my authority to let a passenger on the boarding platform after the prescribed hour of departure." He proceeded to lock the gate.

I tried physically to stop him from doing that, but he was considerably larger than I was and gave me that "How would you like to spend the night in jail?" look. I backed off and began walking away. I noticed that the gate on the next platform was wide open. I casually looked over my shoulder and noticed the official walking away. And then I dashed through the gate, jumped down onto the empty tracks, threw my suitcase up on the platform where my train was leaving from, climbed up, and began to dash down the platform. The train was just beginning to move.

Apparently, a Bobby (cop) had been watching my near altercation with the official and began yelling the minute I dashed through the open gate. They both worked furiously to get the locked gate open. Now I had both the official and a cop blowing whistles and chasing me down the platform, and the train was gaining speed. Fortunately, I had spent as much time that year skiing and hiking in the mountains as I had drinking beer, and I was in pretty good shape. I was looking for an open door.

The last car was a baggage car. The train conductor looked out of the open sliding door to see what all of the commotion was. This was turning into one of those Nazi war movies. Instead of aiding the pursuing cop and train official, this big grin broke out on his face, and he motioned for me to come on. I could hear the footsteps behind me and expected to be tackled at any moment. I started swinging my fifty-pound suitcase and threw it in the open door. The end of the platform was rapidly accelerating toward me. I had one last kick left in me to get in the door. The conductor stuck his hand out the door and literally dragged me into the car on my knees as the platform disappeared beneath my dangling loafers. I felt like my lungs were going to jump out of my throat. I lay on my back for some time, trying to get my breath back.

When I finally sat up, he asked, "Where are you going?"

I said, "To Dover to catch the boat."

The grin reappeared on his face, and he said, "I hope you aren't in a hurry. This is the local. The train you were supposed to catch leaves in twenty minutes and gets to Dover an hour before we do."

The last time I second-guessed myself was two years ago. We had just bought a thirty-three-foot sailboat and were sailing it from Cape Cod to our home in New Jersey. We spent the third night in an anchorage on Long Island, New York, Mattituck. I had never anchored the boat before, but I knew how to. I dropped and secured the anchor without a problem. I had been used to spending the night tied up to a dock or on a permanent mooring firmly attached to the bottom. I made dinner, and I was having a glass of wine when another couple showed up in their boat. They tried to get their anchor to set. They were doing all of the right things, but it just would not work. They must have made ten attempts before they were successful. By this time, I was in second-guess overdrive.

I asked my wife, "Do you think we should check our anchor?"

She just looked at me, probably knowing that my angst level had reached the boiling point. I thought of the train chase in London and all of the other strange things that had happened when I was in second-guessing mode.

Finally, I said, "Fuck it! If the boat floats away in the middle of the night, I'll just deal with it then. I'm not going to second-guess myself again."

My life since then has been less exciting but a bit smoother. I had let it go.

Zang! I'll come back to 1968. The draft board was hopping mad when I got home from Europe. I went down there to see what was up, and they told me they had drafted me twice while I was in Europe. They told me I should have requested permission from them to leave the country. I asked if they would have granted it, and they said no. I politely told them that I was glad I didn't ask and walked out. I went home, packed, went out for one more drink with my friends, kissed my fiancée good-bye, and hopped in my VW beetle (the "Wee Hairy Beastie") the next morning, bound for Iowa.

I was back in school three days later, one day before the third time they drafted me. Getting drafted at that time was a death sentence. The Viet Nam War was in full swing, and American troops were being killed in droves every day. The evening news always included a body count, actually two: one for the Viet Cong and one for our side. The only other time I have seen such an absurdity was in a newspaper in Houston, Texas. The tally was between the 7-Eleven convenience store owners and the people who were robbing them. Asian Indians and Koreans owned many of the stores. These people work hard for their money and don't like to give it away. Gun battles were a regular, at least weekly, affair. The newspaper had a running tally of the score, 7-Eleven was forty-two and robbers were twenty-seven, according to who won. A lot of strange stuff was going on in Texas, but I like it there. They keep it interesting.

Zang! I'll come back to 1968 again. There was also the idea floating around that, if you got drafted, you went immediately into the infantry, which meant ultimately spending weeks at a time tromping around in the jungle (the enemy's jungle), where they had lived for thousands of years. They were the 7-Eleven owners, and we were the robbers. There was no way I was going to get drafted.

Boy, is Iowa different from Europe. Nothing in Iowa even remotely resembles anything in Europe unless it was dropped from an Air France jet by mistake. Yellow ice (blue ice), I think, they call it. I graduated the next spring. My grades went from a 2.0 to a 4.0. I made the dean's list. That's when I realized that grades are a study in motivation. I was still in love with that girl I had met in Austria and motivated.

A friend turned me on to marijuana a few weeks after I arrived back at school. I smoked regularly for about fifteen years. It didn't seem to affect my normal life, but like alcohol, you wind up having various degrees of drug addicts as friends. A big difference was that this was illegal, and for the most part, I was a legal sort of guy. I won't recommend marijuana or any other street drugs as methods. We used them for their recreational value, almost a laughable term if you have any brains. There is an expression, "If you remember the sixties, you weren't there." I desperately wanted to be there, to be accepted, to fit in, to be invisible. I'll probably use that expression a few more times in this book.

# METHOD—Learn to Avoid the Traps by Choosing Your Options

So far in this litany, I have discovered and used two drugs, alcohol and marijuana, that seem to have the effect of trapping you into a certain social group. It took me many years to come to the realization that how you behave and what you do determines your friends and which social group you are in. If you smoke, most of your friends will be smokers. If you drink, most will be drinkers. If you are a musician, most will be musicians. If you are a Nobel Laureate, well, I think you get the idea.

I always had friends from a broad spectrum of people. I got along with all sorts of people from archconservative lunch club types in New York to my drug and alcohol group that seemed to be going nowhere. Some of them were what they call highly productive alcoholics or drug addicts, meaning they held good jobs, belonged to a tennis club, and had expensive toys, but they were trapped nonetheless.

What I know now but didn't know then was that I had a choice. I had always thought that life was something you moved through and things happened, just enveloped you. I wish I had known that life is something that is moving by and you can choose things that are passing by. You can become different things. Of course, society puts up hurdles in the form of degrees, certificates, memberships, licenses, and the like to make you prove who you are, but the choice is still there if you avoid the traps. I think I avoided serious traps because I wanted to keep my options open. I wanted to keep them open as escape routes without knowing that options have value in themselves. This method has to be a bit oblique because it was a coincidence at the time that I employed it. Just remember, you always have a choice, and if you drop the excuses, the choice is yours to make and own.

# METHOD—Stick with Small Organizations

To avoid the draft board again, I enlisted in the army with a contract to go to Officer Candidate School (OCS). A few weeks later, they announced a lottery system for the draft, but I had already signed up. The lottery was held about three weeks after I was inducted. The higher your number, the less likely you were to be drafted. My number was the highest number selected. I remember sitting down on a bench near a parade field and trying to figure out how I had gotten here. It was about the lowest I had ever been. I decided I was living someone else's life. My father had drilled into me that you go to college, graduate, join the navy, get a job, save five thousand dollars, get married, buy a house, have kids, walk the dog, get old, retire, and die. He actually left the die part out.

I decided I was going to take my life back. The war was winding down, and they tried to get us to drop our OCS contracts for tours in places like Germany. I had been having an eating disorder and lost fifty-four pounds in six months. I would have a large breakfast and then barf in the bushes. People on the base thought I was a returning POW because I had the same uniforms that I had fifty-four pounds ago. (There's no joke intended there. A few strangers stopped me and asked.) The first thirty pounds were okay, but not the rest. I failed the OCS physical, and I was diagnosed as anorexic. I had anorexia nervosa.

The officers in charge asked me where I wanted to finish my contractual three-year tour of duty, and I said, "home." There was a big hoopla, and I almost wound up suing the Department of the Army for breach of contract. I came close to the brig a few times and almost got sent to Korea for disposal - literally, but a friendly captain saved me. The end result was that I was stationed at my home address, that is, "sent home," until my discharge papers cleared.

I learned a lot from this experience and met some wonderful people, one of whom I still keep in touch with, Mikel. I gained a lot of self-confidence by getting my life back. I had been in the army for ten months.

Six months later, the Veterans Administration advised me that I was a disabled veteran. I didn't ask for this and knew nothing about it. I felt a bit ashamed. All of these guys were rolling around in wheelchairs. I didn't mind though because it would keep me out of any other stupid wars the government would decide to get in. Back then, I was one of those guys who would have jumped in voluntarily had the wolves been at the gate, but I felt the Viet Nam War was a waste of life on both sides. It was a shame in more than one meaning of the word. My veteran's disability papers had one word on them under reason, anxiety.

Now when I first read this, I was very surprised that the Veterans Administration had made me disabled, a terrible term to read about yourself. I should have had the largest light bulb in my life, a nuclear-powered light bulb, go off in my head. Instead there was nothing. Anxiety was not my problem yet. I didn't get it.

The larger the organization is, the smaller their ability will be to deal with you as an individual. If you are different or have special needs, the larger organization will just chew you up and spit you out, like the army did with me. (Actually, I planned it this way, but eventually I would have been chewed and spit anyhow.) This process is good in terms of getting out of bad situations, but bad for your chances of finding stability.

Another way of looking at this is that organizations like high school, corporations, and the army are geared up for only one thing, success. If you are not on the success track and they can't get you on board with a minimum of effort, then you become a nuisance. You are interfering with their success and will soon find yourself in the proverbial spittoon. If this happens enough times to you, then you will become very adept at managing failure, as mentioned in a previous method, with no ability to manage or even accept success. You will win the battle but lose the war, as they say.

Now what to do? I'm twenty-six and married. I can still fit everything I own into my VW van. (I upgraded from the Beetle.) I interviewed for jobs in and around New York, even though I didn't want to live or work there. It was polluted, dirty, and dangerous. I wanted to get back to Europe to find that girl I was married to and to re-create that junior year abroad. One interviewer for an international insurance company suggested I go to the American Graduate School for International Management (now the Thunderbird School for Global Management) near Phoenix, Arizona.

Imagine me, the person who had flunked as many courses as he had passed with a master's degree. What a joke!

I applied to this school, a photography school on the West Coast, and the University of Denver as an undergraduate. My idea there was to go to Denver for one year to get a second bachelor's degree from them and then apply to their law school. Skiing had nothing to do with it, I swear. I had some good recommendations, and I was accepted to all three. The photography school was another stab at the art thing. The law school thing was a stab at reality. My wife convinced me to go to graduate business school. I was thrilled that any graduate school would accept me, but I was bummed out about Denver and the second pass at art school.

There is always a feeling of uncertainty when you make a choice between positive opportunities. I always think about what might have happened if I had made a different choice than the one I actually made. An experience junkie, I fantasize about outcomes. Several motion pictures have been made using this concept. Sometimes I just try to figure out if my choice were made by listening to myself and using my instincts or if another person or persons just convinced me. You can never really be sure, but it is a thought process I cannot escape. I also think that guys always think about missed opportunities. What women think about along these lines, if anything, is a mystery.

When I arrived in Phoenix, I was terrified and studied so hard that I wound up being seventh in my class. I took off the summer and drove back east to paint houses to help pay for school. People were very generous, as they often are with students, and I made a lot of money.

# METHOD—Self-Hypnotism

I had been smoking cigarettes steadily since age seventeen or so and wanted to quit. I scoured around for a method to quit that did not involve willpower, something I did not have a lot of. A hypnotist in Jersey City, Dr. Aronson, convinced me to take a full course in self-hypnotism. This guy was a trip. He even "looked" like a hypnotist. He was thin with slicked hair. His narrow goatee required daily attention, no doubt with one of those magnifying mirrors. He sat behind a huge desk that must have seemed more impressive from his side than from mine. You knew there was some sort of lewd material in that desk. Certificates and pictures of celebrities and politicians were all over the wall behind him. He was stylized. People who are stylized look their part.

I began going there once a week for two months. He was a great hypnotist and a real nice guy. He once hypnotized sixteen people in the front rows of a crowd at a convention. He did this without saying a word, and they didn't even know he was a hypnotist. He hypnotized me in different ways and used machines like brain wave synthesizers. I had hallucinations and wild dreams. He taught me how to hypnotize myself and create positive thoughts. I would write these down on small cards and look at them just before I hypnotized myself. Then I would repeat the positive phrase over and over while hypnotized. An example would be "I find smoking five cigarettes a day to be enough for me." The mind apparently will only accept positive thoughts while in a hypnotic state.

Needless to say, I stopped smoking. He had replaced the habit of smoking with the habit of nonsmoking, a hard concept to grasp. He told me, if I wanted to retain the skills I had learned, I would have to hypnotize myself twice a day. The basic concept of hypnotism, as he explained it to me, is that you only use about 8 percent of your brain's capacity even when you are concentrating. When you are hypnotized, all of the brain's capacity is available to you. After you come out of it (regain full consciousness), you have the full capacity, but it diminishes rapidly. It is something you need to practice.

I made up a bunch of positive message cards and started to hypnotize myself twice a day for fifteen minutes. It was fun, a very positive experience, and I was getting really good at it. When I returned to school in Arizona, I started using hypnotism for studying. About four months after I had returned, I had an interesting experience with language study. The method of teaching language there was to have the student memorize dialogues, real-life situations between two people in a foreign language. You had a partner, and you would recite the dialogue with the partner once and then switch and recite the other half of the dialogue. It was very effective because, when you were in a real conversation in the foreign language, you would always have something to say without having to think it up. You just remembered a phrase from one of the dialogues, and it flowed out. The bad part was that you either got 100 percent on each dialogue, or you failed it. If you did not memorize the dialogue, then you had the added burden that your partner would probably also fail the dialogue. You were, in effect, screwing your partner.

One day I was really late in starting to learn the dialogue. I decided to hypnotize myself to learn it even though I had not been using that method. I hypnotized myself for fifteen minutes and then started working on my dialogue. I memorized a German dialogue with 172 words in it (24 of which I had never seen before) in eight minutes. I got 100 percent on it. I thought I would try it out on tennis.

I was playing tennis every day. Phoenix is perfect for tennis. I played regularly with my next-door neighbor Doug, a good friend. One of the things you must do in tennis to play well is to keep your eye on the ball. I started hypnotizing myself before playing and suggesting to myself that I keep my eye on the ball. After a little practice, I was concentrating so well that I could read the name on the ball as it streaked over the net. I was elated. My game improved about 100 percent.

One day after a game, Doug informed me that he could not play tennis with me anymore. I thought he was joking and asked him why. He told me that I was no fun to play with like I used to be. I used to joke around and do fun stuff on the court. He said that now it was like playing with a tennis robot. I think I was also regularly kicking his butt. That was the last time I hypnotized myself for a long time. I had taken it too far. I have a natural tendency to take something that works and try to apply it to as many things as possible.

If you are going to try out a powerful method like self-hypnotism, make sure it is under control. You need to evaluate it from time to time to see its effect on your overall being. A good way to do this is to keep a journal. I'll have more about journals later.

I still use self-hypnotism from time to time. If I get tired doing something like writing this book, I will hypnotize myself for a few minutes, using a phrase like "I find writing to be fun and interesting" and then pound out a few crisp paragraphs without much effort. If I wake up at night and can't get back to sleep, I hypnotize myself or meditate

By the way, self-hypnotism has a lot in common with meditation and certain types of exercise. I will discuss them as I progress to those points. I have not used self-hypnotism on a regular basis for a while, but I sometimes use it for relaxation. On several occasions when I was particularly upset about something, usually the behavior of someone close to me, I would hypnotize myself for shorter periods, say ten minutes, but I would do this five or six times a day. It was a better approach for me than giving vent to the anger.

After the summer of painting houses, my wife and I flew down to Mexico City to visit a Mexican couple we had become friends with at school. One day I found a twelve-string guitar in the antique section of the city for fifty dollars. I had always wanted a twelve-string guitar. I could not convince my wife to let me buy it. The next day we all left for Oaxaca for a few days. This is about an eight-hour drive south of Mexico City. I kept lobbying for the guitar in Oaxaca and finally won her over, probably by using the guilt trip about her having ordered a solid gold custom-made bracelet the day before.

We set out to return to Mexico City. I was driving. The weather soon turned grey, and it began to rain and then pour. The roads in Mexico are not what we are used to in the States. When it began to get dark, we were still about four hours from the city. We were driving over a pass, and there were rockslides caused by the rain, which was torrential by this time. The authorities had left these little kerosene lamps near the rockslides, which gave an eerie, ominous glow. The others suggested we stop for the night. I was possessed by the guitar and ignored their pleas to stop. I gripped the wheel tightly with both hands and sped through the night with my head bobbing back and forth in time with the windshield wipers. We got home at midnight, exhausted.

At eight o'clock the next morning, I was bouncing around like a five-year-old, making noise to get everyone up to go downtown so I could buy the guitar. Of course, it had been sold the previous day. I was really pissed, but as a guest in someone else's house, I thought it would be inappropriate to start throwing temper tantrums. That is when I started hypnotizing myself to cool off. Whenever my blood would begin to boil, I would excuse myself and hypnotize myself in our guest bedroom. There is also a moral to this story. If you see something you like and want, don't think it over and come back. Buy it now! It works every time.

The actual technique of hypnotizing yourself is fairly simple. You write out a small card with a positive thought on it. Negative thoughts apparently do not work. An example might be, "I find washing the car to be pleasant and enjoyable." You then sit in a chair, look at the ceiling, take a deep breath, hold it for a second, and then exhale as you drop your head to a normal position. You are immediately hypnotized. (Let me qualify that. You are hypnotized if a professional in this technique has trained you.) You then repeat the phrase you wrote down for fifteen minutes. You automatically wake up at the end of the fifteen minutes. You then tear out and wash every nut and bolt on the car while whistling a happy tune. I'm only kidding about that! You just wash the car as you normally would, but the part about it being a chore is removed. There may be many other techniques for self-hypnotism, but this is the one I learned. It would be interesting if there were some way to hypnotize your spouse and tell him or her how enjoyable things like washing the car could be. How about socks hanging out of the hamper? Even better, the toothpaste tube. See the *Stepford Wives* first. I would watch this anytime just to look at Paula Prentiss, but it is a cult classic movie about a town named Stepford where the husbands replace their wives with pleasant, accommodating robots.

# METHOD—Find an Activity That Does Not Require a Lot of Thinking But Takes a Long Time; Use This Time to Let Your Internal Dialogues Play Out

The summer I learned self-hypnotism and painted houses to pay for school and the trip to Mexico, a method just sort of invented itself. Some people hate painting. I love it, and I'll tell you why. I usually have a dialogue going in my head. This dialogue is usually with some person who is bugging me. I have this conversation over and over again. Each time I change the conversation slightly, eventually I gain the upper hand. It is almost like a script.

Painting is fairly strenuous and involves a lot of repetitive actions that you don't really have to think about. What I found was that these internal dialogues would stretch out into full-blown scenarios. They would sometimes last for hours. When they were over or rather complete, the entire thought would just disappear. The problem would no longer be bugging me. I learned several years later, I think in one of Dr. John Lilly's books, the mechanics of this process. He called these repeating, short thoughts "repeating tape loops." It is like a tape recorder that repeats the same thing over and over, like an echo chamber that rock musicians sometimes use. By allowing the long thought to play itself out, I was killing off the repeating tape loop. I can sometimes use this method when I am working in the yard. Perhaps it would work if one took long walks on the beach.

You sometimes hear people like over-the-road truck drivers say, "When I get out on the road, I leave all my troubles behind." Cruising sailors who spend a lot of extended time on the water talk the same way. I have crossed the country five times by car. I have done it in three and a half days, and I have done it in twenty-six days. Driving long distances has the same effect on me that painting does. I remember reading an interview with Robert Redford. He loved to drive long distances and said in the interview something to the effect that he could drive from L.A. to New

York and make a U-turn at the Holland Tunnel to Manhattan and do it all over again. You would think that a person like Robert Redford would have more exciting things to do with his time. I have a feeling that a lot of truck drivers and sailors have anxiety problems. Maybe Robert Redford does as well. Think about that.

# METHOD—Crafts and Knots

I have to talk about crafts a bit. If I don't, several people will think I have overlooked a vast resource. Crafts and art are different, even though some crafts involve art. Some people think that anything you determine to be art before you start doing it is art. So if I decide to make two macramé belts and decide that one will be a belt and the other will be art, that one will be a belt and the other will be belt art? We have all seen our fair share of dumb art.

Actually, I was reminded of my involvement with crafts recently when an old friend emailed me and mentioned she was spending a lot of time crocheting. I have watched my mother do petty point and my grandmother, Bubba, sew stuff. Bubba was a consummate professional, having won the Vogue prize for design several times. They seemed absorbed in their task. I also had a friend at graduate school whose wife was a veritable knitting machine. It seemed like she could knit a fisherman's type of sweater in about an hour. Actually, it took about a week. She could do just about anything while knitting, especially talk.

During my summer break from school, I took up macramé to earn a little extra money and to kill some time. We were living with my wife's parents, and I needed to get away from the intense three-child-driven family banter. My mother-in-law owned an upscale dress shop, and I had a ready place to sell my wares. I also got 100 percent of the sale price. Being a poor student has its advantages.

Macramé is a system of tying knots in cord or string and, in the process, joining the cords to adjoining cords, thus making a pattern. A belt, for instance, will have typically sixteen different cords that are all tied together. There is a bit of planning necessary as, the more knots you tie in a cord, the shorter it becomes in relation to the other cords. I was making a lot of belts and chokers. I could make a belt in about four hours. I started off doing this for money but wound up doing it for the relief it gave me. I was able to think about things clearly when I was tying the knots. I kept this up for about a year. There are all levels of this and other crafts. Some well-known artists use macramé in their works, and I have

58

seen some remarkable pieces that must have taken hundreds of hours of planning and production.

On a lighter note, I heard a wonderful insult on the Imus morning radio show the other day. He was referring to a certain celebrity as having a macramé plant hanger hairdo. You don't have to see it to get the picture. He is a genius with insults.

Knots always fascinated me. There is a knot for everything. In sailing, you use knots that will untie easily for one purpose and knots that will not become untied under almost any circumstance for other purposes. There are knots for joining different thicknesses or rope and for hauling overboard sailors out of the water. I found a great knot tying learning aid in a yachting store. It is called the "knot tying game." It is about the size of a pack of cigarettes. You get two cords, two sticks to tie knots onto, and a bunch of cards with knot names on one side and how-to pictures on the other. Knots are rated numerically according to the level of difficulty.

Now I can't imagine sitting around on the floor somewhere and actually battling it out with an opponent, bowline against surgeon's knot, but I bought the game because of its compact size. It is small enough to carry in your briefcase. People look at you with raised eyebrows when you pull this out on an airplane or train, but I figure that ultimately, they will come to the realization that you are smarter than they are.

"Care for a game of knots?" After all, people pull out their knitting all over the place. Perhaps knot tying will gain that level of acceptance someday. Knot tying is a good anti-angst way of passing otherwise static time and results in practical knowledge, especially if you have hobbies like sailing. In one of my next lifetimes, I am going to go to MIT and get a PhD in knot tying. My dissertation will be on the theory of knot creation. I have a feeling that several knots came into being by some higher intelligence acting on a length of rope that was simply dropped on the ground. When the owner picked up the rope, this higher form of intelligence created this splendid knot. I could spend my graduate years and perhaps make a career out of dropping lengths of rope from different places and evaluating the knots that were created. I could invent the Wise Knot that would keep shoes tied for the lifetime of the owner. I think they have a place for people like this, the nut house.

I got this wild idea in my second year of business school, commonly referred to as T-Bird, to get a PhD. There are many reasons. I was counseled by a very influential economist, Dr. Bronson, and another PhD who married my wife's best friend. He was a professor at a major state university out West and invited me to join his program as a PhD candidate. Through Dr. Bronson, I was invited to talk to some people at the Rand Corporation in L.A., a think tank, and I was very impressed that they were getting paid a lot to solve problems. The PhD was an entry ticket into this world and the world of government grants. I also had that fear of working in New York for a huge organization although I did not have a very good handle on why. I had a job waiting for me with a large international insurance company and an "in" with a large international bank. I had not learned enough about myself yet, but I could feel the fire on my face when I talked to businessmen in New York. I didn't think I would do very well in that environment. I was wrong, of course, but I had blown the opportunities I had.

You don't get asked twice in New York. I had made my decision to continue with school too late to apply for schools for the following academic year so I had to take a year off. Shucks! It was another opportunity to be irresponsible. I packed up and moved to Lake Tahoe, ostensibly to be near the university of my choice. I really believed my own BS. I never even formally applied even though the department head encouraged me to do so. There was no coincidence that major ski areas surrounded Lake Tahoe. I felt confident after getting the graduate degree. I wanted to follow my own path rather than get involved in some corporate training program.

I got a job in the Sahara, a casino, as a dishwasher. Their dishwashing machine needed eighteen people to run it. I actually jumped up and down in the parking lot when I got that job, the only time I have ever done that. I felt a lot of accomplishment in just picking up and moving somewhere and getting a job. I was elated. Things were going well. After three nights, the steward approached me and offered me the job of head dishwasher. I had to promise that I would stay for the summer. Hey, I was really getting somewhere.

Two weeks later, my wife came home and told me that the cook had quit at the restaurant where she was working and she had thrown my name into the hat. I interviewed, and they offered me the job. They were all people like me, and it was one of the "in" places in town. I went back to the steward and told him about this. I said I would keep my promise to him and stay there if he wanted to hold me to it. He said he believed you should never keep a person from advancing himself and released me from the promise. It was such a small job and such a big idea. It is not a method, but it's a story I wanted to tell.

Tahoe had the highest unemployment and VD rate in the country, according to local legend. That may not be a fact, but everyone sure acted like it. A lot was going on. I could write a whole book on that one year. When I closed the kitchen at night, I had a choice. I could make a left, go out the door, go home, and go to bed, or I could make a right, take four steps to the bar, and join the party that was already in full swing. If I went home, I could go skiing the next day. I loved skiing, so Monday through Friday, I was standing at the lift when the lift operator arrived. I had no problems when I was skiing. Part of this is because I was an expert skier and I could concentrate on the nuances, minor improvements. I skied fifty-five days. I was a ski bum. Cool!

# METHOD—Choose a Sport Where You Don't Have to Compete with Others But One Where You Can See Measurable Improvements in Your Ability

I suggest skiing, golf, pool, swimming, ice skating, bowling, some martial arts, jogging, archery, or target practice, all sports like that. The reason I recommend individual sports is that you are not going to run into someone who is not as good as you are but can beat you because that is his or her prime interest in the sport, beating someone. Beating someone inflates his or her ego. Improving personally at a sport deflates your anxiety. It is also good for your body. I even invented a game where I could keep score against an imaginary opponent, which was of course me. You can pretend you are Jimmy Connors, one of my heroes, trouncing McEnroe or just hit the ball. I would go up to the 92nd Street Y in New York, suit up for racquetball, and go into a racquetball court. I used a children's tennis racket and a tennis ball and whacked my way through an hour using tennis rules. Because I was in such a small space and the ball could ricochet off side walls and corners, there was enough chance in the game to keep it interesting. I might have gotten the idea to invent my own game from Joe Sobek, the inventor of racquetball and the pro who gave me my first tennis lessons.

I have one warning about golf. It is a very complicated game that involves the training of both your brain and about every muscle in your body. In my caddying days, I saw people who were playing golf ostensibly for relaxation but, on occasion, were so angry that the veins in their neck were ready to pop. I have seen golf clubs thrown into lakes, bent over knees, stomped on the ground, and wrapped around trees. Be careful and think about whether it is good for you. Some of the most beautiful places on earth are golf courses, and the players are generally a social group. There is a lot of yin and yang in golf.

Jogging is generally accepted as a good aerobic exercise. You have to be extremely careful about jogging if you are out of shape, sedentary by nature, or over forty. My best friend Bob called me up one day and said, "Remember what you said about things starting to fall apart when you turn forty?"

"Yeah, vaguely," I replied.

"Well, I started jogging on my fortieth birthday, and everything fell apart."

I had a forty-ish neighbor who dropped dead one day after jogging for a few weeks. It was too much too quickly. I know another fellow who is an all-around great athlete who damaged his knee so severely running a long distance that he had to give that and skiing up. Jogging and running are potentially hazardous to your health. You will need these joints when you get older, especially the knees, so take it easy. You also have a fair chance of getting run over if you jog outside on the road. I prefer walking. I'll have more on that later.

# METHOD—Throw Out Any Human Scales in Your House

These are the ones you weigh yourself with. The reason is simple, as Steve described. If you lose weight, you are happy. If you gain weight, you are depressed. Who needs that kind of a seesaw on the bathroom floor? I don't own one. I have read a lot of books about diet, nutrition, and exercise. You would have to exercise so long to lose any weight that you would practically have to devote your life to exercise to make any real progress. Exercise of the right intensity and duration will burn off fat, but you may lose only minimal weight. (See METHOD—High-Rep Low-Pound Free Weights for an explanation.)

Trying to lose weight is a dangerous thing for anxiety-prone people. I have tried a few popular diets and, in every case, suffered some dangerous side effects, including a blockage in my colon, and I'm not even a blimp. My doctor told me that I almost had an impaction that would have had to be removed surgically. This is where your stool gets so dense that it is like wood. It took me three and a half painful agonizing hours on the toilet to pass it. Afterward I felt like I had been cornholed by an elephant. I have a genetically supplied fat stomach that I anguish over, no matter how much I weigh. It was there at 136 in the army when I was anorexic, and it was there at 220. So it will probably always be there. If the diet mongers who bombard us in every type of media with diets would forget the words "lose weight," we could make some progress. Every person with at least two functioning brain cells knows that fad diets generally result in a net gain in weight over time, yet we as a nation spend literally billions on quick fixes, ones that don't work.

(I have to zoom forward a few years for the following, but I will return.) Here is a quick explanation of why diets don't work. I must add, "all other things being equal." I had heard this many times but needed to get two certifications as a personal trainer to have it finally penetrate my thick skull. There is so much misinformation out there that we are really brainwashed on this by the diet industry. Sometimes they overload us with information to confuse us and then sell us on their way. Note that this is my explanation and grossly oversimplified, so just follow the main points. Let's say you are on a 2,000-calorie per day diet. You decide to cut back in a drastic way to lose weight. You drop five hundred calories a day. This sounds reasonable enough, right? Much less than a banana split or a Twinkie and a classic Coke. Wrong! Your body tells your brain, "I'm starving." After all, you have cut out 25 percent of what is coming in. What if that happened to your salary? Would you freak out or what? Your brain is like the guy that sets gasoline prices, quick to overreact but slow to adjust to reality. The price goes up quickly but comes down slowly. Just because you decided to lose weight by using your brain, don't think that your brain has any idea of what you are trying to do. The brain adjusts to starving by lowering your metabolism, which lowers the number of calories you need to not starve. This is why the major amount of weight loss on a diet is so dramatic in the beginning but soon tapers off.

The second thing that happens is that your body runs out of fuel. You need fat and sugar as fuel, and you have stopped eating these, so yada, yada, yada, you are low on fuel. The brain decides to convert some protein into fuel. The protein in your body is mainly muscle, so the body converts some of that into fuel. So you lose weight, let's say ten pounds, before you stop losing weight and get disgusted and start eating again, or the holidays roll around and give you a ready-made excuse. Let's say you go back to your old eating habits like the last five times you tried to lose weight. Let's also say that you lost six pounds of fat and four pounds of muscle total during your diet. Muscle burns forty to fifty calories a day doing nothing. Fat burns ten to fifteen calories. So, you gain the fat back in two weeks. Do you think you will gain back the muscle without doing anything? Of course not! So four pounds of muscle times forty calories equals 160 calories a day that you are not going to burn off because you went on a diet to lose weight. A pound of body weight is generally believed to be worth about 3,500 calories. These 160 calories a day that you are not burning off because you decided to lose weight and went on a diet add up to about a pound a month. That is twelve pounds a year, folks.

What about your metabolism? Remember the guy setting the gasoline prices? He is going to be slow to return that metabolism back to the 2,000-calorie-a-day burning level because you cannot be trusted not to attempt to starve him again! So, when you gain that ten pounds of fat back, expect to gain a few extra pounds of fat because of the price-fixing guy. So a year after deciding to lose weight by going on a diet, you have gained fifteen to seventeen pounds.

This is why diets do not work. Forget diets and losing weight. Learn what diet really means in terms of food value, and erase "losing weight" from your vocabulary.

When someone remarks, "Hey, you look like you lost some weight," say, "Okay, waddyawant?"

No, you should really say, "No, I actually burned off four pounds of fat and added one pound of muscle mass to my glutes."

They will probably say, "Whaddayatalkinabout?"

(Remember the "all other things being equal" quote? Remember that. I will return from the future to my timeline and give some ideas.)

Being overweight can and is a cause for anxiety in people prone to anxiety. If you are concerned about weight, first throw out the scales. Then nude up and take a good look in the mirror. The older you get, the more you look like your parents, right? Well, there is a small force at work here called genetics. No matter how much weight you lose, you are going to look like a skinnier version of your parents. Sorry about that, but it is true. Now that we have defined one term that determines what you look like, let's try another.

How about percentage of body fat? That is more important than calories, diets, losing weight, carb-loading, and all of that rubbish. Go to any gym, find out what your percentage of body fat is, and determine with a professional trainer and your doctor what the ideal percentage of body fat is for your body type. The next thing you do is to develop a diet—or the real meaning of the word, what you should eat—and an exercise program that increases your muscle mass and decreases the ratio of fat to your lean body mass. You may not have to lose any weight at all. Your percentage of body fat will decrease over time and will be sustainable. Your anxiety will decrease proportionally, both due to the exercise and the toning of your body.

Dieticians are probably the most underpaid and overtrained people in our society. You should be able to find one at a reasonable cost that will design a diet for you, one that fits your lifestyle, body type, and metabolism. The exercise program can be provided by most exercise clubs at a modest cost and are often free of charge. I pay thirty-nine dollars a month for my family, which includes the whole exercise club and counseling. What you want is a program designed for you, not something that is hawked on late-night TV by over-the-hill personalities.

# METHOD—Try Not to Get Upset about Anything You Don't Have Control Over

This is another short one. It is not easy to do. I have been using this one for a long time. It is also like a mantra to me now. When I was a kid, I was sure in my heart that we were headed for nuclear war. They were going to "drop the bomb." (The Japanese would add "again.") I used this as an argument when anyone would try to get me to do anything I did not want to do. What a pain in the ass I must have been. The government has proved me wrong so far by not dropping the big one. Let it be known that I am still on the case. Hollywood, with their incessant stream of doomsday movies, and I are going to be the dog with the bone on this one as long as the military has nukes.

Some examples of things you have no control over are how other people think, the government, bad drivers, show-offs, the French, and your mother not getting along with your wife. Pretty much anything that a comedian covers in a routine falls into this category. If you could control it, it would not be funny. Watching something you have no control over career out of control and crash can be anything from amusing to wildly entertaining depending on the amount of disdain you have for it. Great comedians like Bill Cosby, Johnny Carson, and George Carlin look or looked at the world from a slightly different angle than us mortals, and they are able to translate the inherent humor in uncontrollable things into words we can understand. Others like Don Imus exercise their attitude on everything. Their attitude allows them to also look at things from a different angle.

I'll return to Tahoe. Besides all of the fun I had, the skiing, hiking, recreational drugs (yup, tried them all), and the amazing people I met who were also extremely sensitive and talented people who had also dropped out, I began to learn about my spiritual side. If, at this point, any readers are thinking, "Okay, here it comes," relax. It is not. I had been reading the light works of philosophy ever since my philosophy 101 class at Parsons College. The professor was from the Oort cloud, where comets come from. He really stimulated me. For his first lecture, he climbed up on a table, assumed the cross-legged yoga lotus meditation position, and spent an hour telling us how to score well on his tests. I was the only one who took notes. I got a ninety-eight on the final. The light philosophy was, for example, Herman Hesse, Camus, and Aldous Huxley. I had an interest in the German philosophers because of my experiences in Austria where I had met extraordinary people ranging from Cistercian monks to defeated Nazis. Kant's *Critique of Pure Reason* finally stopped me in my philosophical tracks. In order for me to read philosophy, I have to be able to keep track of what is going on, to keep up with it. It is not unlike a tennis match. Tactics change throughout the course of the match, mainly due to the influence of the score. When I watch a tennis match, this is what I am concentrating on. Kant doesn't seem to follow the rules and left me in the dust. That's not the point though.

# METHOD—Meditation

In Tahoe, people were into things I had never imagined, no less ever heard of. Part of this must have to do with Tahoe being partly in California. Out there, you have to be "into" at least three things to even have a conversation with anyone. I had a lot of conversations with people who were into different things, like the fourth way, meditation, Kundalini, gurus, yoga, Gurdjieff, astral projection, transactional analysis, I Ching, numerology, Sylvan mind control, the Divine Light Mission, various religious sects, and a multitude of other things I have forgotten the names of. These were all philosophies in their own right but also were things you did rather than just read about, which differentiates them from the type of philosophy I was used to reading. A lot of these things required direct teaching by and interacting with others.

I talked at length with the believers and the curious. I tried a lot of the techniques but did not involve myself with complicated lifestyles that involved stuff like not talking for six months to learn how to communicate using methods other than speech. I picked up some interesting information. What I found helpful for my anxiety were transcendental meditation (TM) and Hatha Yoga.

A bunch of us in the restaurant where I was the cook with the master's degree in international marketing decided we were going to take up TM. This was popular and would give us something to be into. The leader of this type of meditation was the Maharishi Mahesh Yogi, an Asian Indian holy man. During the initiation, you are given a mantra, what you repeat over and over for fifteen minutes twice a day. Does this sound familiar?

What I learned about this process is that the mind is a progressive thought machine. One thought always leads to another. Imagine a bubble that starts at the bottom of a large fish tank. It is compressed at the bottom because of the water pressure. It grows as it rises to the surface and finally pops open when it breaks into the air. This is like our thought process.

Our conscious thought is on the level of the surface. The person meditating is trying to have his or her consciousness move down to the origin of that bubble where the center of all creativity, love, and goodness is. I realize this is a vastly oversimplified version of TM, so don't send me emails. I am trying to make a point. The way you reverse the progressive thought process is to repeat a mantra, in my case, a two-syllable phrase with no meaning. You get this from the yogi, and this is your connection to him. He is connected to God. Repeating the mantra reverses the thought process and allows your consciousness to go toward better places. Eventually you stop thinking altogether, an enlightening experience in itself. This is an extremely good way to dispel anxiety and refresh yourself. I still use it, especially when I wake up and can't get back to sleep.

One great use of meditation is that it usually identifies what is bugging you the most. By repeating a mantra, you are trying to stop and reverse the normal thought process. When you first begin, random thoughts and concerns interfere with your efforts. Usually with practice, you are able to concentrate on the mantra and move beyond the interfering thoughts. Sometimes you are not able to get past them. The most persistent thought is usually the one you are the most concerned with. I am sometimes surprised at the one that turns up. I would guess that I am surprised because I am in denial, as we all are to some extent about some aspect or issue in our lives. By denying that something is bugging us, we don't have to deal with it, at least for the time being.

TM is only one form of meditation. There are more advanced forms like Kundalini where you concentrate on opening the various chakras, energy centers, in the body. This requires a lot of time and study. There is no rocket science to basic meditation. You can even make up a mantra and give it a try. Just make sure it doesn't sound like anything real, or you will think of that. It should be two nonsense syllables like sta-mo. Sit in a comfortable chair without folding your arms or crossing your legs. Close your eyes and begin repeating the mantra to yourself silently. As thoughts spring up, just try to get back to repeating the mantra. Don't try to analyze what is going on. Tell yourself when you begin that you are going to meditate for fifteen minutes. Your brain can calculate this to the second. You will always feel better after meditation than before it.

Coincidentally the teaching center of the Maharishi Mahesh Yogi is my old alma mater, Parsons College. Parsons went out of business primarily because of an article in *Life* magazine, a very popular and influential magazine back in 1965, that was entitled, "The Wizard of Flunk-out

U." It was about the president of the school who had taken it from a small Midwestern church-affiliated college to the nation's largest business school in about five years. The school had a reputation of accepting almost anyone. They wound up with a lot of rich underachievers, flunk-outs from better schools, and social misfits. Its reputation as a party school was well deserved. Every other house in town was a party house, which was exclusively reserved for that purpose. Ours was the Fairfield Yacht Club, of which I was the commodore. Our yacht basin was a cast iron, claw-footed bathtub in the driveway. I had gone from flunk-out U to transcendental U.

# METHOD—Hatha Yoga

The other major thing I was introduced to in Tahoe was hatha yoga. One of the waitresses at the restaurant, Priscilla, a physically and mentally beautiful person, was into yoga. One night she showed me the sun worship exercise, a sequence of twelve positions, all linked, that return you to the first position. It was one of the most beautiful things I have ever seen. She followed an Asian Indian named Swami Vishnudevananda. He has a book entitled *The Complete Illustrated Book of Yoga*, a wonderful book with a good basic written description of the principles of yoga and pages of photos.

I started the next day. I bought a paperback version of the book, spread out a towel on the floor, and began imitating the photos in the book (Note: This book may be out of print. I found one in hardcover a few years ago, at a used bookstore on Cape Cod. I have given away many of the paperback versions.) The *Complete Illustrated Guide to Yoga* became my spiritual bible and main anxiety fighter for the next twenty years. Hatha yoga is the physical side of yoga, the exercises you do to bring your body into balance with nature. It is based on various positions, "asanas," most of which stretch muscles.

To the beginner, some of these asanas look like the work of a contortionist. Actually, like anything, practice will bring you closer to the perfect ideal even though you may never attain some of the more advanced positions. You can actually gain a great deal of strength from practicing these asanas. One set of muscles must usually contract to stretch another set. An exception is where you are using gravity to stretch muscles. In this case, there is usually still some contracting tension to maintain balance. You also gain a lot of flexibility, especially in the spine, and your balance will improve.

If you practice yoga an hour a day, you will avoid most of the usual muscle strains associated with advancing age. When you complete what I call a "round" of yoga, which usually takes about an hour, you are completely flatlined as far as anxiety goes. This is also a form of repetition and reversing of the thought process. Meditating after yoga can send the anxiety packing for quite a while.

I also found that yoga helped me quite a bit in later life. In my business career, I traveled back and forth to Africa for two years and wound up living there for another two years. This was a hard time for me for both business reasons and unresolved issues between my second wife and myself. During this very angst-ridden time, I practiced yoga virtually every day except when I was on an airplane. Those four years were probably the most anxiety-ridden in my life. I credit yoga with basic survival in my life during that time. Many days it was the only thing I looked forward to, and many days it was the only good thing that happened.

One of the most important aspects of hatha yoga is breathing. Yogic breathing is an important aspect of a lot of the meditative arts. You breathe in by relaxing your stomach, as opposed to heaving or expanding your chest. You exhale by compressing your lower stomach and visualize the breath going out through your chest. Your breaths are long and rhythmic. One of the first signs of my getting anxious is shallow breathing. These short breaths are confined to the upper part of the chest. I have noticed that even animals breathe like this when they get anxious. They pant.

Different practitioners inhale and exhale differently as far as the nose and mouth are concerned. Most inhale through the nose, and some exhale through the mouth, but all use the area about four inches below the navel as the point of concentration when inhaling and exhaling.

In several instances, usually after a round of yoga, I have had experiences that I can't explain. I can't produce these effects at will, but I suppose they have something to do with the effect of proper breathing. In one instance, I was doing a headstand, one of the last exercises in my round of yoga. I was alone. I felt a presence of someone outside of the two-floor house I was in. She didn't belong there. I was living with two guys, and we didn't usually lock the house. This person gained entry pretty easily. I could not hear anything, but I could follow her movements through the house, up the stairs into the hallway. At this point, I leapt out into the hall in my underwear, brandishing the machete that my father had brought back from Cuba. I still can't explain how I could almost see that person through the walls and floor of the house.

The person who was there had come to warn me about an impending bust at a neighbor's house with SWAT teams, helicopters, and all that. Her intentions were good, but I could not pick up on the positive aspect of it. I just knew there was someone in the house.

I just returned from a yoga class at my local gym. Boy, was that hard. I realized that, in all the years I was practicing yoga, I never took a class. I was using the training tables in the back of *The Complete Illustrated Book of Yoga*. I also realized I have never practiced yoga with anyone else even though I have demonstrated the sun worship sequence of asanas and some intestinal manipulation to others. The latter are some weird-looking stomach muscle contractions. I would suggest taking a class to get the idea of what you are trying to accomplish and also to ensure that you are practicing the asanas in the proper way.

I also experimented with fasting while in Tahoe. I usually did this with one or two other people. It was more fun that way, and we could give each other support when the hunger pangs would set in. Actually, I have never had a hunger pang. I get headaches if I don't eat, but I can't understand it when someone says he or she is starving. I just never feel that way. I have read that hunger has something to do with the vagus nerve. Maybe mine is missing a connection somewhere.

When I was growing, my mother used to say that I had one meal a day, all day. I once went for seven days with only a cup of coffee and water. I got pretty sick, and my body temperature rose to dangerous levels, but I never got hungry. One of my friends, Priscilla, had a method to avoid the hunger pangs and still get the benefits of a fast. We would go to the supermarket and buy all sorts of fruit juices. We chose the cheapest ones because they usually have little or no sugar. This is a good general food tip if you are concerned about sugar. There is sugar in almost all processed foods. It makes things taste good, but it still costs money, so they eliminate it or drastically reduce it in cheaper brands.

In the fast, which lasted for three days, you could drink all of the fruit juice and water that you wanted. On the third day, we would go for a good vigorous hike in the wilderness. The theory we used was that your body would start to eliminate toxic substances when it ran out of the usual stuff stored in the cells for energy. This was a very unsophisticated approach, but it seemed to work. We were all smoking cigarettes at the time. And sure enough, what appeared to be nicotine started oozing out on our skin in the third day. You would feel light-headed but still have a lot of energy. I did this about five times.

If you are going to try fasting, I would suggest you do some serious reading before trying it and only do it with people who are experienced. I would tell my doctor if I were going to fast again. I don't think many medical doctors would recommend fasting, but at least if they get a call in the middle of the night that you were unconscious, they could give a quick diagnosis. I carry three things in my wallet all the times, the business cards of my MD and lawyer, and a listings of my medications and supplements. I didn't see any benefit from an anxiety standpoint from fasting, so it is not a method. I'm sure it could be argued that the elimination of toxins from your system would help, but there are probably other ways to do that. I stopped smoking, which probably had more positive health implications than any amount of fasting could.

One important thing to remember is the importance of liquids when fasting. Even people on hunger strikes drink water and take some soup for basic nourishment. Dehydration is extremely dangerous.

# METHOD—High-Rep
# Low-Pound Free Weights

While I'm on the subject of exercise and repetition, let me redefine a sport and use it for the great anxiety battle. I am going to take an anaerobic sport that is used primarily for the sake of physical appearance in our culture, weight lifting, and change it a bit. Actually, weight-bearing exercises are necessary for older people to keep up the calcium levels in their bones. Free weights give better benefit than machines primarily because more muscles are used to try to control the weights while you do the repetitive exercises. I have lifted weights off and on since my teens, and I would recommend machines like Nautilus or Cybex, like those found in most health clubs, for beginners. You are less likely to get injured with machines because the movement is controlled, and you isolate the muscles you are working on. As you progress, you can move to free weights and get more muscles involved in each exercise. Your core muscles will also benefit from free weights.

I don't recommend using the heaviest weights that you can lift for the magic two sets of twelve repetitions required to fatigue your muscles. This is the "biggest and baddest" attitude promulgated by most health club trainers, and while it may puff you up, it will have no effect on anxiety. One of the objectives of weight lifting is good muscle tone, which can be maintained by using much less weight than the maximum you can lift if you increase the number of repetitions and schedule one or two more short visits to the gym per week. I spend about an hour per visit. I suppose you could use smaller weights on the machines if you don't care about everyone thinking you are a wimp.

That is what I do. I concentrate on slow, complete movements with twenty to forty pounds less than my capacity rather than short, macho blasts with heavy weights. I make sure I stop at the beginning and end of each motion. I actually let the weights touch the unused weights on the machine, like they would if you let go. This assures that you are not using a muscle bounce to aid the contraction, that is, using your muscles like rubber bands, which is nutty. Stopping ensures you get a full range of motion.

It would stand to reason that the slowing down of the weight to come to a full stop is harder than just going from one motion to another like a yo-yo and being the extra effort would be more beneficial to your body. If you use a ratio of 1:2 contractions to relaxation, relaxing slower than contracting, you will actually lengthen your muscles, which is beneficial for relaxation.

You can contract your muscles as much as possible, but you should not let your joints flex to the point where they are stretched to the full extent of their motion when you are lifting weights. An example would be exercising your biceps, the muscles on the front part of your upper arm. When you contract those muscles, you can come up and touch your shoulder, but you should not let your elbow stretch out flat when you lower the weight. Leave the stretching for the yoga session. I try to work the machines quietly.

Some people, like me, think of weight lifting and weight machine use as a form of meditation. A person who is grunting and smashing weights is either basically inconsiderate or trying to draw attention to himself (usually) or herself (rarely). A session or two with a personal trainer is recommended.

My free weight method works best at home. Get some light hand weights, the kind that you buy when you are going to turn over a new leaf. The cheapest ones come in fixed weights like five or ten pounds and are just plain old steel. They used to be called dumbbells. They even come in designer colors. These cost a lot more and are a lot more noticeable when sitting in the corner collecting dust. Keep your weights out where you can see them. It is a good reminder to use them.

I started with five pounds even though I can probably bench press two hundred pounds. The weight is not the point; the repetition is. Because you are using light weights, you will be able to do more repetitions, "reps" in gym slang. Take a part of your body that needs some work because, after all, we are going to fatigue the muscles, which will decrease intramuscular fat, that which resides within the muscle, and increase muscle mass.

I exercised the shoulders, arms, and chest when I first began this form of exercise. There must be fifty ways to exercise these muscles. I'm not going to describe them all. Just think about all the ways you can move your shoulder joint and muscles with a small weight in your hand. If you have a lack of imagination about muscle movement, tune into one of the cable TV exercise shows like ESPN 2's "Flex Appeal." It's hosted by Kiana Tom, a bubbly, well-shaped Hawaiian. She has more variations on each muscle than Arnold Schwarzenegger. She probably dissects cadavers on the weekend looking for new muscles. She is particularly good at cross-training, using a lot of different exercises and sports to keep the muscles guessing. There is something called the "waitress syndrome" in fitness training. Why does a waitress who probably covers three miles a day at work not lose weight? The answer is simple: the brain will find the most efficient way to do any physical movement that is repeated a lot. It might have something to do with the brain learning to fire the least amount of muscle groups to get a movement done, conservation of energy (to the detriment of a body that has more than enough caloric intake.)

The point here is to develop a series of movements and try to do a lot of reps of each. Count as you are going along. Breathe out when your muscle is contracting and in when it is extending. Do this for about twenty minutes. Now what was I obsessing about before I started? A thought that was driving you nuts just disappears. There's one more thing about weight lifting. If you go slow, you will build strength. If you go fast, you will build bulk.

One important thing to do when exercising with weights or weight machines is to think about the muscle(s) you are trying to exercise. This causes your mind to focus on the muscle and away from extraneous thoughts, including the ones you are trying to dispel.

If you do weight lifting in a gym or machines for that matter, you will undoubtedly be confronted with what I call the hamster element. These people skitter about from weight to weight and machine to machine. They puff and groan a lot, sweat, and bang down weights to draw attention to themselves. Some of them are in stupendous (looking) physical condition. I have built up a resistance to them over the years, but I would imagine they would be intimidating to a neophyte. Just think of them as hamsters spinning around on their little exercise wheels. Hamsters frequent my favorite machine, the treadmill.

I actually had a female hamster in Cambridge say to me, "With those long legs, you should be able to do better than that."

I said something like, "I'm recovering from a plane crash where my entire family and golden retriever died."

I have been using the treadmill off and on for years. I find it has all of the things I need to fight anxiety. If you have a machine that has a heartbeat-measuring device or you have one that you can wear on your wrist like I do, you can also bring great benefit to your heart. You have to keep your heartbeat to within a certain training range for twenty minutes. The best explanation of this theory I have found is in the excellent book, *The New Fit or Fat* by Covert Bailey. I have been carrying around the formula in my address book for twelve years. You subtract your age from 220. In my case, this equals 165. This is the maximum heart rate. Your training range should be between 65 and 80 percent of this maximum rate. There are exceptions, so read the book. You keep your heartbeat within this range for twelve minutes. (I have had some aerobic trainers use twenty minutes.) If you go longer than twelve minutes, it is still beneficial, but the benefit it has for your heart greatly diminishes compared to the first twelve minutes. You will be surprised at the slow speed that you have to walk on the treadmill to keep within your ideal range. For a full description of the method I use to take advantage of the treadmill, see METHOD—Power Walking further on. Covert Bailey gives lectures on his methods. I have seen him a few times during public television fund-raisers. He has a great wit and is a good motivational speaker.

There are several other theories of percentage of heart rate; maximum; reserve; the Karvonin method, which includes average resting heart rate in the formula; and another that calculates the percentage of maximum oxygen uptake, but the above method is easy to remember and is close enough. The important thing is to get out there on a regular basis and do it. I try for five days a week. There are many ways to get your heart rate into the zone, including jumping rope, bicycling, rowing, or walking, none of which necessarily involves a trip to the gym.

# METHOD—Take a Day Hike

Something I should not leave out—and something I spent a lot of time doing in the mountains—is hiking. If you are near some mountains or even some good hills, this can be a real treat. I always feel great after a good day hike. I usually take along lots of fresh fruit so I won't have to carry water or risk getting giardia from polluted water. Giardia is a diarrhea-type illness caused by a parasite that exists worldwide in the colons of people and animals and is found everywhere in untreated water. It is one of the most common sources of waterborne disease.

Anyhow the best kind of hiking to feel better involves going up and down hills or rocks. This really stretches your muscles and gets your lungs working. I even made a few day hikes in my bare feet. Tahoe is great for this because there is a lot of exposed granite you can walk on. I found myself using my feet like hands gripping the rocks. You also don't have to bend over all the time to examine things. You just use your feet to explore things. There were no rattlesnakes there, so this was okay.

The great thing about hiking is that you get to know your body. You can pace yourself and see how far you can go before you tire. I feel like my batteries have been recharged after a good hike. I don't camp out because I don't like what comes crawling out after dark. When a UCO—an unidentified crawling object—goes streaking across my neck, that is it for the night. I'm up. I also don't like to start fires in the forest. It takes a nice place and makes a great mess out of it. If I started a forest fire, I would feel bad for the rest of my life.

The benefits of a good day hike last well into the following week. If I go out hiking on the weekend, it gives me something nice to think about well into the workweek. Most areas I have visited have books of trail maps for day hikes. You can find these in bookstores and libraries. Ski areas are a good place to hike in the summer. Get a trail map. Some ski areas have slopes that do not go back to the lodge. If skiing, you have to take a lift back to the top. If you are walking, that would mean a climb back to the top.

# METHOD—Learn to Control Your Breathing

Breathing is so important that it deserves its own method. It is a fundamental aspect of so many different parts of our life and is the first thing to get interrupted when we get anxious. This is because it is automatic, controlled by our unconscious brain like our heartbeat. Any chemical change in our body or reaction by our nervous system will trigger what the brain considers to be the appropriate change in breathing and heartbeat.

A woman I met at graduate school told me that, when she started running with her husband, an inveterate runner, she had trouble with stamina. She could only run short distances. She thought she would be able to run longer distances with practice and was disappointed when she could not. Her husband thought about it and discovered, when he first began to run, he would start breathing deeply. If he waited for his body to signal his brain to change his breathing to get more oxygen, then he was already too far behind for his breathing to catch up. His wife tried this technique and, to her amazement, was able to run much longer distances. She described this as "learning how to breathe."

I have noticed that I often wound up in the same situation during job interviews or important meetings, even though I am not exerting a lot of physical energy. I begin to breathe in shorter, shallower breaths because I am anxious. This deprives my system of oxygen and, in extreme cases, leads to sweating, tunnel vision, a ringing in my ears, blood pressure changes, chills, and even a change in the pitch of my voice. What I think is happening is that my primitive brain, the one that controls all of the automatic functions in the body, is trying to figure out what is going on and is making all of the adjustments it can to compensate. It thinks you are having a life-or-death battle with a ten-foot boa constrictor when you are just sitting there having a conversation with a potential employer. I have had this happen so often that I can actually detect a blood pressure change in my body by listening to the ringing in my ears. When there is a change in pitch, I know the blood pressure is changing. The only way I can avoid this sequence of overreactions is to control my breathing.

I have to say over and over to myself, "Keep breathing. Keep breathing."

It works best when I have the foresight to say to myself, "Now this is going to be a stressful meeting. Let's start breathing now and continue through the meeting."

Write it down on a card next to the name of the person you are meeting with. I usually look at people's names on a card just before I meet with them because I am so bad in remembering names, so this is where I put it. "Mr. X" or "Ms. Y" and "Breathe." The type of breathing is the Yogic type, slow, rhythmic, and deep, expanding the stomach as you breathe in and pushing up from your belly button to exhale. You will not believe what a little oxygen can do to dispel anxiety.

If you are trying to learn how to control your breathing, try this simple exercise. Assume a comfortable position while standing or sitting. If you are standing, bend the knees slightly. Put your thumb in your navel, and drape your hand naturally over the area below your navel. You concentrate on this area. Relax your stomach muscles. Breathe in through your nose, and let the area under your fingers expand. Count to six while inhaling. Hold your breath for a count of three. Now exhale through your mouth, pushing up and contracting slightly the area under your navel. Count to six while exhaling. Think of your breathing. Listen to it.

If you get thoughts about anything other than breathing, let them go. Start with ten breaths, and increase the time you spend on this every day. There is a way to completely pack your lungs with air. I don't know what the purpose of this would be unless you were going to dive down to try to get someone out of a sunken car, but here goes.

Inhale per above. When you have inhaled to the maximum, think of filling the area just below your rib cage. This will require lifting the chest slightly. After this, think of filling the area behind your collarbones. This will require a further lifting of the chest. This three-part inhale will show you the different areas that can be filled with air. Most people just use the top one or two areas when breathing normally.

I have a good example of how quickly breathing—or the lack of it— can affect anxiety. A few weeks ago, a couple at our boat club asked my wife and me if we would go out sailing with them on their new boat and give them a few tips. They had bought the boat last year and were new to sailing. There was a sailboat race that day so we sailed out to join. Therry, the wife, was steering, and her husband, Mart, was working the lines that controlled the sails. My wife and I were passengers handing out advice and explaining the cause and effect of what was happening.

As we approached the starting line, Therry became agitated, and her eyes were darting all over the place, watching the other boats darting about and jockeying for position. She asked me to steer, but I refused and offered to talk her through it. I told her when to turn and gave advice to Mart about the lines. She was doing well mechanically but was getting more and more agitated.

I leaned over and said gently in her ear, "Keep breathing."

With that, she let out a huge breath that she had been holding for about a minute. We had a good laugh, and things went smoothly after that. So in sports, like so many other endeavors, a conscious effort to control your breathing will help you succeed.

I have one caution about deep breathing. I used to think it was cool to practice this Yogic breathing for a minute or two and then see how far I could swim underwater. I remember doing fifty-plus yards a few times. This is definitely not cool. I was packing my blood and lungs with as much oxygen as possible. This defeats the normal response of the body to the buildup of carbon dioxide in the lungs, which triggers normal breathing. In the most extreme case, holding your breath in this manner can lead to blackout. I would have then been underwater, unconscious, and I would eventually have inhaled a lungful of water. This would have made me heavier than water, and I would have sunk to the bottom of the pool and stayed there. Even if there were someone there to haul me out, I would have been dead weight and full of water, a challenge for any lifeguard. And there was no lifeguard there for the fifty yard-plus swim.

One of the best examples of this cascade of overreactions is when I am faced with the prospect of public speaking. I would rather take off my clothes in front of a crowd. I avoid public speaking like the plague. As you get older, it becomes harder to avoid this type of thing. My wife is great at public speaking. She can get up in front of four hundred people, often without notes, and talk for a half hour. Her method is to know the subject she is talking about. It is more complicated than that for me. I developed a few methods to make the public speaking ordeal a bit easier. Breathing, of course, gives me a head start.

Knowing my subject helps also. Usually you have to introduce yourself when you are part of a seminar or meeting. I have had trouble even describing myself, probably because I didn't know myself that well. I have a stock description prepared. I never try to memorize anything because, if you falter in remembering one thing, then everything that follows disappears. I try to remember a sequence of several words that are key to the ideas I am trying to express. You also have to think of it as an opportunity to tell others about yourself or your ideas rather than "why would they be interested in what I have to say."

I have had some hilarious things happen when I have been speaking in public. Usually people are forgiving in their criticism and don't bring up embarrassing moments after they happen. One time I was giving a toast in Holland in Dutch. I had sat in my in-laws' backyard, going over my Dutch toast for the evening. I remembered a sequence of words to keep me on track that evening. I delivered the toast okay, but my voice dropped about two octaves, and I forgot about my hand holding the glass with red wine in it. As I spoke, I proceeded to dribble a stream of wine on the person sitting next to me. People thought it was hysterical and, at the same time, got the emotional point I was trying to make. If you have to speak in public, get that breathing under control before it's your turn.

# METHOD—Leave Yourself Ample Time to Get Places

Last week I took the ferry in to New York to have dinner with some close friends. It was cold and windy, and my wife was going to be waiting outside on the dock for the ferry to arrive. Just as we got within sight of the dock, the captain announced we had to keep out of a certain zone, which included the dock, because the president of the United States, as he put it, was coming in by helicopter. We waited about fifteen minutes before the flotilla of menacing-looking choppers arrived and another ten minutes while the motorcades pulled away. After I met my wife, we managed to hail a taxi by some miracle and got caught in the ensuing traffic jam caused by the police closing down the entire Lower East Side of Manhattan so the president of the United States would not have to wait for any traffic lights.

I was getting really anxious. I hate to be late and have people waiting for me. I reminded myself to start deep breathing. I managed to contain my anxiety. This was good for two purposes. Being late is a pain, but when you arrive in an anxious state, it changes the whole tone of the meeting. Breathing deeply when pushed for time or performance will always lower your anxiety.

In the example I just used, I really had no control over the situation, so that was okay. Things happen. I just happen to care about getting somewhere on time, and others don't care or are just chronically late.

When someone says, "Hey, let's go to the movies," and the movies are fifteen minutes away and the movie starts in twenty minutes, I just say, "Have a good time." It is just not fun to be burning rubber to get anywhere. Everyone else is munching popcorn and trying to figure out what the movie is all about, and I am deep breathing under my jacket in my armpit, trying to get myself back under control.

# METHOD—Sing

Singing is dependent on knowing how to breathe. I was asked to join the glee club in junior high school. I was just too afraid of performing in public, of losing my invisibility, so I declined. The music teacher had tested all of us and said I had a great singing range. I did go to a practice to get the teacher off my back. I thought the members looked like puppets with their perfect posture and smiles. I later learned that the posture had more to do with breathing, to free the diaphragm to move, than with appearance. The smiles were because they were enjoying themselves. I had my family doctor also recommend I join the glee club. He was looking at my internal organs through some sort of antique machine and said my diaphragm had one of the greatest excursions he had ever seen. This is the distance it can travel. He thought, rightly so, that I could hold a note for a long time. I regret not joining the glee club. I should have suffered through it. I decided one day after I had started to work in New York, sixteen years later, that I was going to teach myself how to sing.

My immediate boss, Ralph, was a great singer. We were both working for a ship owner who owned fifty-three ocean going vessels. Our job was to find cargoes for them. Whatever situation you got into, Ralph had a song to cover it. I would be sweating over a piece of business, the mighty axe of the ship owner hanging over my head, and millions of dollars at stake, and he would break into a song that was vaguely apropos. Most of the songs he knew were classics. This would crack me up. He would have songfests every time we would get together for a Christmas party or someone's birthday. Ralph finally retired and bought a bar in Fort Lauderdale that had an open mike for anyone (and especially him) to sing.

For me, singing lessons were out of the question because I didn't want anyone to know about it. As soon as you announce something like that, people are clamoring for a demonstration, and they expect to hear Pavarotti. I knew scales from grammar school and just started singing in the car on the way back and forth to the train station. Other drivers often looked askance at this behavior, but I didn't care unless I was at a stoplight. Now that cell phones with microphones are popular, everyone appears as though they are talking to themselves anyhow. Musical scales are a bore, but I remembered from my guitar playing that I could not remember songs, so scales it was. I was after the effect anyhow. Singing is totally dependent on breathing. An acquaintance of mine told me that he had taken singing lessons, and the beginning was all about breathing. After only a few lessons, his range had increased dramatically. I kept at it over the years and have developed a voice that makes me feel wonderful when I employ it. It is a magical thing that comes from within your body and resonates. It is like controlled yelling. You get so much energy out of your body that it deflates that big bag of worry we all carry around.

Singing is another of those things that you don't have to be good at to get the effect. It is such an antique thing with humans, as old or older than talking, that it is part of our spirit. Give it a try. The only time I have ever sung for anyone was the song I used to propose to my wife, Marilyn. True to life, I forgot how to play it, but I still have the words.

Last year I was at an outdoor party standing alone, or so I thought, at the condiment table trying to decide which condiment would ruin my hot dog the quickest, and a friend said to me, "Nobody should be that happy." I looked at him perplexed at first and then realized I had been singing to myself. Of course, I blushed and then looked at my wife, who was in stitches. I felt wonderful afterward. Imagine that! Me just singing away at the condiment table.

If you don't like the singing idea, you can get a similar feeling in your body and the same overall effect by humming. Just make sure you are breathing correctly.

I have taken several group exercise classes like "Dancersize", step, and aerobics. I didn't get much out of it because, when I am not on skis, I am a total clod. I had hip problems when I was in grammar school. I was growing amazing amounts every year, and my nerves were just not stretching as quickly as I was growing. (An MD actually told me that.) My hips would dislocate on a regular basis under strain. Actually, they would start to pop out and then snap smartly back in. It is incredibly painful. Once in fifth grade, I hit a baseball so far over the left fielder's head that it took him about two minutes to catch up to it. (The field was on a slight slope, I must admit.) I was rounding second base, and the hip let go. I was still lying there two minutes later when they tagged me out. The medical community wanted to put me in a full body cast for six months until the cartilage in my hip joints ossified. I promised I would not do anything that would pop my hips for a year. I begged; I groveled. They let me off. The hip joints ossified, but the nerves never got there.

One basketball coach called me spaghetti legs. I'm glad that didn't stick. I was picked early on as a future basketball star because of my size. When we got to junior high, we finally got to meet some African American kids. One who became a good friend, Sammy, was a tremendous athlete. He could take a basketball away from me from twenty feet away. It got so bad that, if I saw Sammy coming at me on the court, I would just pass the ball to him to get it over with. Basketball was not my thing.

I'll come back to dancercise. I would stay at the back of the class and try to duplicate all of the movements. Every now and then, the class would hear a dull thud or clomp, clomp, clomp. Then they'd turn around to see me either sprawled on the floor or chasing my balance across the room. I even took classes about the classes. I see people at the gym bouncing around on the steps in step class. When they come out of the class, they all look the same, red and sweaty. They don't look calm like people coming out of the water. It must be great for the body, but I don't see how it can do anything for the brain because of the constant dum-da-da-dum-da-da-dum-da-da-dum music that they play to keep everyone in step.

I bought a book for a friend in a bookstore in Tahoe. It was entitled *The Center of the Cyclone* by Dr. John Lilly. It was one of those odd happenstances where I just reached out and pulled the book off the shelf. I had no idea what it was about. Dr. Lilly is a medical doctor, an LSD researcher (back when it was legal), a dolphin researcher, a mathematician, and inventor of the isolation tank. If you are not claustrophobic, you might want to find an isolation tank. I looked for one for years but never found one and gave up. I would still love to try one.

An isolation tank is a dark chamber that keeps light and most noises and vibrations from reaching you. You get in and float around in a saline solution, which neutralizes your weight. Your senses stop feeding a lot of information to your brain, and it is very relaxing.

*The Center of the Cyclone* was the most revelatory book that I had ever read. Dr. Lilly made an exhaustive study of metaphysics and combined this with his own self-experimentation and research to come up with some amazingly unique views on consciousness, among other things.

Metaphysics, according to the Metaphysics Research Lab at Stanford University is as follows:

Whereas physics is the attempt to discover the laws that govern fundamental concrete objects, metaphysics is the attempt to discover the laws that systematize the fundamental abstract objects *presupposed* by physical science, such as natural numbers, real numbers, functions, sets and properties, physically possible objects and events, to name just a few. The goal of metaphysics, therefore, is to develop a formal ontology, i.e., a formally precise systematization of these abstract objects. Such a theory will be compatible with the world view of natural science if the abstract objects postulated by the theory are conceived as (possible) property-patterns of the natural world."

My definition is that stuff that cannot be proved scientifically. Many of the methods in this book cannot be proved scientifically, but we all know they work. Theories like meditation, Tai Chi (where energy flows around in your body), and hypnotism are from a scientific standpoint just that, theories, ways of looking at things. So be it, if metaphysical things can help in my battle against anxiety, which is at least in part theoretical, then I'll use them.

Lilly also wrote *Programming and Metaprogramming in the Human Biocomputer*. If you want to learn more about how the brain works, this is a good source. He also has some interesting thoughts on high protein diets and tons of other stuff. John Lilly is still one of my heroes. Another good book about the brain is *The Origin of Consciousness in the Breakdown of the Bicameral Mind* by Julian Janes. Janes deals with the actual physical brain in human development and brings reality to such things as oracles and déjà vu.

# METHOD—Set Your Low Limits

Another great book that led to a method is *How I Found Freedom in an Unfree World* by Harry Browne. This is a brilliant book. I think that books are brilliant if they look at things in a fresh and new way. The main method I got from this book—and one I expanded into many aspects of my life to deter anxiety—was his concept of setting limits. I believe the main example he used, and one which we can all relate to, is money. You have to pick an amount of money that you don't care if you lose. I chose ten dollars.

You then have to say to yourself, "No matter what happens, I am not going to get upset about anything that costs less than ten dollars."

It is like magic. You are free from worrying about any amount less than the number you chose. No more kicking soda machines or pay phones. I almost got arrested in London for beating up on a pay phone that had consumed an entire pound sterling, about $2.25 at the time. That was before I read the book. I remember a time when I was driving from Phoenix to Mexico for the day with some fellow students. We stopped in a pancake house for breakfast. Everything came with pancakes. One of our group ordered some eggs and asked them to leave off the pancakes. The pancakes came anyway. He was incensed because of the idea that he was paying for something he did not want. When we left, he stood at the cash register, arguing with the manager until he got his thirty-one-cent refund. This is a guy who has a trust fund that will enable him to live without working for the rest of his life. I was very embarrassed by this episode, as were the others.

After reading the book and choosing ten dollars as my minimum, I noticed there were other things in life that were similar to the money. The mere fact of setting limits, lower limits, just evaporates a lot of anxiety for me. It is not that I don't care about the principle or the pancakes that my friend did not want forced on him, but I don't want the anxiety that goes with getting the thirty-one cents back. You can still keep your principles, but just apply them to items that cost over ten dollars. If a tire manufacturer guarantees that a set of tires will get 55,000 miles, I set my target at 45,000. I know I am not good at checking the tire's inflation all the time so I am not disappointed when I have to buy new ones at 45,000 miles. Sometimes it is a percentage. A pound of fish is the same to me as 0.8 pounds or 1.2 pounds (a little more or less). I'm not going to feel ripped off if I order a pound of fish and only get fourteen ounces. Some stores have a tiny bit more fat on their pork chops than others do. So what? If the amount is less than ten dollars, I don't care.

There is a song that goes, "Sometimes you win; sometimes you lose," but that is all I can remember of it. In business, this can be described as "take care of the downside; the upside will take care of itself" (quote by Steve).

In 1974, I decided I would move back East from Tahoe. It was a great lifestyle, but it had some drawbacks. I looked at some of the people who had been there for several years, and the boredom was setting in. They would wind up moving to a different ski area and doing the same thing all over. I was almost thirty and had not had a real job yet. I figured that the cutoff in business for hiring entry-level people had to be thirty. I separated from my wife that spring. We were friends, sort of. I had the summer off because the restaurant was being remodeled and I decided to stay for the summer to lick my marriage wounds. I rode my bike eighteen miles a day, hiked in the wilderness, swam in Lake Tahoe and my favorite Fallen Leaf Lake, played Frisbee in the mountain meadows, and hung out with my friends. I was so broke I could not afford gas for my VW bus.

It was a great summer, but California was starting to get on my nerves. You can't do anything alone in California. If you tell anyone what you are going to do, when you get there, it's like a tour bus just pulled up at your picnic site. I had more close friends in eighteen months than I had in my entire life. They were very nice people, and I still have a few friends from that group, but it was getting to be too much.

Let me say a few words about being alone. I am a firm believer in the fact that, if you can't be alone, then you can't be a full partner in a relationship. I have been in relationships where I was the dominant person and ones where I was the bug that eventually got stepped on. The ideal, of course, is the one where there is an interdependency that grows from sharing your best attributes, not your worst. My invisibility factor taught me how to be alone. I can be alone with no one around and alone in a crowd.

I'm not talking about ignoring people, but being independent of them. It allows me to go places that would otherwise cause me anxiety. It's like entering the water and becoming a part of it rather than just swimming in it. You can be in a crowd and become a part of it or be part of an empty field. It is hard to explain, so I will leave it as a comment instead of a method. I think it is something that can be learned.

I just took a break from writing and saw Charles Barkley, the former basketball star for the Phoenix Suns, being interviewed on TV. He said that, during a game, he always felt he was alone on the court. If he can feel that way with sixteen thousand fans yelling, ten players on the court, and a television audience of several million all watching him, I suppose that being alone in the crowd of sixteen thousand fans watching the game is highly possible. Once you accept this perception, you can be calm whether alone or in a crowd.

So I abandoned California and all of my friends out there. I started interviewing for jobs from New Jersey to New Hampshire. There are cycles in the business economy. One year, lawyers are in short supply, and they get high salaries. The next year, lawyers can't find a job, and everyone is hiring engineers. It is cyclical. My degree was in an international marketing. I contacted 224 companies in four months, and all I got was a lot of yawns. Marketing was not in the good cycle.

Finally in desperation, I turned to my father's industry, the shipping business. This was something I swore I would never do. I had better luck in this field. I was hired as a trainee ship broker in two weeks. A ship broker puts ships and cargoes like grain and coal together for a commission. You compete for business with other ship brokers. The company I worked for had brokerage contacts all over the world. Over several years, I worked hard learning the business, developed my own contacts, and became good at it. A few key elements allowed me to succeed at this job. The industry relies on trust and friendship. I worked for a small company with very supportive colleagues. Most importantly, almost all of the work was done on the telephone and the telex (a machine, pre-Internet, like a typewriter that can send messages to similar machines in the same city or worldwide using standard telephone lines). I did business with people I never met in places I had never been. The phone and telex were impersonal to a degree. They kept me one step away from the face-to-face meetings that were difficult for me. I was semi-safe. The worst situation for me would have been in some sort of sales where I had to present a product to an endless stream of people on a face-to-face basis.

# METHOD—Find a Way to Keep Score

After a few years of competitive brokerage, I was offered a job with a Greek ship owner, the biggest and baddest one. I jumped on board, doubling my salary. I didn't meet with him, but he knew my skills via my reputation, and I knew him through his immense success. (Actually I did meet him in my parents' house several times at dinner parties, but I was very young and probably in my pajamas.) Suddenly I was the person who everyone wanted to do business with because I was the one paying the commissions. I had power, money, and hockey tickets.

I once told a friend and colleague of mine, Ricardo, that I was not interested in all of this, especially the money. He convinced me that money was the only way in business that you could determine if you were playing the game well. It was a way to keep score. It became okay for me after that, one of those things I accepted instantly. I studied hard, worked hard, and played hard. I learned I was a natural negotiator and I could accept authority and use it. It was strange stuff for an anxious person. I learned a lot of business techniques working for that company. The person who coined the phrase, "You can't have it both ways," never negotiated with a Greek.

For three years, I worked with the Greeks, chartering super tankers. These ships can carry up to 340,000 tons of oil. That is about 99.96 million gallons, or about 7.14 million tanks of gas for my VW. After three years, he started selling off his fleet of ships. I knew there was an end to this idyllic work and lifestyle, so I started looking for a job.

The money example above worked in that particular instance by allowing me to keep score, but overall money is not that great of a measuring stick because of inflation. I'm not talking about inflation of the currency, but inflation of your ego. I learned a better way to keep score from one of my shrinks, Dr. Gray. He suggested I visualize two clear plastic tubes next to each other. They are just wide enough to hold quarters, which stack up neatly when you toss them in. When a good thing happens, toss a mental quarter into the good tube. And when a bad thing happens, toss a mental quarter into the bad tube. Every now and then, take a look at the tubes. You will be surprised at the result.

My brother likes to use the baseball batting average as a way to keep score. A good batting average in major league baseball is .300. This means that, for every ten times the player gets to bat, he gets a hit and gets on first base three times. The batter tries to have a high efficiency in his decision making. He can't always be swinging for the fence because the chances of getting a hit and a home run at the same time are less than getting a hit by itself. A homer only counts as one hit. If the player is playing the averages and strikes or grounds out, he can put it in perspective because it doesn't have that great of an effect on the overall average. I don't use this method because I am usually batting about .600, but don't feel like I am getting anywhere.

All the while I was succeeding at business, I was avoiding women. Because of my failure at my first attempt at marriage, I figured that the thing between women and me would not work out, that I would be alone for most of my life. I was living in a cottage in Greenwich, Connecticut, with two other guys. One was gay, and the other one was one of the horniest heterosexuals I have ever known. He could pick up a girl from across the room. I, on the other hand, would look at a girl in the lunchroom for three years before even saying hello. I had other gay friends in New York that I used to hang out with and realized that, although they had a healthy and interesting view on life (in this pre-AIDS life) and I had a great time when I hung out with them, this was not the lifestyle for me either.

This is the time that I practiced being alone. I took guitar lessons at Eddie Simon's school in New York, cut down dead trees with my outside alter ego Tony and split the wood, raced sailboats, and hiked the bridle paths in Greenwich, Connecticut. There were a hundred miles of bridle paths in Greenwich. I spent so much time in the woods that I could whistle at certain places and dogs would appear. I would play with them, and they would follow me for a while and then depart. I never met their owners. I have a thing with animals. I'll have more about that later. I also spent a lot of my time in bars, both in New York and Greenwich, and I was smoking marijuana on a regular basis, so my alcohol and drug crew were still intact.

After working for the Greek ship owner, I found the ideal situation with a small mom-and-pop oil trading firm. The owners were younger than

I was and very supportive. I could really be myself in that environment. We were buying and selling cargoes of gasoline and diesel fuel and other petroleum products all around the world. As an example, I would find a supplier in Singapore that wanted to sell twenty thousand tons of diesel fuel. I would find a buyer in, say, the Philippines. If I could charter a tanker to carry the cargo at a price that would allow me to make a profit, then I would confirm the buy, sell, and shipping all at the same time. This is called the "spot oil market." I would take trips to Asia or Europe whenever I wanted to meet people or search for new business contacts. My negotiating skills were getting sharper. I don't know how I did it, but I learned later that it was intertwined with my anxiety.

Sometimes I would get so anxious while negotiating a buy or sale that I would have to take walks around the block to cool off. I slammed phones. I intimidated ship brokers (like I used to be) and maritime lawyers. I nailed ship owner's hides to the front door of the brownstone we worked out of. I closed bars and once woke up at 3:00 a.m. in the train yard in North White Plains in my tuxedo. I was taken out to the best restaurants. I was a young … er … middle-aged Turk. This will all fit in later.

# METHOD—Turn Off the TV Where They Feed You Junk, Buy a Good Newspaper Like the New York Times, and Learn Selective Reading

One of the owners of the oil trading company, Steve, gave a big boost to my sense of humor and a general appreciation for looking at ordinary things in a humorous way. On the back of the New York State driver's license, when they were made out of paper, is a place where you can check off if you want to be an organ donor. I guess they would look for your wallet in your mangled car and mangled body, and if you were still warm and had checked the box, the medical folks would start carving out parts to help someone who needed a transplant. It is a good thing. There was a place next to the box where you could write in "special instructions." He wrote in that space, "Make sure I'm dead." He also taught me how to read the newspaper in a creative way.

One day in a major New York newspaper, there was a story about a couple in their late nineties who were getting a divorce in Florida. They had been married for close to seventy years. The judge granted them the divorce and then asked why they had waited so long to get the divorce. He was curious.

They replied, "We wanted to wait until the kids were dead."

Steve could find things like this in any newspaper. I asked how he did it. He called it "selective reading." The concept is simple. You find what you expect to find. I found it a fascinating way to avoid all of the bad news and sensationalism that everyone complains about. My wife is a newspaper and political junkie. She will read a section of the *New York Times* over breakfast and then pass it over to me. I will find this hilarious stuff and read it to her.

She looks at me and asks, "How do you find that stuff?"

If we sit next to each other at the diner, she is always reading my paper. She wonders why my paper is always more interesting than hers.

She reads several editorials. These are a good source of keen insights and some outrageously clever humor. Most editorials are about politics, economics, international relations, and other current events matters that affect our lives in an oblique way. There are editorial writers from every background, far right to far left. They are all biased in some way and are usually sitting on the edge of their chairs, waiting for their favorite targets to screw up. You will have to try a few to find out which ones you like. It will give you something to look forward to, like the lottery ticket. My wife's favorites are Maureen Dowd, Gail Collins, and Tom Friedman. Maureen Dowd has a knack for cutting through the BS that politicians spew out, the spin, and replacing it with what they really meant, usually in the most disparaging terms. Some of her columns are hysterical. Gail Collins is single-handedly responsible for keeping the story alive that Mitt Romney tied his dog Shamus on the roof of his car and drove the family to Canada for a vacation (a true story). Tom Friedman has actually lived in hot spots like Jerusalem and Beirut as a reporter and has a unique way of deciphering what is really going on internationally. Paul Krugman is another great columnist. He is also a Nobel Prize–winning economics professor at Princeton and can easily pick apart any nonsense that a politician will spin with authority. These examples are of liberals. There are some good ones on the other side like Pat Buchanan. I don't care much for his politics, but he is as smart as a whip and knows his stuff.

You will have more fun between anxiety attacks by reading selectively and following your favorite columnists. If you are addicted to TV, then let someone like Don Imus do the selective reading for you. Don has a book reading list, like Oprah Winfrey used to, that major booksellers support. Don is all over the place with his books, but Oprah seems to be leaning toward the self-help angle. Both are great intellects. A favorite TV personality of mine for political stuff is Chris Matthews. He also writes a column for the *San Francisco Chronicle*, but I have never seen it. My brother thinks he is an angry person. I know a little bit about his background, and I would venture a guess that he is probably one of the ten happiest people on the planet. He is just the kind of kid who always had his hand up in class yelling, "Me! Me!" He's one of those overachievers. He interrupts guests in midsentence and often gets so keyed up that he is almost yelling. He is parodied on *Saturday Night Live* on a regular basis, and he gets such a kick out of this that he plays the skits on his program, *Hard Ball*.

While I'm on the topic of reading, I will try to describe a type of reading that I have used to get away from myself. I call it "reading up." It is basically reading above your level of understanding. You have to figure out what the author is trying to say. Straight philosophy is the purest example, but I am not recommending that because it can be frustrating. I have always been interested in science, especially science about the universe. I read light science, that which is either aimed at the layperson or edited by a good writer so the layperson can understand it. An example of this kind of writing is work by the late Stephen Jay Gould, which can be found in a variety of places. He writes articles for several publications and every so often comes out with a book reprinting them. He can explain the most complicated topic in a fascinating way. Two of his books are *Hen's Teeth and Horse's Toes* and *The Panda's Thumb—More Reflections in Natural History*. A few good sources for day-to-day reading up are the *New York Times*, the *Science Weekly* section on Tuesdays, and *Natural History*, the magazine of the New York Museum of Natural History. They both have regular articles that explain what the latest findings are in science. The articles are just long enough to get your brain cells thinking about just that topic but not long enough to be boring. *Smithsonian* magazine is another good one, but the articles are too long for me and are often too esoteric. If you have to look that word up, forget the magazine.

# METHOD—Read Up

An alternative to reading up is to read old novels. Our house at Cape Cod is full of them, left behind over the years. You can find old novels at any tag sale or used bookstore. The writing style of the 1800s and early 1900s is dramatically different from what it is today. Rules of grammar were adhered to, and everything was more formal. This was back in the times when coal miners would work all day in the mines and, after cleaning up, would put on a tie for dinner. I can even remember everyone dressing up to fly on an airplane. The language used in these books is fascinating. The attention to detail is marvelous. The topics that people wrote about are bizarre by our standards. The covers and paper even feel different. My favorite find is *Istar of Babylon*, a phantasy, by Margaret Horton Potter. It was printed in 1902. I used to read this aloud to my wife after we got in bed. She has no trouble at all sleeping, and I hoped that, as she slipped away, these antique words would carry her to a different place. She naturally slips into a very deep sleep. When you describe someone as "being able to sleep through a rocket attack," you are describing how soundly my wife sleeps. Actually in Viet Nam she had a person assigned to wake her up during rocket attacks and bring her over to the main bunker. Now that is world-class sleeping!

I have my cat, Fernando, sitting on me, attempting to block my writing of this book, so now is as good a time as any to write about animals. I have always had a thing with animals. Some people say that animals love me. I don't know about that. I think it is the other way around. I like animals, and I have spent a lot of time with them. I pay attention to them, and they appreciate it. When I hear a bird whistling, I whistle back. I can whistle back and forth with chickadees and have them wind up sitting on my hand picking out sunflower seeds. It's very relaxing, by the way, and wondrous. I have read that people tend to live longer if they have a pet, especially if they live alone. Of course, if you have a pet, you either take care of it, or it dies or leaves. I suppose that this caring for some other being has its own therapeutic value, but I am after the anxiety diminution angle. I have had dogs, cats, snakes, hamsters, mice, tropical fish, goldfish, eels, crabs, flying squirrels, guinea pigs, and birds. In my opinion, the pets that do the best job with anxiety are cats, rabbits, and rats. I have heard that ferrets are good also.

When I ordered my flying squirrels, I called the Railway Express office in New Rochelle and warned them that they were coming. They thought my call was a prank. They took a few weeks to arrive, and I called back every few days to check.

"Sorry, guy, no flying squirrels yet," was the usual reply in a gruff voice.

One day the same person called up, this time with a meek voice, and said, "Uh, Chris, your, aaah, flying squirrels are here."

I'm sure he then loaded his shotgun and put it under the counter in case I turned out to be a lunatic.

There is nothing like taking a nap with a cat. They seem to be made for it. Wild cats sleep about 90 percent of the time. This is because they expend so much energy in catching dinner. House cats have a more leisurely time of it and are awake slightly longer. Not any cat will do. Cats that are not handled a lot when they are very young and feral cats that are not caught and socialized very early will barely tolerate people. You will never get a feral cat to be friendly in the same way that a real house cat will be. I find that purebred pedigreed animals are more uptight than mixed breeds, with the notable exception of Labrador retrievers. Sometimes cats will just show up on your doorstep. It is hard to evaluate these animals. They may be lost or hungry. They are sure to be very friendly at first but may have habits that will drive you nuts after they move in. One good way to determine if a stray cat will adapt to you is if it lets you pick it up and if it relaxes in your arms while being petted.

# METHOD—Get Adopted by a Cat at the Pound

If you want a cat, I would suggest going to the pound. You will be doing a great service to the animal world in saving these cats from destruction. You can't pick out a cat; they have to pick you out. The way to get picked out by a cat is not so easy. First, you have to find a pound that will allow you to interact with the cats. They should have a room where the socialized cats can roam around freely or a room where you can take cats to see if they like you. You have to get on their level. That means getting down on the floor or sitting on whatever contraption they have made for the cats to climb on.

In the case of Fernando, who now has my left arm immobilized and is snoring, I was sitting on this carpeted apartment-like structure, watching my wife play with a cat on the floor. I got head butted in my right ear by this huge black, gray, and white tabby. Head butting is the way cats let you know that you are acceptable to their world.

I said to my wife, "Hey, sweetheart, watch this."

He bashed into my head again, as if on cue. I had her sit down, and he gave her a good head butt. We were in hysterics by this time. She gave him the pickup-and-get-the-hug test, which he passed with flying colors. We were adopted. We had spent over two hours looking at cats, and finally Fernando had picked us out. Fernando is named after Fernando Bujones, a ballet dancer that my wife admired. If it were a female, I would have gotten to name her Sophia, who autographed my book with a beautiful smile, years ago. Fernando will climb up on you whenever you stop moving for more than ten seconds.

If you have an affectionate cat, you have an effective way to dodge anxiety. Just scratch and pet it, and your anxiety will dissipate. I keep my cats inside. I happen to like chipmunks, snakes, mice, squirrels, and birds crawling about in my yard, not brought home and unceremoniously dumped on the doorstep. Cats will kill anything they can. They also have shorter life spans when let outside, especially if there are coyotes or great horned owls in the area. They can contract feline leukemia from other cats and rabies from raccoons. They will also surely bring home lots of fleas, ticks, and other vermin.

Rabbits are similar to cats in size, fuzziness, and affection. They do their business in a cat box and are very clean. I have not had all that much experience with them, but I know rabbit owners, and they confirm my perceptions. I did have a rabbit living in the house when I was a child, but it was not mine. It was kept in a cage. I feel they should be free to roam around the house.

I was in a woman's apartment once in Holland. She had this huge Dutch lop-eared rabbit. He was a bit shy. I did the laying-on-the-floor routine, and within fifteen minutes, I got myself adopted by the rabbit. They love to be petted and scratched and will sniff in your ear and climb on you like a cat. The downside is that they are more fragile than cats are, and you have to always watch that they don't get outside or dogs don't get inside.

Rats may seem like a strange choice. I am talking about big laboratory rats, not edgy mice or gerbil-type animals. The main reason is that they are super intelligent and like interacting with people. From an intelligence standpoint, rats make dogs and cats seem like furniture. I had a roommate who had a real lab rat, a white one. He had worked for a company that raised lab rats. He mistakenly dropped one on the floor and had the choice of either euthanizing it or taking it home because it was contaminated, having made contact with the floor. This was a huge rat, about a foot long, and the smartest animal I have ever dealt with. He loved to be rolled back and forth across the bed. You would place your forearm on him and slide it back and forth, and he would roll like a log. We used to set up mazes that he would figure out and then repeat at blazing speed on the second try. You can nap with rats, but you have to be careful not to roll over on them.

A friend Pietr buys feeders, rats bred to feed to snakes. Pietr's ex-wife didn't like his rat Rathenry on the chaise lounge. When Rathenry heard her footsteps coming down the stairs, he would streak over to the chaise and jump up. She would put him on the floor, and Rathenry would jump up again. This would go on until she tired of the game and left the room. Rathenry would then climb down and go back to what he had been doing before the wife had appeared. The rat was playing with the wife!

I have only had one cat instigate play, a Persian. She would look at you from behind something and then disappear. Slowly the head would come back out until you made eye contact and then pull back. She would do this until you went after her, and then the chase was on. Try this with a cat or dog, and you will get the same reaction. They can't resist.

Why not dogs? I love dogs dearly and have had some very good dog friends. I have had dog friends where I had never met the owners, both in Greenwich and Tahoe. Different dogs would come visiting during their daily rounds. I used to think that I didn't have a dog because I was away at work too much. I didn't want the dog to be alone. It was an excuse. Another excuse was that I didn't want the responsibility. The real reason, from an anxiety standpoint, is that dogs are a lot of work. They need to be walked, rain or shine, and groomed. I don't want an animal that is too much work because I don't want to resent it. Resentment destroys the possibility of you lowering the anxiety through relating to the animal. Also all I have to do is make a relationship with someone else's dog and I still get to play with them.

There are fifty million dogs in the United States alone. If I wanted a dog, I would also look for a mutt at a pound and stay away from pedigreed dogs, especially terriers and beagles. You will also be able to avoid the terror of having a puppy destroying your place by getting a mature dog. Puppies and certain adult breeds like Portuguese water dogs live by one rule, play with me or I will play with everything you own. If you get a dog and take it out in your car, you are going to need a lot of Windex and paper towels. When I was a kid, our Dalmatian would smear every window in the car within five minutes of setting out. I was in charge of cleaning them. I guess that is why I hate cleaning car windows.

Llamas, probably the oldest domesticated animal, would be a good choice, but you can't take naps with them. If you have more than one llama, you may get glommed occasionally because, like camels, they spit at each other to settle disputes. Horses, very spiritual animals, and other large animals take an inordinate amount of care.

One thing you must get in the habit of doing is to touch your animal every time you pass by. If you ignore them, you will lose the bond that will help you reduce your anxiety. Give them a pet and a kind word, or give a tug on the old tail. All of my large pets loved hugs.

# METHOD—Spend Time In or On the Water

I have mentioned water a few times in a circumspect sort of way. I love water. Some people hate water or fear it. What I have noticed about myself and most other people who use water for pleasure is that, when they go in or on the water, they are in varying states of animation and mood, but when they come back on land or out of the pool, they all seem to be on the same level. They are moving in a more graceful manner without jerky movements and usually slower. They are quieter and friendlier. They are usually smiling. Water seems to be a universal cleansing agent.

I grew up around boats so I am fortunate that being on a boat or on land is pretty much the same for me. For some who are not familiar with boats, it must feel as different from land as I feel in a commercial airplane, uncomfortable with a little anxiety. Boats are an ideal way to feel the water. I'll deal with boats in a different section.

The important factor is the water. We need to be in it or on it frequently. I try to swim four or five times a week at my exercise club or the Y. I really feel great when I am swimming regularly. Swimming laps has all of the meditative, repetitive, and physical aspects that work. It is also good to learn to control your breathing. If you don't have breath control, you will wind up inhaling water. Some clubs have whirlpools. I am fortunate enough to have one at home, and every time I use it, I am amazed I don't use it more. Many people I know, including myself, have become certified scuba divers. With this equipment, you can dive below the surface for periods of a half hour or even longer. You need certification to be able to dive at most resorts around the world. The best thing about scuba, apart from the beauty of the water and the colorful creatures living in it, is that you are weightless so it is wonderful for older people. Free diving or snorkeling is also fun and a lot cheaper. You are restricted pretty much to the shoreline, but there is often more there than in deeper water. I don't remember ever not having a mask and snorkel. I have spent hours underwater or floating along, just watching. I have even taken people who do not swim out on air mattresses with a mask and snorkel on to let them see and feel what it is like.

You can be active or passive in or on the water, and it will have the same effect, but I feel you have to cross the barrier to get the full effect. Sitting near or walking along a body of water is nice, but to me, it's not the same. We live near Sandy Hook, part of the national park system located in New Jersey. It is on the Atlantic Ocean and has long stretches of untouched beaches. If we walk there, I have to at least get my feet wet to get that connection. The simplest way to enjoy water is to take a warm bath, especially a Jacuzzi or whirlpool bath. I find that, when I cross the barrier, into or onto the water, that is the only thing I am thinking about.

As mentioned before, boats are an ideal way to feel the water. The type of boat is important as some can be intimidating. If you are not driving, you are at the mercy of the person who is. If a person owns a boat that is noisy and fast, at some point on the boat ride, the boat will be going as fast as it possibly can. You don't need a license in many places to drive a boat. A person can buy a boat that is capable of going fifty miles an hour, get in, and jam the throttle wide open and go fifty miles an hour. He or she can do this, even if he or she has never been on a boat in his or her life. Unfortunately, there are a lot of people driving boats who don't know much about them.

It is a thrill for me to go fast on a boat, but it always gets my anxiety level up. Stick to slow, clunky boats, or go out on a head boat, one that charges by the head to go out for a ride. They usually follow a set route or go out for a specific purpose, like whale watching. By law, head boats have to have a licensed captain and adhere to Coast Guard safety regulations. These are usually larger boats. You can also take a ferry ride. When I worked in New York, I used to frequently take the Staten Island ferry back and forth during my lunch hour. It was the best thirty-five cents I could spend. It is now free. If you are driving somewhere, see if you can make a detour or go on a different route to get on a ferry.

I had anxiety problems with one boat. I always had access to family boats but never owned one. Again I did not think I could handle the responsibility, but it was really the anxiety. My wife does not have the anxiety problems that I do. We both love boats, and one type in particular is found mainly around Cape Cod, a Herreschoff 12 ½, named after the designer, a famous naval architect. It is a pretty, antique (1907) design that is twelve and a half feet long on the water. He designed it for his children of ten and twelve years of age to be sailed safely in any weather conditions. It is substantial and rugged.

We had one made. They are very expensive, so that added to the responsibility. I freaked out. Everything had to be perfect, from the varnish to the sails. I was afraid of damaging the boat when we were sailing. There were races every Saturday, but I never participated because I didn't want to damage the boat. I also went to Cape Cod to relax, and sailboat racing and relaxing do not mix. There was a lot of fun but a lot of anguish.

Now that I am on medication, we have a thirty-three-foot sailboat that is seaworthy enough to sail to Europe. We sailed it from Cape Cod to Maryland in the first year. It is just a wonderful way to travel. It is slow and peaceful when you are only under sail power. If you plan your trip well, there is no hurry. When you approach a town from the water, it is an entirely different place than the one you drive up to in a car.

Because of my problems with owning a boat, I am not going to recommend getting one, even though boats can offer all of what we need to suppress or release the anxiety. There is another way to get out on boats, other people's (OP).

People who own sailboats are always looking for crews to help them sail and enjoy their boats. Put up a sign at a sailing club with the words "crew" and your phone number. You don't have to know how to sail. The person steering the boat is in charge and will tell you what to do. Just let him or her know your skill level or lack thereof. There are two kinds of sailing, sailing for fun and enjoyment and racing. I raced out of Larchmont, New York, for four years. I was crew. Several top racers are in that area. The races are run according to strict rules. If someone looks like he or she is going to break a rule, the first thing you do is start yelling the rules at him or her or worse. He or she usually yells something back. If he or she actually breaks the rule, you can protest him or her. If you protest someone, he or she has to meet with you and the judges after the race and defend his or her actions. He or she can also withdraw from the race, which involves hurt feelings and bruised egos.

There is a lot of tension on a racing boat, which is magnified if one of the crewmembers or the skipper makes a mistake that costs time or position. Sailboat racing is all about winning and competing. I have seen some intense outbursts of anger. From my anxiety standpoint, sailboat racing is not a good way to get out on the water. You do learn a lot about sailing, which is important if you ever want to own one. I wanted to get involved in ocean racing, and most good ocean racers start out racing in smaller boats.

I just read that last sentence over, and I thought, *That doesn't seem to make any sense.* I thought about that for a minute, and what draws me to the ocean, aside from the water factor, is weather. I love weather, especially severe. It is thrilling to be outside when there is a heavy snowstorm, especially when I have my skis on. I am in my own bubble of a world with a muffled snow scape passing by. I love to hike in windstorms in the mountains. I can't get enough of electrical storms. I have been out in the ocean during magnificent blows where the waves are as big as city blocks tumbling all over themselves. Now I just read that over, and it still doesn't make any sense from an anxiety standpoint. Maybe it is because it is natural and gets me away from myself for a while.

I'll return back to boats. Many kinds of boats will allow you to get out on the water. These are self-propelled boats. Rowing or paddling is an acquired skill. In the beginning, you feel like a complete klutz, spinning around in circles while learning about the liquid medium. Some people try it and give it up because it is too difficult. This is too bad because it is one of the best ways to feel the water and to enjoy nature. I love rowing. It is strenuous if you are trying to get anywhere, so it involves heavier breathing. It also involves balance. The repetitive swooshing of the oars stops my active thoughts. If you just sit in a boat on the water, you will soon be accepted as part of the scenery, and wildlife will appear from everywhere. If I see a school of fish feeding, I just automatically go over there and sit in the middle of the activity. Fish are darting, and birds are swooping, diving, and making a racket. This is heaven. Canoes, kayaks, and rowing sculls are a bit more difficult to learn how to use than flat rowboats, but they are designed to cover a lot of territory easily and quickly.

A former colleague of mine would not ride in helicopters. He said, "Airplanes are designed to fly; helicopters are designed to crash." If you look at a canoe or kayak, they look like they were designed to turn over rather than stay upright, and indeed that is what happens regularly to the novice.

My first real experience in a canoe was on the Delaware River near the Delaware Water Gap in the spring. Most rivers are full of water in the spring. About a mile after we got started, a park ranger paddled up in a kayak and told us to get down in the boat as we were approaching rapids. It was actually more like a waterfall, Skinner's Falls. As we were being sucked through this field of boulders, a canoe in front of us overturned. It was either run over them or crash into a boulder, so I crashed. All of our stuff, including our bodies, tumbled into the icy water. People were throwing ropes to us to haul us out. We lost everything except what we had on and were relegated to having to mooch beers for the next ten miles down the river. That crash was understandable, but the other two were not. We were just floating along. Some turbulence appeared ahead, and we decided to avoid whatever it was underwater. My partner zigged, and I zagged. And just like that, we were in the water with no warning. Just plop! This happened twice. I didn't mind this. It was a beautiful, warm day, and the dunkings made the trip memorable. Boats are great. If you can't find one to get out on, an air mattress will do.

Most sailing clubs and rowing clubs offer instructions, often to nonmembers. The fees are usually low as they feel it is part of their responsibility to the general public, and several clubs are actively seeking new members. This is a good way to learn about boats. The only group that has regular courses about powerboats that I know of is the United States Power Squadrons and the Auxiliary Coast Guard. Yacht clubs also usually have a very active social schedule. You see the same people at all of the events, so the anxiety level is not as high as at other social gatherings. Most of my friends I have met are at boat clubs.

# METHOD—Build a Fish Pond

There is one notable exception to crossing the barrier into water. Fish ponds are really ornamental bodies of water created just to sit and look at and into. I dug one in my yard down at the Cape. It is six feet by nine feet. Designing and building the pond is a fun but not necessary part of the process. My wife and I had been doing a lot of gardening, and the neighbors had even been given to taking people on tours during the week when we were not around. We had been toying with the idea of a pond for a few years. We had done some reading on the subject and visited a few ponds that others had made. A lot of people are into ponds, and if you spread the word about your interest, you will be found and taken to their pond.

I had put about fifteen rocks on the ground where the pond was going to be. Every weekend for two years, we rearranged the rocks into different patterns to see what we liked best. Every weekend I would carefully move the rocks to mow the grass and then put them back where they had been. In the end, we wound up with the most standard and boring shape in the history of ponds, kidney-shaped. What a laugh. My alter ego Tony dug the hole by hand, piling the dirt up next to the pond for an eventual ornamental grass garden. I assembled some old pumps and fountains from my parents' home in Larchmont and bought a rubber liner. The pond was terraced so we could put ornamental water plants around the edge.

After installing the liner, the pumps, and fountains, I got a pallet of New York river rock at the local rock store and placed them around the pond with some of them hanging over the edge. It looked like it had been there forever. This was a monumental effort in planning, digging, and finding supplies, but it felt good to have it. I was even a bit anxious because everyone knew we were building one and I was going to lose some more of my invisibility. The magic moment came when I bought a few dozen feeder goldfish and snails at the pet store up in Cambridge, drove them down, and put them in the pond. Suddenly the pond transformed into this magical, anxiety-free spot in the yard.

I have spent numerous hours feeding and watching those fish, all of them positive. Everyone who knows ponds ask the same question. "Did you get frogs yet?" We live several miles from the next pond, but sure enough, several weeks later, the nicest frog I have ever seen showed up. I quizzed everyone in the neighborhood to find the wise guy who had put the frog there, but no one had. Birds show up and leave all sorts of eggs and seeds in their droppings. A chipmunk even showed up and started digging a nest and kicking the dirt into the pond. I put a piece of wood there to catch the dirt until he was finished. He would sit on the wood and look around, no doubt the only chipmunk in Massachusetts with a deck and lake. We have battled with raccoons and herons, both of which love to eat goldfish, but it is all good fun. I even go in the pond a few times a year to tend to the plants, especially the water lilies that need to be fertilized. The goldfish love this and then chase me around and bite the hairs on my legs. You can buy preformed plastic pond kits at gardening centers, Home Depot–type stores, and on the Internet. These have all the benefits of our pond but can be assembled in an afternoon.

If you live in an apartment or don't have a yard, you can build a mini fish pond in a large ceramic pot. Most pond books have good examples. The pond I am building now is nine foot by eleven foot, replete with fountain with a smaller pond next to it with a butterfly beach and bird bathing area. Yes, I am possessed, and to think I was embarrassed about the first one.

I'll return back to the chronological path. It was 1980, and I was working in New York City after having left California. I was a commuter, living outside of the city. I needed the woods and the water. I needed to get my batteries charged every now and then. In one case, a friend came out for the weekend. He had not left Manhattan for fourteen months. I found him sitting on the terrace staring at the trees. I asked if there were something in the trees.

"No, I'm just looking at the trees. I haven't seen trees in so long that I forgot what they looked like."

That was not for me. I had changed jobs a few times. This is normal in the shipping business. It was my problem, and something that caused me to change jobs was that I felt a pressure build up whenever I did anything for a certain period of time. It was not boredom. I looked to some of the spiritual clues I had learned and came up empty-handed. I read *Psychology*

*Today* and other books looking for information. It was like I had the seven-year itch about life.

One of the things I learned in my analysis of my behavior was very disconcerting. I noticed that, when I went to a play or a concert in New York, as soon as it started, I wanted it to be over. Imagine seeing Jimmy Stewart twenty feet away doing a revival of Harvey and wanting it to be over. It was idiotic. I was being analytical rather than living in the moment.

If you think about it, every planned human activity has a similar rhythm to it. Church services are similar to Broadway plays, which are similar to rock concerts, which are similar to Hitchcock movies. They all follow a pattern that is closely related to our concept of time. When there is not enough action, more is added. When there is too much action, we get a break. Near the end, things build up to a crescendo, and then it is over. Life is ritual—school, work, marriage, kids, and retirement. And then it is over. Why wasn't I doing any of that? I was cutting everything short, realizing that there was an end before I was supposed to. Part of this may be the abandonment problem, but I suspect that anxiety was at the heart of it. This was serious stuff. I was making a mess out of my life and others' lives as well. I was having a lot of interesting experiences, "been there and done that" stuff, but was this what life was all about, a series of short experiences?

When I got a job, I was thinking of the next one. When I got married, I started thinking of what the next one would be like. When I went to a movie, it didn't mean anything until it was over. Yet I would not go to a movie if I missed the beginning. Movies are so efficient and expensive that they can't afford to include anything that doesn't contribute to the whole. Everything is important. I was waiting for everything to be over, and everything did end. I felt trapped in this cycle, but I had no control over it. This created endless possibilities for anguish. It was a fire feeding itself. My concept of time was out of whack.

I ended my dating hiatus and ran into serious trouble on my second date. People were always trying to fix me up with women they wanted to date but could not because they were married. I was their surrogate penis, I guess.

"Hey, Chris, I met this girl in Boodles the other night, and she is hot. I know I could get her in bed in a flash. Why don't you ask her out?"

I was able to stave this off for a couple years, but then I thought, *Here you are, a guy who can't ask a girl out on a date, and these guys are flogging these women at you. Are you nuts?*

I would say, "I'll buy the turkey; you invite us over to dinner."

I fall in love easily, sometimes three times a block in New York City. Some of this must come from the fact that I am so shy (anxious) that I can't approach people on my own behalf. Anyone who notices I am alive gets my full attention. I wasn't having the severe self-esteem problems that I have had at other times because of my success in business. I generally believe that you should not judge yourself by your work alone, but being successful at work sure helps.

So I was only on the market for two turkeys. She was fresh, a traveler from Holland, half-Indonesian, who was looking for a place to land. She was younger than I was. I had never dated anyone out of my age range. Perhaps this was an opportunity to make up for the mistakes I had made, ten years ago. She hadn't made up her mind about a lot of things. She would never begin a conversation with, "What do you do?"

We were in love. We were so much in love that couples who were thinking of splitting up would give it another try after spending some time with us. I knew it would be over, but I didn't know when. That was such a hideous thought to appear in the middle of this bliss, but I couldn't help but analyze it. I recalled times in my life when I had made a good friend and then looked at him or her and said to myself, "There will be a time when this person will no longer be my friend." On my merry-go-round, it happens with everyone. It is the loneliest feeling I know.

We married. She developed a great interest in astrology, past-life regression, movement, and other metaphysical type of stuff. She even participated in a few psychic fairs. We took seminars in the city in voice dialogue and a few other things that we were mutually interested in. She, like I, had some problems with her Catholic upbringing. She tried to solve hers by joining a spiritual church. This had a great effect on our lives. I guess now is as good a time as ever to talk about religion and how it may fit into this whole picture.

First of all, when I use the term "spiritual," I am referring to personal internal matters of the spirit and soul, which have no direct connection to the physical world and also no direct connection to organized religion or

114

God. If I am connected to God when I meditate through the Maharishi Mahesh Yogi, it is great, but I don't feel it. I am what is known as a half-baked Catholic. I was baptized but nothing more. I went to public school, and we were allowed to leave school on Wednesday afternoons to go to religious instructions at the church. I was a little behind the group because I had never studied the religion, so one of the young priests, Father McNamara, took me under his wing. He is now a monsignor. We spent hours, one on one, discussing the religion. My questions were always about why we have wars and cancer if God is omniscient and why big kids beat up on little kids if God is omnipresent. A little slap on the ass, and it is over. The answer and the difference in my world between spiritualism and religion is faith. I have been in some of the most holy places on earth, and I have never felt God there. I have also not felt God in nature. I have felt my own spirit.

Some people have said to me in an almost offhanded tone, "You really don't have much of a problem. Just give your life to Jesus, and you will be happy."

This reminds me of the time I was talking to a lifelong friend of mine, Wade, about the physiology of getting drunk. As far as I was concerned, being drunk boiled it down to a simple salt and sugar imbalance. He was a recovering alcoholic who was going to AA meetings every day.

His response was simple, "Cliff, it is a little bit more complicated than that."

Acceptance and faith are either too complicated or simple for me. I can't figure out which. Father McNamara finally released me from my perplexed state by telling me that, if I didn't have faith, Catholicism was not for me.

The best quality I got from my years as a half-baked Catholic was a firm sense of guilt. Catholics and Jews both have a healthy dose of guilt. They even argue and joke about who has more guilt. Any amount of guilt, as far as I'm concerned, is enough. My guilt manifested itself in a quest to find the perfect religion. I needed to fill the hole that society said I had. I thought I would learn about a lot of religions and then choose one. This is a fairly naïve idea, but part of the guilt is that you have to have a religion.

I thought I could intellectualize all of this and began reading the major religions texts. I had studied the Bible and the book of the Acts of God at Presbyterian-affiliated Parsons College, so it was off to the races. I read the Essene Scriptures, the books that were left out of the Bible concerning afterlife, reincarnation, and the like, to round out the Christian thing. I read about Zoroastrianism, the Bhagavad Gita, the Upanishads, the Vedas, the writings of Confucius and Lao Tzu, and what I could find on Shinto, modern Judaism, and the Animism of Bali. (There is a door to heaven somewhere on Bali.) The most difficult for me was the Koran, but I read it.

I also carried around the Koran for protection. This was during the time that airplanes were being hijacked and all of the passengers with Jewish-sounding names or American passports, which I had both of, were getting shot or beaten and tortured. I wore a chain around my neck with a medal that had a likeness of the Virgin Mary embossed on it and the inscription, "I am a Catholic. Please call a priest." I carried the copy of the Koran in my briefcase. If they were going to shoot me, I would ask for my holy book to hold while they blasted my brains out onto the tarmac. Of course, they would see the Koran and arrange for a first-class ticket out of there on Swissair. I can still remember the twinge of guilt when I bought that medal from that nun in New York.

The result of this multiyear reading binge was a sense that the major Western religions all came from the same place, but one had the Democrat point of view, one the Republican, and the other the Independent. They seemed to be made up from stories and oral traditions. The Eastern religions were more animistic. They seemed to grow from the real world. I thought that Taoism made the most sense, but Taoism is something you do, a way of living your life in balance. It is not something that you worship, per se. I got a lot of points of view, but I was still lost. I still am. At least I expunged that particular guilt by taking a good look around, if only in books.

One of the features of a spiritual church is the quiet part of the service, the important part of the service. This was when the person who was conducting the service contacted those who had passed over, the dead, and gave messages to us, the living. The closest I had ever come to anything like this was sitting in the dirt parking lot of a tent revival in Oklahoma. People were listening to the preacher and waving back and forth, clutching their Bibles. They had a look on their faces that was somewhere between enthrallment and terror. They seemed entranced, almost possessed by another spirit.

Around the same time, I saw the movie *Marjoe* about the life of Marjoe Gortner, a child evangelist. The movie was an exposé that dispelled any magic that ritual possession had for me. But here I was in Old Greenwich, Connecticut, and the spiritual church seemed real. I got a message from my passed-over uncle the first time. One time my wife concealed her passed-over father's watch in her pocket and attended a private session. The watch was discovered immediately and was running! It had not been wound in ten years. Probably running from body heat, you say? The disturbing fact about all of this is that, when I would go to a service, it would calm me down to the point where I would not want to talk. I'm not one of those people who are afraid of silence. If you want to meet some people who are, just go to Spain. If you stop talking for five minutes, they ask you if you are feeling all right. They are lovely people but very chatty.

The effect the spiritual service had on my wife was the opposite. She would become very animated and want to discuss everything. I would go into the service with a Dutch-Indonesian and come out with a Spaniard!

I have spent a lot of time in holy places. I always feel nice there. I have spent pleasant time in Hindu temples. I have lit candles for my Irish Catholic grandmother and now my Aunt Elma in every church from Oaxaca, Mexico, to Abidjan, Ivory Coast. I feel good when I leave after lighting the candles, but I don't feel God. Or do I through the peace I feel?

# METHOD—Learn How to Wait

This actually comes from a movement class that my wife took in New York, taught by Mr. Milton Feher. I attended some of the classes myself and picked up a lot of stuff. The whole idea of movement is something to look into, but this method is the one I find the most useful. First, I have a bit of background on movement. If you want an instant image of a person who is good at it, think of Sean Connery. He studied it for five years. He had an audition for the Bond character and really did not catch the director's eye until after the audition when the director looked out of the window and noticed Connery walking across the courtyard below. The director thought that he moved like a cat. He was called back and got the part. Sean Connery feels that a love scene is really a dance between him and the woman.

The teacher we had in New York was a former member of the Ballet Rousse. He could do things like see with his feet and encouraged people to learn to do things like walk up stairs backward to analyze their movement and then try it forward and change it. His technique for waiting was simple, and it works every time.

You first think of your feet and feel them on the ground. After you are totally aware of your feet, you concentrate on the sounds around you. You will soon be able to separate the sounds. With practice I learned how to separate traffic noise from birds singing. Time passes not more quickly but in a more pleasant way. You will have enjoyed your wait.

# METHOD—Never Wait for Anyone More Than Fifteen Minutes Unless Her Name Is Sophia

I used to really get steamed when I had to wait for someone. I hate to be late for anything. I especially don't like to have people waiting for me. This may have something to do with my basic disbelief that anyone would want to spend time with me. Not wanting to be late must have been something I translated into a dislike of waiting for others. I can remember standing in the snow in my Italian loafers (those with thin soles that are like having nothing on at all), waiting at the Greenwich train station for my wife to arrive. I was getting so cold that I pressed my feet and legs together to keep warm. I must have looked like a bowling pin. Dutch people are invariably late, about fifteen minutes. It is not that they are late, but when they say a time, they really mean fifteen minutes before or fifteen minutes after, usually the latter.

When I recognized that this was a Dutch trait and I knew that nothing I would do could change it, I fished around for a method to combat it. "Combat" might be too strong a word, but that is what usually happened when the person I was waiting for finally showed up. How I got around this trait was to wait for fifteen minutes after the agreed-upon time using Mr. Feher's waiting technique and then went on to the next logical place that I would be. She had to figure out where I was. This caused some confusion on her part at first, but she soon caught on, and we never missed each other after that. If she were more than fifteen minutes late, she would just have to find me.

You may have to adjust the time for people of different nationalities or those who come from Texas or the South. My parents used to have dinner parties for a lot of international people. If they set a time for dinner at seven, the Norwegians would show up at six forty-five, the Italians at eight, and the Greeks at nine. They solved this problem by inviting different nationalities for dinner at different times, and they would all show up at the same time.

# METHOD—Make a List of Your Weak Points

I remember a gubernatorial race in Massachusetts that pitted the Democrat Dr. John Silber, the president of Boston University, against the Republican William Weld. The race was neck and neck. Dr. Silber had a lot of great ideas, and he was a great speaker. On the night of the election, he appeared on a very popular news program, and interviewer Natalie Jacobsen, a fixture on the Boston TV news scene, asked him to tell her some of his weak points.

Dr. Silber bristled and gave Natalie a minor chewing out for asking such a dumb question. He lost the election the next day. If he had a list of his weak points and had answered the question in his usual eloquent manner, there is no doubt in anyone's mind that he would have won. On a smaller scale, yours and mine, because I don't think that any of us are going to run for governor, a list of our weak points may keep us out of trouble.

Let's see how this works in the workplace. I have a nigh need for what my brother terms "closure." I need to have things finished, or I start to get anxious. The worst thing that can happen for me is to have a bunch of projects lying around unfinished. The second worst thing is to have to guess at components to have a project finished. My usual method is to over-research something and to be dead sure that all of the facts are right before I turn in something for scrutiny. You can't guess at finishing kitchen cabinets, so I am referring more to a thinking or written project.

A thinking project would be, "Let's try to increase our sales by 30 percent next year, or let's figure out how to do business in Korea next year."

An example of a written project is this book. It is hard enough to keep your personal projects in order, but when you are dealing with others, bosses, or teammates, the problem is compounded. The solution to this is not very easy. You may be in a situation where you can't choose the people you work for or with. A nice, cozy, friendly workplace can also be turned upside down if a company is sold or restructured. I have found that the size of the organization has little to do with the internal stability. Positive corporate culture, what the management wants the company to look and feel like, can be defeated on the personal level by one lousy boss or colleague.

The people who bug me the most, those who cause me the most anxiety, are the ones who need chaos to survive. I call it management by chaos. No matter how serene, how planned, how well-oiled, and smoothly functioning an operation may be, they will screw it up because they can't operate in a calm, organized environment. What they do well is manage chaos. Normalcy is not exciting enough for them. There is a new term called a "seagull manager." This is one that flies in, makes a lot of noise, craps all over everything, and then leaves. They should all be kindergarten teachers, only that doesn't pay that well.

There are others who can only participate in something if it is spur of the moment. They don't like to study manuals or do any research. They refer to themselves as hands-on people. What that really means is that you do all the work and then explain it to them. I took a large format photography class in Boston and had a partner that was like this. I had to show him every time how to assemble the various parts of the camera, tripod, lights, flashes, film containers, and electrical equipment to charge the flashes because he would not read the manual. He was hands-on. I soon tired of this and began arriving at class early. By the time he got there, everything was already assembled. The bastard also took better photos than I did, which really annoyed me.

There is another person who has such a short attention span that he can't do certain basic tasks, like reading. Because he can't concentrate on something long enough to read it, I feel that he is really a functional illiterate. To me, it doesn't make a difference why he can't read something. It matters whether he can read it or not. You can spend weeks preparing a plan or report, and it will sit there like an old Archie comic book waiting for others to read it. The corners will become curled, and then it will disappear.

My college sweetheart taught me a great method of checking to see if something were read or not. Right in the middle of the term paper, she would type, "My room is brown." This would stand out in a chemistry paper if it had been read. She never got a comment on this.

Referring to the previous paragraph, my apologies to anyone with attention deficit disorder (ADD), in case you think I am specifically referring to you or only to you as a group. This may be the cause of a small amount of what I call functional illiteracy, but I feel that most of the practitioners are people with lack of training discipline or those who are generally lazy.

I am very detail-oriented. I look at things from as many angles as I can before I make a decision. This way, I usually have the odds in my favor as far as being correct is concerned. It is an inoculation against screwing up and looking like a fool (and blowing my invisibility). This behavior drives short attention span people nuts.

I had one manager who would ask my opinion on a piece of business. I would disappear and do about four hours of calculations and research. Then I would come back with the full and complete answer. Often he had already forgotten what the question was. Annoyed by this habit of mine, he would ask my opinion, force me to make a guess, and then release me to do my research and calculations. He was trying to get me to trust myself and to build up my self-confidence. I was right 80 percent of the time using the first guess method because I worked in and understood the oil market every day. This number, 80 percent, of course, was not good enough for me.

Another person I worked with often asked my opinion on business matters. I would give an answer. He would go ahead and proceed with the business, and then when it didn't work out, he would blame me. This went on for several months. Finally, I started answering his questions in three ways. I didn't have responsibility for short answers. Medium-term answers, those I could think about overnight, I had half responsibility for. And long-term answers that I could research and calculate, I was fully responsible for. This worked for me. He found it difficult to deal with, but those were the rules.

The point here is that people use many different methods to get things done and to control their world. Many of these methods can and will cause anxiety for most of us. People who are trying to control their environment may actually seek out the things that cause us anxiety and employ them selectively to control us. This can be true of managers or people who report to you. It may not even be a conscious effort on their part to do this. The best defense in this case is a good offense. Write down your weak points. By knowing what they are, you can sometimes avoid conflict with others, either by not associating with them or not working for them. If you are thrown in with a group of people, it will make it easier for you to figure out what is happening on the personal level because you will be aware of half of the interpersonal equation. Having control of half of the equation should lower your anxiety to a level where you can deal with difficult people without getting all tied up in knots.

My brother is a big fan of the *Dilbert* comic strip by Scott Adams. This strip covers all of the above situations and more on a regular basis. If your paper does not have the strip, buy one of his books, and soon the dynamics of ineffective management bureaucracy and people attempting to take charge of their lives will come to you in a humorous and cynical manner. This guy knows how to hit the nail right on the head.

# METHOD—Think of Yourself as a Mirror

If you mirror another person's behavior, it tends to subdue his or her obnoxious or abrasive traits. When I was using this method, I did not try to emulate the other person or playact. I just had to think of myself as a mirror. Don't ask me why it works. It is such a simple concept and works so well that I'm not going to take the chance of screwing it up by elaborating on it. I feel that this is an ancient Eastern philosophical technique, but I don't remember where I got it from.

# METHOD—Make a List of the Traits You Dislike Most in Other People

The things that people dislike most in others are usually what they dislike the most about themselves. This was, at first, an embarrassing concept because I felt like a simple tool when I learned it. I don't like Johnny because he is a loudmouth and he always laughs when he is talking, like everything he says is automatically funny. That night after two beers at the bar, I am shooting off my mouth and laughing while I am talking, like everything I say is funny. I don't know where I got that one from either, but I have been carrying it around in my tool belt for a long time. This may almost be a reverse mirror. It keeps the playing field level.

# METHOD—Start Learning
# a Foreign Language

During my years commuting to New York, I spent a lot of time on the train. I watched my father commute for thirty-eight years, that is, when he was not traveling on business. If you assume that he commuted an average of three hours a day for only thirty years, then he was on the train for about one and a quarter years. That is about 10,920 hours. When I first started commuting, I used to look out the window like I did when I was a child. I did everything I could to avoid thinking about work. I also tried to leave everything behind when I left work at night by taking off that imaginary coat as I walked between the office door and the elevator. On the weekends when I first started working, I would sometimes think of my desk in New York on the eighteenth floor of one Whitehall Street and freak out thinking of what I had to do the next week. As I got more involved and started trading more ships and cargoes, I basically wound up working twenty-four hours a day. I noticed that most of the people on the train either read the newspaper or slept. I was anti-newspaper at the time. I had not learned selective reading at that time, and most of the articles depressed me. I had not found the science section in the *New York Times* yet either. My philosophy books were okay, but I got strange looks. This was still the early seventies, and several businessmen were still longing for the McCarthy days when you could get rid of someone if you just thought he or she were a "pinko." Pinko was code for Communist. Philosophy was dangerous stuff to pinko haters.

One time I was standing in line at the subway token booth with a book on numerology in my hand. A Hassidic rabbi walked up to me and demanded to know what I was doing with that book. I answered that I was reading about numerology.

He practically shouted at me, "You can't learn numerology from a book!" and stomped off.

I decided to drop the philosophy and spiritual books on the train. I still needed something that would give me some relief from thinking about work. I started studying German. I had studied German using a memorization technique in graduate school and in Austria. Memorization works well in a train as there are few distractions, or at least there were few until cell phones were unleashed on the public. I started reading German novels and noting words that I did not know the meaning of by writing them down in the back of the book. I learned this from Scott, a friend I made in the army. He would write down any word he did not know the definition of. He would then look them up later. He had a pretty impressive vocabulary.

During my eleven years of commuting, I studied German, Dutch, and French and reading music. This was interspersed with the science section of the *New York Times*. The language study consisted of some reading and mostly memorization of lists of words. This was satisfying because I was able to stop thinking about work and actually learn something that was useful while lowering the anxiety level. Learning new things also does something for your brain from a chemical standpoint. I get the feeling that learning new things creates good chemicals.

Nothing could be more foreign than a language different from yours. True to my nature of not being able to finish anything, I have never become totally fluent in any one language, but I have been able to have conversations in four languages other than English. When I was divorced, I found that meeting someone in a foreign language and having an affair with her is about as good as it gets. I made attempts at learning Italian, Swahili, and Yoruba, a Nigerian language, but I never got far. I'm saving Italian for last. You can say things in Italian that would sound so idiotic in English that you would jump off the nearest bridge in shame. You could actually play a guitar under an Italian woman's balcony and beg for her undying love. Italians are great. Proposals will be accepted at my email address. A German friend of mine is learning Arabic. She likes to travel to Petra in Syria and visit with the Bedouins, and she wants to learn to speak to them in their own language.

Foreign languages are especially helpful if you are traveling, even in New York. In most places, if you even try to say a few words in the local language, you will be treated much differently than if you only speak English. I'll give you an example. During my junior year in Europe, I decided to spend my Christmas week skiing in Cortina D'Ampezzo, Italy, where the 1956 Olympics were held. I traveled there by train from

Austria. I stopped in Bolzano in South Tyrol for the night. South Tyrol was part of Austria prior to the Second World War, but it became part of Italy afterward. Most signs were in both Italian and German, and most people spoke both. I was looking for a hotel that I had found in *Europe on Five Dollars a Day*, a popular book back then. I was carrying all of my ski gear and a suitcase of regular clothes that was heavy, and I was lost. I saw a policeman directing traffic on a pedestal at the middle of a busy five-road intersection.

I put down my stuff, and dodging the seemingly mad Italian motorists, I approached, asking him in English if he knew where the Hotel Miramar was. He looked at me, shook his head, and shrugged his shoulders. I then asked him the same question in German. He glared down at me and shrugged his shoulders again. All the while he was directing traffic. I had been studying Italian because I was in love with an Italian woman in Rome.

I asked him in Italian, "Excuse me, sir. Where is the Hotel Miramar?"

He looked down at me and smiled. He climbed down from his pedestal and motioned for me to follow him. He casually stopped a whole line of traffic, walked over to the sidewalk, flagged down two old Italian women in heavy overcoats and scarves, and requested that they escort me to the hotel. By this time, the traffic at the intersection was hopelessly snarled, and there were Italian drivers yelling and gesturing at each other. The policeman could have cared less, and he stood there watching me and my two escorts amble down the road toward the hotel. I had asked him in Italian. Try it! You'll like it.

# METHOD—Determine If Physical Problems Are Causing Imbalances in Your Body and See If They Can Be Changed Using Dramatic Physical Therapies

Several interesting things came my way during the nine years of my second marriage. The first was Rolfing. My wife had a small scoliosis in her spine, a curvature. This can cause a lot of discomfort. She also had temporomandibular joint (TMJ) problems. This is the hinge joint for your jaw. More women than men have this problem, and a lot of people suffer without ever finding out what the problem is. I found out about TMJ by reading a poster in my dentist's office. The scoliosis of the spine cannot usually be fixed after childhood. The dentists have had good success with the TMJ with retainers and capping teeth to relieve the stress on the joint. To relieve her pain, I used to massage her shoulders, neck, head, and scalp a lot. I am very good at massage, but I will deal with that as a separate method. She had very dense muscle tissue, like most people with Indonesian blood. The massage helped, but it was not dramatic enough to give her any permanent relief.

I had been reading a lot about Essalen Institute in Big Sur, California. A lot of very fine psychology and real-world methods for improving life had been developed or perfected there. They still, to the best of my knowledge, have residence seminars in all sorts of positive stuff. One of the people I had been reading about was Ida Rolf. She had developed this theory that an outer layer of fascia surrounded all of the muscles. Think of fascia as a bag that holds the muscle tissue. She felt that, by using a method of very deep massage, muscles could be lengthened permanently by literally moving the muscle tissue around in the fascia. Certain muscles would be lengthened to correct imbalances in the body. Ida Rolf even used to Rolf racehorses and other animals.

After a few years of trying to convince my wife that this might help her and following a trip to Asia that the scoliosis and TMJ problems almost ruined, she agreed to try it out. We interviewed several Rolfers on the phone and finally decided on one named Owen. It is important to feel comfortable with any person who has the level of responsibility that he or she has. The process is very painful for the person being Rolfed and exhausting for the Rolfer. I have not been Rolfed, but I have seen firsthand what it can do. After the process was complete, about twelve to fifteen hours of deep massage, it was like a heavy rock had been lifted off her. Many people suffer from physical problems that cause terrible anxiety. Some can be fixed by dramatic treatment like this. Balance in your body is a basic tenet of most of the healing arts.

I also have another personal example of how a physical problem can cause anxiety. I crashed badly on my bicycle when my second set of teeth was just coming in. I chipped both of them. The dentist ground them down to smooth points and left it at that. They didn't look like fangs, but I was very self-conscious of them. From the inside looking out, they were fangs. I talked with my hand in front of my mouth, mumbled, and generally kept my mouth closed. People with nice smiles invariably have nice teeth.

When I saw my first shrink in college, I mentioned my teeth. He asked about that, and after hearing my tale of woe, he made me promise that I would go back to the dormitory, telephone my parents, and demand to have them capped. I did. They said okay. That Easter break, I had them capped. For three hundred dollars (now about eighteen hundred dollars), I erased something that caused me great anxiety. I am all in favor of cosmetic surgery, teeth capping and straightening at any age, nose jobs, liposuction (which I am thinking of now), and so on, if—and that is a big if—you are convinced that the procedure will lower your anxiety. The important thing to consider is what impact the cosmetic surgery will have on your self-image and if that will, in turn, lower your anxiety. Good or better looks are no substitute for a pleasant personality, interesting character, or a nurturing attitude in a relationship.

# METHOD—Biorhythms

My general readings ultimately led me to learn about biorhythms. This is based on natural rhythms or cycles that human beings have. They are not unlike menstrual cycles, which are predictable once the starting point is established. There are three major cycles: physical, emotional, and intellectual. These cycles are all different in length, and they sometimes coincide to produce dramatic effects and occasionally balance or complement each other.

In Japan, the belief in biorhythms is so strong that, in some major companies, employees wear different colored tags to show to the general public that they are in a critical day range. This means they are near the top or bottom of one of their cycles. The color of the tag designates which cycle it is. Colleagues try to avoid contact that could cause the sensitive person trouble. I would call them "anxiety badges."

I bought a Biomate, a small plastic calculator that shows your biorhythms using three plastic wheels. Most biorhythm calculators I have seen work from the birth date of the individual. You set the Biomate on your birthday and adjust the revolving wheels, and you can then spin it to any date. It will then tell you where your cycles are and whether they are going up or down. There must be some deviation from this for each individual, but this is something you will have to figure out through observation. I already knew something about cycles from my regular depression cycles. I could tell if I were going up or down just by thinking about it.

I used my Biomate for about nine months. The interesting thing about watching biorhythms is that it makes you aware that the different cycles are there, meaning extent of and the differences between them. You may be low emotionally and high intellectually. That will give a different result from the opposites.

As I became more aware of the cycles, I used the device less and less. In my opinion, using biorhythms as an exact science sort of thing is impracticable unless you are in a group of like-minded people. This might be the case in Tokyo but certainly not in New York. It is worth investigating biorhythms to learn more about yourself.

# METHOD—Learn Massage; Apply Learning

Learning how to massage occurred naturally when I was very young, from age six onward. This coincided with the development of my brain. It was fortunate that massage was always something I thought was part of the natural scheme of things and I came to it at such a young age. That imparted some sort of natural understanding in it for me. My mother was born with her thumbs tucked into her hands. If you want to know how that looks, hold one of your palms up and touch the tip of your thumb to the base of your pinky. Her mother spent hours massaging her hands when she was a child and managed to get her about 75 percent use of her thumbs. She could live a normal life without the stigma of a birth defect. I imagined that the limited use of her thumbs was very uncomfortable from a physical standpoint.

Whenever I was within reach and not doing anything, she would ask me to massage her hands. I don't know how many times I did this, but it was a lot. She enjoyed it, and I enjoyed giving her pleasure in such a natural way. I would start with each finger and joint, moving them in all directions, pulling and pushing. I would work the joints in the hand and wrist in the same way and massage the muscles. I paid special attention to her thumbs. After several years of this, she told me that I had given her the full use of her thumbs. I thought it was wonderful. I occasionally massaged her hands after that. The die was cast.

The only body I worked on after that for a long time was my own. I could usually massage an injury or stiffness caused by anxiety and aid in the healing of the injury or diminish the anxiety. I don't know why, but the teenagers I hung out with were not at all touchy-feely, even girls I dated. It was all or nothing, sex or not, with little or no cuddling or just enjoying each other physically without the sex. When I first started working in New York, I began to have problems with what they call tension headaches. Things would be normal during the week, but on the weekends, usually on Saturday afternoon when I really started to relax from the week, I would get one of these tension headaches. My neck and shoulders would tighten up progressively until they felt like steel bands. This tightening would then creep up my neck to the base of my skull. It was so tense that it felt like the reaction you have after a sprain when the swelling and pain starts. The stiffness would then move into my scalp and begin the inexorable creep toward my forehead. By the time the creeping stiffness got about halfway across my head, I was in intense pain. It reached my hairline a few times, and I was barely able to move or talk. It happened every weekend.

Once when I was driving up to Connecticut to visit some friends, I could feel the tightening in my shoulders, and I was tempted to turn around and return home. Instead I decided to fight it. I pulled off the road and began giving myself a vigorous neck and shoulder massage. I'm glad no cops came by. It would have been hard to explain. It was a very painful way to combat these headaches, but it worked. I battled the headaches for about six months, every Saturday, and finally started giving myself daily shoulder and neck massages. Eventually my weekend headache problem vanished.

When I married again, as mentioned before, I started to massage my wife to relieve tension caused by scoliosis and TMJ. I found it easy to spot and fix a problem, despite the density of her tissue. I credit this to my early training. When someone complains of a stiffness and I start to massage, I can usually find the source very quickly, and it is often not where the subject thinks it is.

I enjoy massage because it is a form of intimacy that you can't have any other way. You are exploring the interior of someone's body. I get as much enjoyment from giving someone a massage as she seems to get from having one. There is a connection that is different from sex or cuddling. It is a concept that I can best explain using a movie analogy. In the 1970s, I went to the West Coast premiere of movie in Los Angeles entitled *Claire's Knee* directed by Eric Rohmer. I thought there would be several celebrities there, but there were about twenty people in the theater. Still I got bragging rights, which I just exercised for the first time. The movie was one in a series of what he termed "moral tales." I felt the movie was about passion. The lead actor, an adult of about fifty years, was infatuated with the teenage daughter of a friend of his. He wanted her but did not want to seduce her. That would have cheapened the feelings he had for her. He wanted to experience his feelings without her knowing about it. He concentrated on her knee as the object of his passion.

Later in the movie, after the young girl was disappointed in love, he sat with her in a gazebo overlooking a lake in Europe, consoling her as she sobbed by rubbing her knee! It was the most intense love scene I have ever seen. Now if I apply that to massage, you are going to think I am this incredible lecher giving random massages to unsuspecting victims. I should probably include watching French and Italian films as a method as they are so bizarre and convoluted they take you away from your current scene, but I like doing things rather than watching them to work with my anxiety. It doesn't stop you from going though.

Actually what I feel is very intense, but what I am feeling is that I am absorbing energy from the person's body. It can be an exhilarating experience. It can wear me out mentally, long before my hand muscles tire. In New York City, the home of most new ideas in my opinion, they even call masseurs and masseuses as energy vampires on occasion as they take so much energy from people. Touching some people is like handling an electric fence. Sometimes my hands feel like they are on fire. Occasionally they ache. I often have to use my knuckles to protect my fingers. I tell the person that the pain in her body is a release of energy. I have her imagine that her breath can be moved around in her body. I position my fingers or knuckles over the spot, apply pressure, and have her breathe into that spot, pushing up and creating as much pressure as she can stand. (The person also can't blame me for the pain).

The usual case is that the individual holds most of her negative energy in one place, like between the shoulder blades. After several weeks of repeated massage in that area, the energy level drops, and the muscles are not as quick to return to their tense state. Eventually the negative energy leaves that area, and the individual feels long-lasting relief. Soon the energy bundle reappears in a different place. You just keep chasing it around.

When I massage someone and find an energy spot, I usually feel around to all the places where that muscle goes and all of the adjoining muscles to find the center of the problem. I then go to the extremities of the muscles and begin working on the dense connective tissue. This tissue usually does not get much blood flow.

Usually the person I'm massaging will say, "That's not where it hurts."

I try to explain that I am trying to get to the problem in a way that will give longer relief. I then move along the muscles until I get to the main energy point. Sometimes the energy is gone by the time I get there.

This is not a mechanical process. Actually I am just letting my hands move around. They have their own way if finding the energy. In a way, I am the observer.

I like animals a lot. I usually start petting them, and within five minutes, I am massaging them. I have gotten some quizzical looks, and sometimes they get up and walk away, but they are back in a few minutes and settle in for the full treatment. Sometimes they have to be carried out to go home, like my old buddy Duke, a basset hound. The next time I go to where the animal lives, it plops down in front of me and gives me the look. I got this idea from Ida Rolf, who used to massage racehorses professionally in the sixties, something that is a common practice nowadays. I'd like to try a big cat sometime. I do house cats all the time.

Actually I recently almost had the opportunity. I was visiting my brother-in-law in Burns, Oregon. This is about as in the middle of nowhere as you can get. I gave him a list of animals I wanted to see. (We got to see all of them except bighorn sheep.) He found someone who had two cougars and a snow leopard as pets. I had meditated before going out there, and I was visualizing getting along with the cats. I wanted to be projecting good cat vibes. When we arrived, they were out back, making those eerie cougar sounds. They knew we had arrived. The cat owner and I approached this feisty ninety-pound female. He scratched her through the bars and introduced me. I was just about to reach out and start petting her when my wife walked over to take a look. The cougar went wild and tried to attack and kill my wife, hissing and spitting. Apparently the owner had a girlfriend a while back, and the cat resented her so much that she took a dislike to any females. The snow leopard would have been a better choice. The owner went in the enclosure with her and roughhoused a bit, but by that time, the cats were all on high alert. Maybe some other time. The best thing about relaxing an animal—or a person for that matter—is that you see it happening and that in itself causes you to relax.

I read a few texts on Shiatsu, which some are touting as being the massage equivalent to acupuncture. Shiatsu consists of applying pressure to energy points all over the body, usually for one breath or about six or seven seconds. These are the same spots where the acupuncturists insert the needles. I tried this on myself for a time, pressing points all over my body in sequence. I didn't really feel anything from it. The one technique I did pick up from Shiatsu was to press a muscle for that magic six or seven seconds. I combined this with the breathing technique mentioned before and developed what my wife calls "knot patrol."

When I find a muscle with a knot in it, I curl my hand into a massage weapon. This is identical to giving someone the finger except the finger next to the index finger, the "finger" finger is folded down between the index and third finger, and the thumb slides down to hold the three together. This is the same weapon used to deliver "Noogies" in grammar school. I apply this to the knot, and once it stops sliding around, I tell her to inhale against my massage weapon. The knots disappear with their tails between their legs.

Another thing I like to do for a partner is to take an area like the hip joints and massage all around through the buttocks and pelvis to free the energy in this area. You eventually run into the sciatic nerve, which also relaxes the legs.

Feet are another prime target. There is a system of foot massage named foot reflexology where you massage certain parts of the foot and you are indirectly massaging different organs in the body. I figure that, if you massage the entire foot, then you are getting everything. So I never bothered much with formal foot reflexology. I even massage the heel bone, which is actually a separate bone in the foot and can be moved around. Women who wear high heels, like my wife does, love to have this bone manipulated because that is the bone right above the heel spike.

When I first met my wife Marilyn, I asked if she wanted a foot massage. She thought that I was a bit nutty but said okay. Twenty minutes later, I finished and asked her to take a walk around the room. She didn't think I was nutty then. She said she had never felt her feet before like that. She felt like she was walking on pillows. She was an instant convert. I have also massaged the feet of a friend's wife when she was pregnant. She thought she died and went to heaven. I massage feet the same way I massage hands, one joint at a time, and then one muscle at a time slowly.

The ideal massage is using massage oil such as jojoba oil or a fragrant massage oil around the hands and arms, feet and legs, hips, back, neck, occipital lobe, scalp, face, ears, front of neck shoulders, and chest. I like to massage the neck with the subject lying on her back. After the massage, I go over the body with a very light touch and lighten this touch until I am barely touching the skin. I finish with figure eights over the skin (not touching) to harmonize the energy. Sorry, guys, I only do women. My wife thinks I could make millions massaging. I'm really thinking about going to massage school to become a licensed massage therapist.

Seriously though, massage is a gift. Learn to massage yourself, your partner, old people, people in the hospital, pregnant friends, babies, dogs, and cats. I have used a number of devices, vibrators, and things that have balls that you roll around. I don't see any benefit of these things over fingers and knuckles unless you just like the way they look hanging on the back of the bathroom door, where they will hang unused for years.

I have read that crack babies, those born to addicted mothers, benefit greatly by being held and being massaged. I called a couple hospitals in Boston and volunteered after explaining I had a special talent.

The usual reply was, "We already have people who do that."

Can you imagine that?

There are courses given in massage in almost every town I have been in. They usually call them workshops or seminars. On the lighter side, I met a woman from Swampscott, Massachusetts, who had taken a weekend seminar in foot reflexology and thought it was fantastic. The only problem was that her boyfriend and she had split and she didn't have anyone to do it with. Mutual massage can reduce anxiety, and it is great if only one person in the relationship is anxious.

Massage can be practiced alone, with a partner, or just by one on the other. Back scratching is something that really needs another person. There is something about the touch of another person that is so different from your own touch. My mother had long, hard nails that spoiled me from the outset. I realize that some people have very soft nails, and for them, back scratching is not a pleasant experience. Some people have very short nails due to constant clipping or biting. A proper back scratch involves the use of nails with the hand in a semi claw position, so strong nails are important. Back scratching is such a fleeting pleasure that I can't make a method out of it. All I can say is, for the time it is happening, that is all that is happening for me. It is a good thing to do for someone. If you have soft nails and really want to scratch your partner, go to a guitar store and buy some finger picks. These are different from flat picks and fit over the tips of your fingers. You could scratch someone's back with feathers, but watch out. Things could easily get out of control.

While I'm on the subject of things requiring a partner, you can do another simple thing to stop your partner's anxiety for a short time. Play with his or her hair. Of course, he or she has to have some. When I had my first haircut, I fell asleep in the chair. Whenever someone plays with my hair, I just travel to a different world. The technique I use is to spread apart my fingers and move them across the scalp, starting from the hairline and moving toward the middle of the head. When I get a lot of hair in between my fingers, I close them together and pull my hand straight up away from the scalp, letting the hair fall out as it passes through my fingers. You can repeat this many times without the subject getting tired of it. I call this a "hair rub." This stimulates thousands of sensitive nerves each time. This is a good method to put someone to sleep who is having trouble doing so. You can even brush someone's hair in the morning just after he or she wakes. For some reason, having this done to you feels better by magnitudes than doing it to yourself.

# METHOD—Make More Love

I could have entitled this method as "have more sex." I don't mean to make a distinction. I always find it amusing that parents blanch at the idea of words like "screw" being on a CD that their kids listen to, along with a whole raft of other verboten explicit words and phrases, but they think nothing of a track that has phrases on it like, "Baby, I want to make love to you all night long." What do they think the artist means by that, sitting ten feet apart and cooing at each other? So "make love" it is.

Sex causes me a lot of anxiety. I enjoy it, but in ways, it has been a curse. If you take medication to fight anxiety, you may experience a lowering of the libido as a side effect. A friend of mine does not take this type of medication, but he has experienced the same problem with blood pressure medication. Still another friend, Pietr, has reported that his libido has all but disappeared. He has felt a great relief because of this side effect. He enjoys not having to think about it or do anything about it. I have experienced a lowering of the libido and a diminished amount of fluid that is ejaculated. The lowered libido manifests itself in a decrease of thinking about sex. In the past, there were times when thinking about sex was a pleasant experience, just in itself. I especially enjoyed this when awakening after a good night's sleep. When I try this now, it seems like the fantasy is detached from me in a way that it was attached before. It seems unreal and only vaguely stimulating. The decreased amount of ejaculate means that particular part of sex does not feel as good and indeed often feels uncomfortable. This is all perplexing to me because I thought that most of the antianxiety drugs, the serotonin reuptake inhibitors, left more serotonin in your system, and we all know that serotonin is the natural stuff that makes you feel good. Serotonin is what your body's nervous system produces to aid in transfer of impulses between nerves. The body then absorbs the used serotonin. At least this is my understanding of it. The drugs prevent the (reuptake) absorption. Some anxiety prescriptions can increase or decrease libido depending on the individual. I don't know if I am one of the lucky ones or not by having mine decrease. It sure is different though. Your physician should be able to tell you which drugs have the greatest chance of affecting your sex drive. Because love and sensuality reduce anxiety in most people, keeping up your libido can be an important consideration.

My doctor gave me a trial prescription of Viagra. I tried this and found that my problem was not with getting and maintaining an erection. It was the thought process that went along with it. I never knew that the thought process about sex had so much to do with the actual act. Sex is such a complicated issue, and the effect of medication just compounds this. I don't understand the whole process and never have. I will leave the topic to someone more qualified. I just didn't want to not say anything about it.

# METHOD—Meet the Personality within That Is Causing You Anxiety

One of the more interesting seminars we attended in New York City in the 1980s was about voice dialogue. This was very popular at the time. I believe it is an outgrowth of transactional analysis, something I believe was developed at Essalen Institute, which I mentioned before. Everyone will recognize the stereotype of someone talking to a pillow and pretending it was a person to get to his or her real thoughts. Hollywood gets a big kick out of taking these methods and exploiting them for laughs. Voice dialogue is a method developed by Doctors Hal and Sidra Stone. The basis of voice dialogue is that all people have the same basic personalities, yes personalities with an "s," and if you separate these, then the person being facilitated will be able to see which personalities are causing the problem.

You need a facilitator and a person to be facilitated. Others can be present in the room. We sat in chairs facing each other. The person being facilitated had two chairs. A conversation would begin with the facilitator being the questioner. The questions would be general questions about the person. Soon the questions would take a natural personal turn as they always do when one person is trying to find out about another. Suddenly there is a resistance to answering any more questions. This is one of the personalities, usually the police officer (person), stopping the conversation. At this point, the facilitator would identify the police officer and ask if he or she could speak with the person being facilitated. The police officer, being recognized, would usually accede. The facilitator asks the person being facilitated to move to the other chair. This gives the person a sense of separation from the police personality. You then continue the dialogue. You will soon encounter the child; the adult; the controller; the meek, controlled person; the sex fiend; and a myriad of other people. Facilitating someone is interesting and fun, but being facilitated is a blast.

When I was finished, I felt like I was one of those dog walkers you see in New York City with ten or fifteen dogs, except you are the dog walker and the dogs are your personalities. It is amazing that a process this simple can bring so much to the surface for you to take a look at. Imagine actually being to talk to the personality causing your anxiety.

Voice dialogue is one way to do this. Talking to a shrink may work if he or she understands that you are interested in defining the part of your personality that is causing you the most anxiety. Most shrinks I have met do not specialize in quick fixes like this. If psychology is their only way of making money and they are not affiliated with a large hospital program that feeds new patients to them, then they would probably go out of business with quick fixes. An alternative would be group therapy with a group of like-minded people. I have not participated in group therapy, but I know several people who have. The important thing is the feedback you get from the other people in the group. The psychologist acts as the facilitator.

# METHOD—Visualize Events That You Are Anxious about as Completed, Fun, and Enjoyable

I was having sex problems in my second marriage. It was not unexpected. I learned this after a strange skiing trip to Switzerland that included staying with a particularly strange couple in a flat because they did not have enough money for a hotel. The male was very argumentative, and this led to a nightly battle with my wife, usually about the philosophy of relationships. These types of arguments are very stressful for the other people trapped in the same room with the participants because it is more a battle of wills than an argument about two opposing philosophies. It is not a group discussion. If you try to butt in, you get flattened and told to butt out.

After a week of skiing and staying with this couple, I wanted to spend a day in Geneva, Switzerland, one of my favorite cities, before returning to the States. I thought it would be relaxing to walk around, look at the lake and fountain, shop, and have some lunch. My wife was so strung out by this time that the day and night in Geneva turned into a twenty-four-hour-long argument in which I was informed that I had a sex problem and I had to see someone about it. See someone? Like go to a shrink? Unthinkable. There was nothing wrong with me!

I finally agreed to see someone. I personally thought I was having too much sex rather than too little, but this often happens when you have a relationship with a person nine years younger than you are. It is a hormone war. The Rolfer Owen recommended the shrink, Dr. Henry, who used cutting-edge techniques that was very different from what I had expected. There's no talk about your childhood, dreams, or any of that Freudian stuff. What is the problem? And let's try to solve it.

One of the techniques he used is visualization. He would describe several scenes involving your problem. You could comment on them if they needed correcting, and he could ask you questions if he needed more information. He had my wife undressing in the backyard and more, very sensual stuff. This all worked great for the sex in the relationship. The really important thing was my introduction to visualization.

I read something about the American hostages in Beirut a few years back. These guys were held for years. They were moved from place to place, almost daily. They were threatened and beaten, to the point of one of them having brain damage. They spent weeks at a time with garbage bags over their head. This is fairly rough treatment. The press followed them for a time after their release until something more newsworthy came up. Occasionally you would, using selective reading, come up with a blurb about one of the hostages. I read that one of them had won a golf tournament several weeks after returning from Lebanon! How could this be possible? He must have been in sad physical and mental shape (and was).

When he was asked how he could possibly have done that given the circumstances, he said he had spent the four years in captivity visualizing the game of golf. He was a golfer, and he would go over a full round of golf in his mind stroke by stroke over and over again. All he had to do then was to get out and play, the easy part.

I wish I could spend more time visualizing things, but I am too busy doing them. I find visualization helpful when I run out of time. I use it now to visualize my Tai Chi when I do not have time to physically go through the forms. The next time I do the actual form, I have improved. I often do this before falling asleep. There are all sorts of possibilities with visualization. It can lower anxiety when you are going into a stressful meeting, if you have to talk in front of people, or if you are going to ask someone to spend time with you. By visualizing the event in its complete form, all you have to do is get out and play, the easy part.

# METHOD—Learn Several Methods to Aid in Falling Asleep

Sleep and the lack of sleep are important contributors to the level of anxiety you have. I had insomnia and would sleepwalk when I was a kid. I had a lot of trouble getting to sleep and staying asleep. I would often wake up in total darkness in a different part of the house. My grandmother, a light sleeper and midnight snacker, would often follow me around. I did strange things like walk around the dining table and knock down the chairs. She would put them back. We always had dinner together as a family, which was good from a family standpoint, but there was often contention at the table or lecturing, so I guess I was evening the score by knocking down the chairs later on. One time I woke up in the front yard, balls-ass naked.

Having this happen was as frightening from an anticipation standpoint as the actual occurrence. I had no tools to fight the insomnia except George, my half-Siamese/half black alley cat. For years, I would fall asleep with him on my chest. I would be scratching his cheeks with both hands, and he would be purring away. I tried sleeping with my dog, a male Dalmatian, on the bed, but he would bite my legs through the covers if I moved around too much. It is an odd way to be awakened. The cat was best. I was taken to several doctors about the insomnia, but they didn't have any tools either. I was never given any sleeping pills, I guess, because they were mostly addictive back then.

So I know what a drag insomnia can be. Anxiety has to be one of the causes of insomnia, which causes anxiety. This is a bad cycle to get into. Over the years, I have developed or learned a few methods to fight insomnia. The most humorous and one of the best comes from a former colleague, Steve.

He said, "Think about sex."

I can tell you that this works when all others fail. The only problem is that, if you are really anxious and think about sex long enough, it could lead to the problem of having to do something about it, like spank the monkey. The first thing I try when I can't get to sleep is to lie on my back. I usually sleep on my front side. When I lie on my back, I am comfortable for a time, but after fifteen minutes or so, I get the urge to turn over. When I do turn over to find a new position, I usually fall asleep. I use my TM mantra a lot, especially when I can't get a thought out of my mind. This reverses the thought process, and I just fall asleep. The first method I ever learned and still use today in various circumstances is joint-by-joint relaxation. Because this is a method, I will describe it in the next section.

Yet another technique produces varying results. When I close my eyes, I seem to see a black background with red shapes. Sometimes these shapes are an afterglow of things I was looking at before I closed my eyes, but this quickly fades. Eventually the red coalesces into a single spot. If I concentrate on this for a while, the red spot starts taking on recognizable shapes, sometimes whole scenes. These fade, and are replaced by other scenes, faces, or shapes. Once I went through every cartoon character I had ever seen. I don't know if other people can duplicate this. I think it is the most dangerous method because it deals with so-called hallucinations. It is a fact that all normal children have hallucinations and most societies teach them not to have them because they are not acceptable in the real adult world, whatever that is. The short form is that they interfere with the necessities of society.

There is another method I use that appears below under

# METHOD—Thought Balloons

It is good enough to be a method. Lately this red spot method has morphed a bit. At night, you can usually hear your breathing, so I listen to that and focus my eyes on the back of my eyelids, very close. There is a faint red glow. Next thing I know is that I just woke up from being asleep.

I ascribe to the theory that you have a different intelligence for each sense and a memory that goes along with it. I have experimented with this a bit and have even taken tape recorders on vacation to see if I can have as vivid a memory from the sound of a place as I can from photographs. I have found that the sound brings back more vivid memories. I have also found that, the more senses I get involved when I am trying to learn something, the quicker I learn and the longer the learning lasts. They say the best place to learn a language is in bed. Think of all the senses that are involved there. An entirely different method involves visualization to some extent and remembering a specific sequence of events.

If I can't get to sleep or back to sleep, I try to remember the entire sequence of a motion picture, including the sound. Motion pictures are mainly visual and auditory so I am invoking two senses. My favorite is *Terminator II* starring Arnold Schwarzenegger. This movie had a lot of memorable scenes and sound bites. I find I usually get to the scene where he is jumping off the road into the drainage canal on his Harley in L.A. before I fall asleep

Some of the methods I use to combat anxiety involve time that has to be spent alone. Examples would be hatha yoga and meditation. If you are answering the phone or trying to feed the baby, these methods are not going to work as they should. Sometimes you have to make time, and not everyone's lifestyle supports this. The main dilemma is the one of sleep versus the beneficial method. I feel that, if you take a half hour of time usually reserved for sleep and use this time for a method, you are going to sleep better and get more benefit from the sleep that you get. If you are tired, a slow physical activity that does not produce a lot of sweat is preferable to a meditative activity.

For example, one thing you will not fall asleep after is lifting weights.

It excites the body. I feel that I sleep more soundly after mild exercise. If you want to get up a half hour early, stretching is a good way to wake up. I have read that the mind is most active in the morning right after waking. Meditating would be a good match for that or reading up. I've tried taking a hot bath or shower just before going to bed. This does not work for me. Heat speeds up my body for about a half hour, so sleep is impossible during that period. If I take a shower before bedtime, I plan to read for the half hour I would be awake anyhow.

# METHOD—Joint-by-Joint Relaxation

I admit I have seen this method a lot and explained in many varying ways by different people. It is still a good one because your mind is forced to follow a sequence, not unlike repetition that I find so useful in good methods.

Joint-by-joint relaxation is a way to mentally and physically relax your entire body. It is employed to varying degrees in many of the other methods described in this book, usually after some form of physical activity, to bring the body back to the normal state. I use it after yoga and before meditation and to aid in falling asleep. I first thought of this sometime in high school. As usual, it was a roundabout learning process. I loved the *Tonight Show* starring Johnny Carson. This was back when the show was three hours long. I think I must have watched him every night for three years. I even started acting like Johnny Carson. My parents knew I had insomnia problems so they rarely bugged me about this. It was either lie there and stare at the shadows on the ceiling or watch the *Tonight Show*. Of course, I was sleep-deprived, so that added to my anxiety.

There were several ads on the *Tonight Show*, so I had to fill these with some activity. This was before zappers and cable TV, so you only had thirteen channels and had to get up to change them. I would invent things to do to pass the time. I have long legs and often look down at my feet, amazed they are attached to the rest of me because they are so far away. I saw a movie starring John Wayne once in which he was paralyzed in combat. He was determined to walk again. He was lying on his stomach and had a mirror rigged up so he could look down at his toe.

He used to say over and over, "Gonna move that toe. Gonna move that toe."

Of course, his almost superhuman employment of mind over matter worked, and he finally got the toe to move. It didn't hurt that he was the get-anything-done-that-you-want John Wayne either. John Wayne's toe was about as far away from his eyes as mine is. I could relate to the distance. I decided I was going to learn to move my toe in a different way than it normally moved. My nervous system was intact so it was not that type of a challenge, but a challenge nonetheless. One movement that is not employed to any great extent by the toes is the lateral movement. We have the muscles to make our toes move in this way, but we don't use them all that much, especially since we started wearing shoes.

I decided to learn to wiggle my toes back and forth. At first, the only movement I could get was a splaying of all of the toes. Night after night, I stared down there and worked on my movements until the tiny, seldom-used muscles, torn out of their genetically downward spiraling multigenerational torpor, began to respond. I finally was able to get my big toe to move back and forth. I could also cross my toes, which is the usual way I sit now when barefoot. I am barefoot whenever I can be. (Many times, when I'm minding my own business, someone will exclaim, "Hey, look at your toes." I look down, and sure enough, they are crossed). I finally stopped training my toes because I figured, "Where can I go with this?" The answer was nowhere. I had heard that Houdini could play the piano with his toes. I'll bet it was chopsticks. I was interested in a more conventional way to make a living. This toe moving learning experience made me aware of different parts of my body. I thought about different parts of my body and how things felt. I became aware of the tension in my muscles and decided to work on that rather than learning how to wiggle another dormant set of muscles in my body. I tried to relax different parts of my body in sequence. The sequence part is easy. I separate my body in my mind according to joints. You just start with your toes and work your way up. Sometimes it may help to first tense the muscles in a certain area of your body, say your calves, and then relax them. This may have some physiological effect, but I use it to just become more aware of the area I am trying to relax.

One of the methods that works well is to think of an area and concentrate on your breath. Every time you exhale, you relax that area a bit more. I use three or more breaths on each area. Also, think of the surface you are lying on, and think of it as a surface that your body can penetrate. Let your muscles sink a bit below the surface. You may feel like you are floating. I have done this on stone and on a soft mattress with equal success. Most of the meditative arts and self-hypnotism recommend that you sit in a chair rather than lying down to avoid falling asleep. In this case, sleep is the desired effect.

One good effect of this method is that you will learn to identify areas of your body that are the reservoirs of your anxious energy. An aspect of this was described under the massage method in case you find this interesting or skipped over it.

I learned another good way to relax your body in a sequential way in a Tai Chi class. We were standing, but I see no reason why it would not work sitting down. Imagine that water fills your body. Start from the highest point, and imagine the water draining out of your body very slowly. Think of the different parts of the body and limbs as the water drains out. Think of your breathing as replacing the water with fresh air. When you are empty of water, you will feel light and at rest.

As an aside, there is also a way to wake up from bad dreams. You become aware that it is just a dream while you are still in the dream. You tell everyone it is a dream, and you can wake up if you blink your eyes really hard. Nobody pays attention, so you blink one time hard, and you will wake up in your bed. The bad news is that your companions who didn't listen get eaten by dinosaurs, stung by huge spiders, or attacked by lechers or whatever else was chasing you in the dream. Schwartz, Treg, and Dennis, I'm sorry you had to suffer, but I hate being chased by dinosaurs.

I am going to digress and move back to the present. There is an opposite to falling asleep, staying awake of course. I took a course in coffee business and bean basics in Portland, Oregon, because I wanted to start a coffee business when I retired. I am a trained barista and can make cappuccinos with Christmas trees or antlers on top, but that is beside the point. I learned a lot about coffee. One thing I found out that the older you get (for most people), the greater the effect that coffee has on your sleep. In college, I could drink five cups of coffee studying and going directly to sleep. Now if I have a cup after three o'clock in the afternoon, I will invariably wake up at two in the morning. It is not a slow wake-up, but more like that Japanese soldier they found in the jungle in the Philippines in the 1970s, who had been living there almost thirty years alone. He was studied, and it was found that he could go from a deep sleep to totally awake in like one tenth of a second. That kind of wake-up. Bing! You are awake.

Because this is my book and I want to write about staying awake or rather being able to sleep, I will give a little history of coffee. The original coffee plant is native to Ethiopia. There was a goatherd named Cheffee (pronounced "coffee" no doubt in Ethiopia). There are over ninety native languages spoken there, so I will not guess at which one it was. He noticed that his goats became frisky after eating certain red berries. He picked some, and they had the same effect on him so he took them to market. Soon the Benedictine monks in town found that, if they ate the beans, they could stay awake easier during prayers. (It's interesting that they find church as boring as I do.) They tried to send some berries to the Vatican, but the fresh berries rotted during the long caravan across the desert. They did not find the solution as the first coffee beans were roasted in Yemen. These roasted beans could survive the trip. The coffee industry was born.

Brazil alone has over five million people working in the coffee industry. Coffee roasting is easy. (I went to a separate school for that in Colorado Springs.) Just throw the raw beans in a skillet and cook them dry, stirring constantly. There are, as I recall, about forty-four naturally occurring plants worldwide that contain caffeine. The jury is still out as to its benefit to the plants, but I think it is a natural insect repellant. The insect starts eating the leaf, gets agitated, and splits. The same caffeine-producing plants growing near each other usually have different caffeine levels depending on whether they are in the sun or shade. The plants grown in shade have higher levels. There are also more plant-eating insects in the shade. So be aware that, if you are buying shade-grown or bird-friendly coffee or tea, it may have higher caffeine levels. Tea has more caffeine than coffee in its dry state. Brewed coffee has more caffeine than brewed tea. Don't drink a cup of tea before trying to go to sleep. Try an herb like chamomile. According to Wikipedia, "There is Level B evidence to support the claim that chamomile possesses anxiolytic (antianxiety) properties and chamomile may have clinical applications in the treatment of stress and insomnia." You will see references to chamomile tea and other teas, but they are really infusions. The only real tea is produced using the leaves of the plant Camellia Sinensis. It's a short digression but interesting.

# METHOD—Keep the Child Inside of You Alive and Well

Childhood is a very complicated subject. Everyone has gone through it, yet nobody can explain what happens. Privileged children can have unhappy childhoods, and children with nothing in Africa can have good ones. One can become a Nobel laureate and the other a mass murderer. My former colleague, Steve, always said, "It's never too late to have a happy childhood." You may have to learn or relearn how to play, if you haven't done this in a while. Asian Indians run the local liquor store. I have worked with Asians Indians and understand a lot about them and their culture, some of them at least as they have many different cultures yet some similarities. They are very polite and service-oriented. They give me a bag for my bottle of wine every time even though I keep telling them that I don't want the bag because it is a waste of paper. I recycle. Most of the guys in the store have learned this, but one kept putting my bottle in the bag.

One night when no other customers were in the store, I growled at him when he started putting my bottle in the bag. I learned this great warning growl from my Dalmatian, Mister, replete with trembling upper lip. He slowly looked up at me, fully expecting to see a German shepherd staring him down. We all broke into uproarious laughter. Needless to say, I no longer have to remind him about my no-bag policy. We have become great friends and lately have been talking about food. I shop every day for food, like the Europeans do. I love Asian food, and they are curious about the stuff I buy, like artichokes.

For this last Thanksgiving, I brined a turkey in a salt solution overnight before cooking it. I also threw in some garlic and Garam Masala, a mixture of Asian Indian spices. It was fantastic. I told my Indian friend about it, and now they all think I am a great chef. It is interesting how many great relationships start with a good laugh.

# METHOD—Do One Thing at a Time at an Enjoyable Pace

One of the worst habits I have is always trying to do several things at the same time. Of course, you can get a lot done that way, but in the end, I am jangled, and I don't have the sense of accomplishment that I should. I believe I read somewhere in a study about people who are prone to heart attacks that doing multiple things at once was one of the worst traits they had, one of the top ten. This makes sense. There are times, particularly in a work environment, where doing one thing at a time is not possible. I have spent a lot of time retraining myself to do one thing at a time, usually a project around the house. Before I start, I plan it out and remind myself that I am only going to do this one thing. I get a great deal of satisfaction when I am successful at spending some leisurely time working on one task rather than just getting it done. Afterward I clean up and then go out again to look at it. It probably even looks different than it would if it were just one part of many tasks. My wife is an expert at concentrating on one thing, and she derives a great deal of enjoyment in doing a project, probably more than she gets from finishing it.

One day she was planting some geraniums in window boxes at our cottage on Cape Cod. Geraniums are de rigueur on the Cape. When she was about halfway finished I, or rather Tony, my alter ego, finished his project and came clanking over to where she was placidly mixing dirt and planting plants. Tony furiously bent into the task, mixing dirt, cow manure, and peat moss; filling boxes; and separating and laying out geraniums. After she planted the plants, he would water them and lift the boxes up onto their holders under the windows. He was quite proud of the efficiency of the operation.

At the end, Marilyn got up and stomped inside, pausing at the door to thank me for ruining her entire day. This is an illustration of the value and anxiety-reduction capability of planning and doing a task yourself. One task at a time for enjoyment.

# METHOD—Write Down Detailed Step-by-Step Plans Before Starting a Major Project

One facet of the last method will make the task even more enjoyable than doing one thing at a time at an enjoyable pace, but it takes some explaining, planning. I spent hours in my childhood and teens building things with my father. He is an engineer and an expert mathematician, obviously not something that can be passed on genetically, and he can figure almost anything out. He also loathed spending money on carpenters and gardeners, things he could do himself. I was the carpenter's assistant. I got to hold things. He was not a very good teacher, but I did manage to learn a lot just by watching him. He often became anxious and frustrated when he cut something wrong or a machine failed to work properly. Plastic was his nemesis.

Plastic was fairly new, and most plastic things broke easily. He was a perfectionist and cut everything with very fine tolerances. Things had to fit together perfectly, not too tight and not too loose. Every so often, usually when he made a mistake, he would explode. The air would turn blue, and often stuff would go flying. He would curse at his ignorance. These were unpleasant times. My adrenaline and other chemicals would flood into my system. This happened with such regularity that I thought that it was normal - that rage was part of the process of building things.

Five years ago, I built our home here in New Jersey. I was actually the general contractor, but to save money and get some exercise, I acted as the laborer for any skilled labor that I hired. I would pay them, and they would yell at me like they would yell at anyone else that worked for them. When the basic house was finished, I set about finishing the trim and the paint and varnish inside. I lost it a few times but got it done. A friend who was a contractor was building a large building nearby and had some wooden floor beams (joists) delivered that were all about eight feet too long. They had to cut the extra eight feet off to use them. This was a tremendous waste of material. He asked if I wanted any. I had dreams of a workshop in the basement and needed shelving for the rest of the basement for storage. The wood for this project would have cost literally thousands of dollars, and I would have had to assemble everything. These pieces were finished. They were not pretty because they would wind up with a layer of sheetrock underneath and a floor on top. They were so strong that you could drive a loaded cement truck over them when they were in place. I rented a truck and loaded about sixty of these wooden I-beams into the truck.

When I decided to make the shelving, I wanted to do it in an assembly line fashion. It was Tony again, but the thoughtful Tony this time. I also wanted to build them with the least amount of aggravation. I built a prototype shelf using the trial-and-error process and kept notes. I then went up to the computer and typed them out. When it came time to build the rest of the shelves, I just referred to the directions I had written. I built an entire workshop and nine sets of shelves eight feet long without as much as one tantrum, and I actually enjoyed it. I stained them the darkest stain I could find. You can cover up a multitude of ills with stain or a coat of paint.

I had been sending my family detailed letters about the progress in building the house, and in the one letter that described the workshop and shelves, I included a copy of my directions. About a month later, my father wrote a letter back to me, thanking me for suggesting to him that he write out directions before building something. He had tried it, and it had really worked well.

I was totally and completely flabbergasted. After fifty-two years of frustration and fear working on projects with my father, he took my advice. Wow! I had learned an important lesson for myself, taught him one, and learned why he was not a good teacher. He was making it up as he went along! How can you teach someone that?

Later when we learn to think things out before starting them, maybe we can dispense with the writing part. One of the toughest things for an anxious person to do is to remember to say to himself or herself, "Now let's stop for a minute and think this through."

When I embark on a project with Marilyn, she will just sit and look at whatever we are going to do.

I finally say, "Let's go. I'm getting nervous just standing around here."

Her reply is usually, "I'm thinking."

When she finally gets moving, she has the entire plan in her head. She doesn't need the writing it down part.

I will get into cooking later, but if you are recipe-oriented like I am, the most important thing to do before starting anything is to read slowly through the entire ingredient list and the recipe. I repeat before starting anything. This is one of the most difficult habits I have ever tried to develop. I often attempt challenging recipes that may have days of preparation. It drives me nuts, but it is absolutely essential unless you want to wind up without the proper ingredients, a broken sauce, or a fire extinguisher in your hand with smoke all over the place.

# METHOD—Keep a Journal

I was talking with my father recently about things we liked and disliked in life. One of the things that he said really amazed me. He said that one of the things he enjoyed the most was making a list and then crossing off items as they were completed. He discovered this while working as a ship repair supervisor in his first job. He was required to make sure that all of the repairs that were being made to an oceangoing ship were completed in sequence and on time. If you miss one sea valve on a ship, it can skid merrily down the ways and promptly sink in the harbor. He thought that was the most enjoyable job he had because of the list-keeping aspect of it. He rose to a very high level in corporate business and traveled with my mother all over the world, but that was the one thing he enjoyed most in work. The methodical nature of making and checking off the list was, of and in itself, a means to its own end. Maybe this lessened his anxiety, gave him a way of keeping score, and freed his mind to think of other things.

The act of recording things, just for the sake of recording them, has been around for a long time. Prehistoric cave dwellers in France drew pictures of their hunting on the ceilings of caves, perhaps in an attempt to preserve their own history. If you go to the Pearl Art store in New York City on Canal Street, you will find a rack with at least a hundred different kinds of journals, nicely covered books with blank pages. People who write for newspapers and magazines are called journalists. I am creating a journal of sorts by writing this book. Young children, especially girls, keep diaries. Some of our most famous leaders like Thomas Jefferson kept journals about his gardens. I visited his home, Monticello, in Charlottesville, Virginia, and saw a reproduction of his entire garden journal in the store. Just keeping that journal would have taken me eight hours a day, eight days a week. Some journal keeping can be for posterity or future reference, but the act of keeping a journal, of writing things down, is itself something of great value. I enjoy getting an idea out into the open. It is a completion of some urge that I do not understand. I suppose that the writing of a song or a poem touches the same need. You learn where you have been, where you are, and perhaps even where you want to go.

You don't need to be a good writer to keep a journal. There are many courses available on how to keep a journal. It is not about the quality of the writing but the act of doing it. Quality is an embellishment. I found a diary from one of my ancestors. It consisted of page after page of comments about the weather during the 1800s.

When I first started reading it, I thought, "What a bore. Couldn't she have written about some Indians or something else interesting?"

She wrote about what she was interested in. It was about the writing. There were a few notes in her journal about other things. I was amazed at the time frames that people had to deal with back then. Making a visit to some friends fifteen miles away entailed a lot of planning, cooking, and packing. You had to get the horses ready and hitched up to the sleigh or wagon. The trip could easily take two or three hours. When you arrived, you had to cool down the horses and put them in the stable for the night.

Many novelists start out by writing about things that happened to them and expand the story to make it interesting and complete. "Write about what you know" is an oft-repeated theme from novelists giving advice to new writers. If you have trouble finding something to write about, start by chronicling your life. You will find a lot of things you didn't know about and remember a lot of things you had forgotten. I sure did. This book is a good example.

I have mentioned dreams a lot in writing this, so this may be a bit redundant. I decided back in the 1980s to start recording my dreams. I read that, if you want to do this, you have to do it as soon as you wake up because that is the only chance you have to remember them. Some believe we constantly dream but can't experience them during waking hours because the flood of sensory input drowns them out. Anyhow, dreams are transitory. I kept a notebook and a pen on my night table and started assiduously recording my dreams just after waking. This practice did not last long because, when I read them later, they were so frightening and bizarre that I started wondering about my sanity again. I would be careful about this kind of journal keeping

# METHOD—Write It Out and Then Take Action

I have the ability to get myself into bad situations or, rather, to let potentially bad situations develop into bad ones. I then have to figure out a way to extricate myself from the situation. In times of greatest anxiety, times when pressure is building up for a major change, I can find relief in writing. Writing is less abstract than drawing, and you can often gain concrete ideas from what appears on the paper. I have written about abstract things like dreams, fiction, and fact. All three have the same effect as far as anxiety goes. Somehow writing deflates the balloon and pushes back the walls a bit. The most constructive writing is to try to describe what is going on at that moment. I'll give you an example.

When I was a Boy Scout, we made a field trip up to the Air National Guard at the Westchester County Airport. They kept some active P-51 Mustangs up there, a famous, very sleek, and powerful World War II fighter. They were propeller-driven planes that made a lot of noise, wonderful noise. We watched them land and taxi over to where we were waiting. After they had gone through their post-flight check, the pilots hoisted us up and let us sit in the cockpit. If time had stopped there, it would have been okay with me. I always felt comfortable around that airport, and later in my teens, I used to drive up there as a place of refuge. I knew ways to get close to the runways, and I would just sit there for hours and let the mind run. If I were in a crisis, I would take a pad of paper and a pen, drive up to the airport, and write down all of the good and bad things that were happening. I would then write down what some of the solutions could be. It was immediately apparent which one I should choose, but I would play with them a bit and try to factor in the effect that my actions would have on other people. Somehow the aircraft coming and going would aid in this process. They could be coming from and going to anywhere. It, sort of, opened up the possibilities of my thought process. I'm sure a view of a harbor or a stream could have the same effect.

I just find that getting away from my usual surroundings and writing everything down helps me to push back the walls and see things as they really are. I usually tell the people closest to me what my course of action is right away and others the next day. I have never had a great deal of anxiety in taking action if I have taken the time to write it out. If I just jump into the ring and try to make changes before writing it out, I just wind up with questions.

The last time I went to that airport, I was forty-one. Shortly thereafter I dissolved the business partnership I was in and walked away. I never once have thought about whether or not that was a good decision because I knew it was.

# METHOD—Practice Creative Writing

The writing of fiction, dreams, and fantasy have a different effect than writing about reality in that they do not (necessarily) have a result. Emotions have an odd way of coming to the surface, especially if they are filtered by the anxiety police somewhere in your brain. I know I have anxiety police from my voice dialogue training. I really can't trust what I think I feel by just thinking about it, so writing it down helps. Writing, for me, is a direct contact with the source. One of my shrinks, Ms. Ortega, always asked me about my dreams, usually at the end of the session. I thought that dream interpretation was very Freudian, that is, not modern. It was surprising how close she could get to what was on my mind.

If I had a dream about trying to find something, for instance, she would relate that to my job search or some problem I had in a relationship. Similarly, if you just start writing, things will often appear that will reinterpret what you are really thinking about. You will gain insight into yourself. My long-term nemesis in dreams is looking for something, including distractions that keep you from finding them. I always wake up pissed off and tired. I would much rather dream about sex, but alas that is a type of suggestive mind control that is on the level above where I am right now.

I have been to psychic fairs, had my astrological chart done (Gemini, double Sagittarius), had my palm read several times starting at age five, had tarot cards and others read me a few times, threw I Ching sticks for a while, talked with psychic healers, taken seminars in sound therapy, and had past-life regression done. None of these seems to have the clarity of talking out a pen and paper or sitting down at the computer and just letting it come out. I mentioned to an old friend the other day that I was writing a book.

I don't tell people the subject, so she said, "Is it about the man in the computer?"

I had forgotten about the man in the computer, one of the dreams I had written down, but I'm sure that story and many other forgotten tales are on a disk somewhere. Actually, it doesn't matter because they are out and served me well when I let them out. I'm going to make creative writing, fiction, a separate method even though we already have journal keeping and writing to take action because creative writing may aid someone more than the other two writing methods have.

Remember, it is not the quality of the writing. You are trying to get something outside that is creating anxiety on the inside. This book is my example of creative writing. It is a catalog of events in my life, ideas, and processes I used to reduce anxiety as I progressed in my life. My experiences bring to the outside things that may be of benefit to others. What could be better than that?

By the way, I have recently joined a novel writing group. It is all women, the best kind of group for me. We read and critique each other's work. It is a lot of fun. The criticism is all positive, and we have a lot of laughs talking about how weird all of our thoughts are when they appear on paper. The next book may be a novel. I'm sure It will contain many of these themes.

# METHOD—Send Away Your Annoyances on Thought Balloons

One method I have been using for a long time and don't remember the origin of is what I call "thought balloons." I use this for general purposes in visualization or meditation and for falling asleep when I am having a hard time doing so. The process is simple and very effective. You just think of something that is bothering you. You visualize that this something has a shape even if it is only an idea. If it has a shape like a chair or person, use that. You take this shape and put it on a piece of material, wrap the material around it, and pull it up, like a stone in a sack. Hook this to a balloon, and watch as it floats away. Watch it for a long time as it gets smaller and smaller and finally disappears. I sometimes have to wrap a particularly difficult something and float it away more than one time, but eventually it works. Keep doing this with all of the annoying things that come into your mind until none is left. It can actually be amusing to visualize your boss floating away while trying to get out of the sack. I have heard of another method where things get tossed in a stream and float away. Balloons are more effective for me.

# METHOD—Compare the Time Frames of Others with Your Own; Adjust to Their Rate as a Conscious Effort

It is time to get back to the chronology. In 1983, I quit my oil trading job in New York and started traveling to Europe and Africa with a business associate. Our business objective was to determine where the best place was to combine our various skills and to start a business there that would make a lot of money. We were reaching for the brass ring. I had done some traveling before but not as extensively as this. I had previously done oil trading and some shipping business involving Africa, but I had never visited there. The first place I went to was Nigeria, a huge country in all respects. It was a great learning experience. One of the things that are important to learn when traveling to another country - or even a different part of the same country - is the concept of time in local terms (distance also). In the United States, it is possible to make a traveling schedule and to stick to it because everyone else in business realizes you need to get on to the next destination. Time is of the essence.

In Africa, the business makes the schedule. You stay in one place until you get done whatever you came to do. They do not have the same sense of urgency that we do. (This is an oversimplification.) We determine how much time something should take and squeeze everything together to make it happen on time. In Africa, you decide what you want to do, and it takes as long as it takes. If you make a stink about how long things take, you lose credibility. If you ask them to explain a delay, they have no answer. You are dealing with a concept.

Many concepts that we have are nonexistent in Africa, and we are thought of as arrogant if we demand them. An example would be hotels. Most of precolonial Africa depended on guesthouses for travelers. These are different from hotels and are considered to be part of a person's or community's communal home. Hotels are different as they are built to attract people for money rather than offer them a place to stay. If you are a guest in a guesthouse, you are aware that there are certain demands you do not make and rituals that need to be performed that are not necessary in a hotel. When an American or European stays in a hotel in Africa, he or she is apt to demand the same level of service that he or she would expect in a hotel at home. The problem is that most of the people working in the hotel do not have the same concept of a hotel as you do. This is a subtle but important difference. I have been invited to stay in private homes and guesthouses many times, sometimes in mud huts with open fires. They could not understand why I would travel over an hour over muddy, potholed roads to my hotel if I were going to return the next day. The two concepts were mutually exclusive. There was no understanding. There are many things in Africa that have no common ground with our ideas. This is all written down in a journal that I kept while there. I'm thinking of publishing that but it is more important that I wrote it, got it out, kept a journal of events. The publishing is a separate issue.

When I first started visiting different countries, mainly on the West African coast, I was very frustrated and anxious because of these differences. When I began to analyze what was going on and talk to some other traveling businessmen, things began to come into focus. As I figured out each difference, my anxiety level would drop accordingly. This was an important learning experience for I was learning how to judge each person as an individual and as part of the culture he or she belonged to. I began to carry this over into my life in general. The result was that I was able to quickly ascertain the timeline I was on almost anywhere, in a diner on West 58th Street in New York City or a café in Bali. You expect things quickly in the New York diner but have to realize that, in Bali, often they wait for the order before killing the chicken. As soon as I got good at judging different timelines, I felt less anxious in most situations.

During these trips, I was in Africa for up to two months at a time. This went on for over two years. This and a general lack of direction was beginning to take a toll on my marriage. Actually my wife didn't have much direction either. She didn't know what she wanted, and consequently I could not provide it for her. I later discovered that she wanted everything, and I could not provide that either. She was developing other interests and friendships while I was away. By the time that I realized I was losing her, it was too late. The abandonment factor kicked in, and it was only a matter of time until it was over. I was feeling generally down about myself. I had trusted the wrong people in business. The business we had set up was going to work very well for them, but not for me. I had not been receiving a salary, and I was getting precariously low on cash. The relationship problems with my wife led to libido problems, and I was feeling worthless. When things get to a certain point, I usually take some time to myself to figure things out. This time I decided to go skiing by myself for a few weeks in Lech, Austria, after one of my trips to Africa. Lech is about an hour and a half driving from where I had spent my junior year abroad.

Back then, going back and forth to Africa usually required a stopover in Europe. I mentally checked my morals and worries at the last mountain pass outside of town and decided to devote the two weeks to having a good time. I really needed a good battery charge. I learned that I was not a social dud, my libido sprang back into action, my German was great, and the skiing was superb. I saw people at night that I looked for during the day to ski with and people that I saw during the day I trolled for at night. I soon discovered that there were two distinct groups, a skiing group and a nightclub group, so I joined both, burning the alpine candle at both ends. I learned I was not the sole cause of the breakup. When it is too late, it is just too late. Friends begged us to stay together. If she had asked me not to leave, I probably would not have left, but she didn't.

When I split, it usually involves a change in scenery. This is part running away from myself in that I don't want to be reminded of the failure. If I hang around in the same place, I am constantly reminded by my anxiety in a unique way. It took me many years to figure this one out. I get a feeling of sadness, sometimes almost overwhelming. Every time I look at something that is familiar, I get a twinge. Every time I shop in a store where we used to shop, I get a twinge. Sometimes I seem almost blocked from opening a door because I dread the feelings that lie on the other side and the memories of happier times. I have this feeling at other times also when I drive around the places of my youth, for example, if I see an old school. I thought it was about lost opportunities or a lack of staying put in one place for any length of time. What it is about really is the anxiety building up. It is just easier to take off sometimes.

As Carlos Casteneda's Don Juan explained, you should keep a short history if you want a chance at growing spiritually. My history was kept pretty short for me by the axe of angst. My change of scenery in this case was halfway around the world, to Dar Es Salaam, Tanzania. I might as well have moved to the moon.

Dar, as it is called, was a shock, even after Nigeria and Cameroon. I had only imagined three worlds, First, Second, and Third. This was the Fourth World. Tanzania is a socialist country. In Africa, that means that everyone owns nothing. I was moving here from living in Greenwich, Connecticut, to starting a business importing wholesale petroleum products and distributing them to neighboring countries. Some of the stories I told my friends in Greenwich about my travels in West Africa were so outlandish that they thought I was lying. I decided not to bring back any stories from Dar in East Africa because they were even more outlandish. I also spent a lot of time in Kenya, Nairobi, and Mombasa and traveled around to various countries like Rwanda and Burundi (before the genocide), learning about the oil market and meeting potential business contacts. I used to drink beer with the owner/manager of the Hotel des Milles Collines in Kigali, the hotel in the movie *Hotel Rwanda*. I did some business and wound up buying an oil tanker in Singapore to use down there for coastal trading. I spent three months in Singapore getting the ship ready to take back to Africa. I worked sixteen-hour days. I am probably the only Western man in history who has spent that much time in Singapore without getting laid.

I looked at this time in Africa as a learning experience. People always ask about the animals. I didn't see many animals. I saw a giraffe on final approach to Nairobi International Airport; a hippo that had been imported from Germany, of all places; and some baboons along the road from Mombasa to Nairobi. That was a curious sight. About two hundred yards before the baboons was a bus stop full of Kenyans. I just noticed them in passing. Then I saw the baboons. They were doing all of the same things that the people in the bus stop were doing. It was like a caricature.

I met my princess in Dar. I had determined as a child that I was going to marry a Nubian princess when I grew up. Nubia was a rival of Egypt in ancient times. It now lies partly in Egypt and partly in Sudan but is not a distinct political entity. I read *National Geographic* a lot as a child, and often they would have maps with drawings of how typical people in each region looked. That fascinated me. I thought the Nubian women were absolutely beautiful. I wound up with a Bantu princess. Bantu is a large ethnic group in Eastern Africa south of Ethiopia and Somalia. Her father was the king of a small island nation in central Africa, Ukurewe. He had also been the ambassador to the several countries in Europe and North.

Stella was probably more well-rounded than I was. She spoke perfect English, Swedish, and Swahili. She was also like a walking history lesson and an activist. I came to confront my colonial roots, my racism, and my lack of cultural finesse and diplomatic skills. This was all new to me. I thought I was liberal and that was enough. We talked for hours about the crushing force of colonialism about power, exploitation, and racism. We in the West somehow accept our behavior, past and present, as normal. We are moving quickly and have developed, with the exception of the Holocaust, the ability to just forget the past. They are still feeling the residual effects of colonialism and are justifiably pissed off at us. I learned a lot from Stella. She also gave me my manhood back, but as they say in New Yawk, "That's a whole 'nother story."

I was heavily into hatha yoga when I was living in Africa. Stella told me when I was forty-two that I was the most flexible person she had ever seen. She said that some of my movements reminded her of a child. I would flop on the floor to put on my shoes and socks or sit on the floor for an hour with my legs crossed reading or fixing something. This is all possible due to the flexibility I gained from yoga. I wanted to combine my journal with a description of her life. She was not interested at the time. It would have been an interesting account of two very different people coming together for a time. I would have entitled it *Princess*. Readers would have been surprised when they found out what it was really about. It could still happen.

After working in East Africa for two years and banging my head against the cultural differences in business, I was getting frustrated. The African time problem was getting to me. I had originally wanted to live in Africa for two to three years. I figured this would give me enough time to get the businesses to a semi-self-sufficient state. I would then move up to Europe and manage the business using faxes and frequent trips down. This was a great plan, but I figured after about eighteen months that it was going to take more like five to seven years down there to get it done. Traveling back and forth to the States to see friends and family was not in the cards because of the time and expense involved. I was getting very involved down there. There is no other word for it. The culture is very powerful and pervasive. It has the ability to absorb an incredible amount of foreign influence and still remain intact. It has absorbed the influence of Middle Eastern traders and settlers, colonial powers, and the remnants of those days in the form of Asian Indians. I was just a lone American.

After beating your head against the same wall over and over, trying to do things your way, you find yourself giving in and doing things their way, just to get them done. I call this process becoming Africanized. In seven years, I would have been fully Africanized. This is not a moral judgment on my part. It is just a reflection of the difference in the way I like to do things and the way they have to be done down there. I wound up my affairs, flew home, dropped my stuff off at my parents' home, and flew out to California to visit with my brother. It was another successful getaway and abandonment. I had two major getaways in two years. The cycle was beginning to shorten. I was deeply confused. There is a top-ten list somewhere of things that will cause anyone high anxiety. I was hitting them regularly with getting divorced, moving, and changing jobs.

My brother and I are separated by four years. We had different upbringings in a strange sort of way. He went to parochial school; I went to public school. He went to summer camp; I went to Cape Cod. He went to military college; I went to a liberal arts college. He was a successful officer in the army; I got to private first class. He got a real job; I went skiing. He got his MBA at night; I went full time. He seemed to be doing everything right.

We had not spent that much time together after he left for college. He was just about to retire when I flopped on his doorstep, practically broke and depressed. I had a real fear of success and proved it by giving everything away. We spent a few weeks there in California, then a week in Hawaii, and two or three weeks in Guam, where he had another business. Then we spent two weeks traveling to places like Bali in Indonesia and Saipan in Micronesia. It was a wonderful time. We spent hours talking about life in general, where we were and hoped to go. He lavished attention on me that I had never felt from another person. We made lists of the good and bad things in both of our personalities. We talked about batting averages. The most important thing he did was to convince me to see a shrink when I got back home. I was very opposed to this at first because

I thought I could take care of my problems by myself. He thought I had some issues that needed to be addressed.

The reality of it is that I was repeating the same destructive behaviors over and over, and I was on the verge of crashing and burning. He had had a good experience with an industrial psychologist who had worked with his company for some time and given him some very good advice on running his company. He had continued with him as a personal advisor/shrink after that. He thought this approach could be of great benefit to me.

When I returned home, I consulted with a family neighbor who was a psychologist. She thought she was too close to the family scene to deal with stuff about my parents objectively and recommended several other psychologists. I decided on a female and started seeing her, Dr. Ortega. We worked together for about a year. She had some good suggestions for me to deal with my strained relationships in business, the next topic in this story. Because I had problems asking for things for myself, she suggested I write notes to people. It worked out pretty well, but it put me a step away from the people I was working with and for. I would get notes back, in my inbox, at some pretty strange times. It disrupted the "normal" flow of information. I highlight normal because some things needed fixing. Some of the notes were so vague that I realized that the other people had no idea what I was talking about. I somehow had expected them to know about my concerns even though I had not expressed them clearly.

# METHOD—Transfer Responsibility Through Notes

There are good and bad things about communicating with people in writing, especially in a close day-to-day relationship. Several years prior to this latest attempt to make myself understood, I had learned about the value of writing notes to people from a casual acquaintance. He worked for a large family-owned import company. They hired a management consulting form to help them streamline their business. The consultants started out by observing each employee and timing what he or she was doing during the day.

At the end of the week, they made their preliminary suggestions and then went back to observing and timing the next week. As the employees tried the new techniques suggested by the consultants, their work became more efficient. The technique that was most amazing to me was the technique of transferring responsibility by using notes and reminders. It is basically a concept. If you tell someone something that he or she needs to do, you retain responsibility until he or she does it. If you write him or her a note with time, date, and all that and keep a copy, you have effectively transferred responsibility to that person to complete the task. You can forget about it and get on with what you need to do. This system relieves a lot of anxiety for me because I have fewer things to keep on my list. Watch out though. There are people who will not work on this system because they don't want the responsibility even though it may be something they should be responsible for.

# METHOD—Use Lists to Organize Your Life

I previously mentioned lists. What can be more frustrating than going out to the store and leaving the shopping list at home? If you try to live your life without lists and you have ten things going on in your mind like I do, you are sure to boost your anxiety level up at least ten points. Lists make life so easy. All you have to do is get in the habit of making them and then looking at them occasionally. I have a habit of making a list and then leaving it somewhere where I can't find it when I need it. Having to look for the lists defeats the whole purpose of having them. I bought three small notebooks. One is for lists, and I have separate lists on different pages for each store I frequent. This one also has the measurements for everything in the house. I bought my wife her personal small tape measure. We take that with us when we go shopping, and if we see something for the house, an ongoing building project, we can refer to the measurements in the book and measure the item before purchasing it. Some of my friends just buy stuff and return it if it does not fit. I have noticed that the customer service/return lines are usually longer than checkout lines—probably by design—and this entails a separate trip to the store so that method would create angst for me. When you return stuff, they always ask you many annoying questions like your address and phone number. If I do return something, I give them the address of the Russian Embassy in Washington. I have done it for years and not even raised an eyebrow. Another notebook stays by the phone in the kitchen. The third has a listing of all of our favorite places and restaurants in New York. Of course, I forget this almost every time I go in. I also use sticky it notes on the front door for medical appointments and the like. The refrigerator is also a good place for lists. I keep the schedules for the gym, Tai Chi classes, and the boat club on the refrigerator along with my hippopotamus pictures. Word processors were designed to make lists, not for any other purpose. Smartphones have modernized all of this, but I still like my lists, analog or digital. Doesn't matter how you do it. Write them on your arm.

Lists also make relationships easier. Both my wife and I are organized. We approach the to-do list from different directions, however. I make a written list, and new tasks go on the bottom. She makes a mental list, and new things go on the top. She has a tremendous memory. She can tell me where we were on this day a year ago, who was there, and what they were wearing. She remembers the items on her list by repeating them to herself, sometimes out loud. I feel pressure because of this even though she swears she is not intentionally doing that. I want to make her happy, and completing tasks is one way of doing that. Sometimes we will take on a project to "fix the broken record," meaning to get her to stop reminding herself, that is talking about it. We designed and built a house (contracted to have a house built) together over the last four years (at this writing), and we are still working on it. We did a lot of the finish work together, including faux paint finishes, baseboards, varnishing, and so forth. If a relationship can survive this level of accomplishment, then you have something good going for you.

We create several lists. We have developed a rule that works most of the time. You can't add anything to the list without first taking off something. Lists are a way of transferring responsibility from your active to your passive mind. You only have to think about things to do when you pass the refrigerator or wherever the lists are. They should be out somewhere where they can be seen, or the passive mind will just forget about them.

Calendars are a form of list. Whether they are boxes or vertical lists, they are still a linear list. We joined a boat club when we moved into the area. Because we are new here, the boat club is pretty much our entire social life in the area. We started missing fun things until we taped the entire year's calendar of events on the refrigerator. If you are a computer nut, you can put your entire life on the computer or cell phone, and it will bong every time you have to do something. I used one in business, ACT by Norton software. Microsoft is now in the market with Outlook, which will manage everything. I am sure there are other good ones out there.

Occasionally you see someone staring into a small device and poking around with a pen on the screen. These small devices are really managers of lists, business and personal. Learn to use lists as your friend, and don't leave home without them.

Now that I was started with Dr. Ortega, I could get on with my business life, not knowing that the two would clash in short order. A former employer offered me an opportunity to start a ship operating company. We would charter ships (rent for a specified period of time, like a year or two) and charter them out again in the spot market (like tramp steamers, an antique term but apropos) or use them to carry our own cargoes at a discount.

This was a great opportunity. I could use all of my skills. All I had to do before starting this company was to buy a small tanker for a ship fueling operation (bunkering) in San Juan, Puerto Rico, and to set up that operation. This was a bad opportunity. There was no time to get involved in planning the operation, and we wound up flying this one by the seat of our pants. The people I was working for were very good at juggling cash assets, but they really had little or no understanding of the responsibilities of a capital asset, exactly what this oil tanker was. Capital assets, like a house, cost money all the time. Things break down, mortgage payments must be made, and so forth. You can figure out what your house is costing down to the minute. This tanker was costing $13,000 a week. I got back into the sixteen-hour day routine and wound up exhausting myself. I was always playing catch-up. There was not very much support from the other people in the company, and I began to get very anxious. The money, personal and corporate, was again running out.

About a year after I started the shipping operation in Puerto Rico, it started going south. The operation started bleeding money. There was some fraudulent antitrust behavior on the part of our competitors. I was getting absolutely no support from the New York office. They were having their own problems.

With all of this going on for a year and a half and seeing a shrink, things were beginning to happen that I had no control over. I was constantly reviewing what was happening business-wise with the shrink. She was interpreting everything in relation to my personality traits, and I realized I had opened a major, large, stinky can of worms. I was finding out things about myself that I did not need to know. I was finding out that the reason I was so good at business was that I was a complete neurotic.

So, what to do? Do I continue making a living and being a neurotic, destined to crash and burn? And I am talking serious consequences health and otherwise. Or do I change some things and lose some of the edge I had that made me a desirable employee and businessman? I chose to bite the bullet. It was sort of the decision not to smoke but on a larger scale. You know it is the right thing to do, but you also know it is going to be hard and unpleasant. You have to go through a series of steps before you can make a major change in your life. The first step is realizing and admitting you have a problem. Another important step is to make a conscious decision that you are really going to change. The actual change is almost a mechanical process after this, like filling in the blanks. I didn't sit down and decide that this is what I had to do. It was not a methodical change. I just did it, but I still followed the steps. In retrospect, it is amazing how close this is to the suicide procedure. Make your decision and then just get on with it. There is no relation here to the AA twelve-step process. The words may be the same, but I am describing a personal process. I have been to many AA meetings and read "The Book."

I started having severe anxiety problems. Panic attacks were slipping into the public consciousness around this time. People were having them in movies. Stars were pulling out their paper bags during guest appearances on talk shows and demonstrating how to breathe in one to avoid an attack. After checking with Dr. Ortega, I got my own paper lunch bag to breathe in. It had "My Bag" stenciled on the side. I took it everywhere I went. It was a very popular item. I never saw anyone using one in public, but if you pulled yours out at a party, suddenly everyone would be holding one.

New Yorkers can be weird. I guess the inhalation of one's own carbon dioxide had a calming effect on the nerves. I have not seen one of these bags in at least ten years. Was it a passing fad, or are people hiding them in their briefcases and pocketbooks? Do they sneak into the men's or lady's room for a few quick hits during anxious times?

My biggest problem was that I could not recognize when the anxiety was building. I'll try to address that later on. If you don't know that it is coming, it is too late for the bag! If you can tell when anxiety is building up, then this may be a good method for you. A paper bag will not change the underlying causes of anxiety, but you sure will feel a lot better. What you do is just breathe into the bag and then inhale what you just breathed into the bag, back and forth. Please check with a medical doctor before trying this as I do not understand what is happening physiologically.

The saving grace in all of this business activity is that, when I went up to Boston to get this oil tanker ready for work, I called a woman I had met through friends some years before on Cape Cod. We are now married.

Marilyn and I were spending all of our free time together. We were the same age and had a lot in common. She loved Cape Cod as much as I did, and I wound up buying a cute cottage on the same street where I grew up. I had played on the porch of this cottage as a child. It was my "Summer of '42" house. I was still working in New York and Puerto Rico and had faith that the business would eventually turn a profit. I was optimistic. Being in a new and exciting relationship can have that effect. The following winter, we ordered a new sailboat, a Herreschoff 12 ½, a small day sailboat that was based on a turn-of-the-century design. The only big ticket item I had bought before in my life of that magnitude was a new car. My landlady was a Ford dealer, and I got a great deal. The significance of being able to buy something like this sailboat was not lost on me. I had trouble with the responsibility that goes along with ownership before. I credited my relationship with Marilyn. She was very stable, nurturing, conservative, educated, independent, and extremely intelligent. She had worked for the government for her entire career. She had volunteered to go to Viet Nam during the war to work in civilian services. She was a great example to me, and through our love, I was able to start moving in the direction of the person I wanted to be. My apple cart had been upset by the shrinks, who I had been seeing for about a year on a weekly basis. This was a chance to get things in order. I often say that my relationship with her is the longest I have ever done anything except be alive. I fought a lot of anxiety and asked for a lot of help to keep this relationship together, something that is extremely difficult for us.

I decided to send the ship back to Florida and put her into mothballs. I made one more trip to Europe to sell the oil tanker I had been running in Africa. I then packed up my stuff and moved to Cambridge. I had always wanted to live in the Boston area. It is a manageable-sized city and near the important things that I liked: sailing on Cape Cod, skiing up north, and, of course, seeing Marilyn. The state was undergoing an economic boom they called the "Massachusetts miracle." I was sure I could find work.

Unfortunately, the miracle stopped as soon as I started looking. The economy was still good, but there was a perception that it was going to slow down. Everyone stopped hiring. I spent months looking around to no avail. Marilyn bought a new condominium in Cambridge, across the river from Boston and invited me to move in. I accepted.

# METHOD—Define Yourself; If You Don't, Others Will

During my last few days working in New York, my colleagues started complaining about some of my behaviors. These were not necessarily the things I was doing at the time, but things I had done in the past. I thought this was odd. When people perceive that a relationship is going bad, they begin to look at the relationship and try to figure out what it was that made it go wrong (other than themselves). They usually do this out loud. To me, this is a turning up of the volume, but the radio is not on a station. It is just noise. There is nothing that this process will do to save the relationship.

I was surprised at some of the things they said. One of the recurring comments I used to get was that they never knew where I was, on a global basis, that is. I would walk in the office in New York, and they would say, "What are you doing here? I thought you were in Singapore." I figured that they just did not remember that I had told them on the phone that I was coming. I started sending my schedule via telex.

I got the same reaction, "I thought you were in Kenya."

I bought a big monthly calendar, put it up on the wall in the office, and personally filled in my schedule. I had the company secretary keep it up to date.

When I called in from Rome with some information, they said, "Rome? I thought you were at the conference in Houston. I've had people looking all over for you down there."

I said, "Look on the schedule board on the wall. You can see where I am."

They had been using that board for themselves and looking at my schedule but had not been seeing my schedule. This is when I realized that they had made up their minds that I was all over the place. No amount of information about where I really was would change their perception. I didn't know if they were serious or joking. Unless I was in Africa, where if you missed a plane the next one might be a week later, I adhered to strict schedules. Everyone had my schedules, but all had this fixed, biased perception that had nothing to do with reality. Even though I had used various techniques of presenting information about my travels to them, I could not change their perception.

People will always try to fit you into a box that they feel comfortable with. If they succeed, then they don't have to put much effort into figuring you out according to the circumstance at hand. They will try to manipulate and define you according to the box they have put you in. If you let them define who you are, they will. If you truly feel different because of anxiety problems or anything else, you have to let them know that that is how you feel. If you don't do this, you are setting yourself up for an increasing series of anxiety-related jolts as they learn your hot buttons.

I know it is hard to stand up for yourself, to be pushy about it, but this is different. It is reacting to a negative attempt to control you. In this case, it's a threat. Learn to take advantage of this. In martial arts, you always learn to use an opponent's own force against him or her. If he or she punches, you pull him or her forward and off balance. I did it by documenting my schedule in faxes and on my schedule board, but it was an uphill battle. It did reduce my anxiety, however.

# METHOD—Take Action or Blow Balloon

I was watching television one night, and there was a news article about a study that was beginning at the Massachusetts General Hospital (Mass General). This hospital has a worldwide reputation for innovative programs and research. The program was to involve people with obsessive-compulsive disorder (OCD). For three hundred dollars, you could get evaluated and, if accepted, treated for free. The reporters gave a brief description of OCD, and I thought I might be a candidate. I had repetitive thoughts and internal dialogues, I was prone to fantasy, and I had all of the usual baggage that comes along with anxiety. I signed up.

A funny thing happened on the way to the OCD clinic. Mass General is a hospital that has grown over the last two hundred and some odd years. There are a lot of interconnected buildings, passageways, stairways, and so forth. I stopped at the information desk and got directions to the OCD clinic. The directions were so long and detailed that I could have driven to Flathead Lake in Montana with less of them. The only thing missing was crawling through the Warp Plasma Conduit on the Starship Enterprise. I finally came to what I thought was the OCD clinic and pushed through a heavy door. I wasn't really paying attention like I should have been and walked right in to an amphitheater, the Ether Dome. This is one of the first places where ether was used in surgery, back in 1846. More importantly, it is the place where several horror films were filmed that I saw in my childhood. Horrible images of Boris Karloff hacking off heads came to mind, and I fled like Frankenstein was chasing me with a scalpel.

After I calmed down, I met with the head of the study for an hour and then with one of her researchers. I was not acceptable. The difference between OCD and my problems (and this is a gross oversimplification) is that I knew what I had done (past tense) and the OCD person did not. A reality factor was involved. I would sometimes get up out of bed and check if the doors were locked in the house. I would then return to bed, assured they were locked. The OCD person would do the same thing, but after returning to bed, he or she would not be sure if the doors were locked or not and have to get up to check again. One poor soul would get to work and think he had murdered his wife in the bathroom that morning. He would call her at work, and sure enough, she was alive and well. About an hour later, he would think again that he had killed her and have to call her again at work. Thank God, I didn't have OCD. They offered to refer me to one of the psychologists on the staff, Dr. Halley.

His specialty was working with people trying to get his patients fixed as quickly as possible. He worked with people who could not ride in elevators or even cars. We decided to work together. He unraveled a lot more of this big ball of string that was my life. For the first time, I realized the main culprit was anxiety. We had a lot of fun together. He was the kind of guy who would laugh if something were funny. With most shrinks, it is like testifying in front of the Supreme Court. I learned many things from him, but one of the most effective methods was simple, "Take action or blow balloon."

I was spending some time in New York looking for work because Boston was so dry. I had a great deal of trouble just picking up the phone and asking people if they had openings or knew of anyone who did. It would get to such a state that I could literally not lift the phone up.

Dr. Halley helped me solve this problem by describing what happens if you don't take action. The pressure builds up and literally paralyses you. I kept a slip of paper on the wall next to the telephone with "take action or blow balloon" written on it. It worked like magic. It didn't really make calling people any easier, but it reminded me of what was going to happen if I didn't. When you take action, you are usually met with a positive or at least neutral response. I cannot recall one time when someone said, "No, we don't have any openings and don't call back and waste our time."

# METHOD—Ask for Something for Yourself Every Day

Dr. Halley noticed I had difficulty asking for things for myself. So did Marilyn. My problem was that I could ask for anything literally for someone else or on behalf of someone else or a company, but I was not able to ask for anything for myself. With my experience, I should have been able to start my own business, but that would have involved a lot of asking for things for me. It was a circular trap. Dr. Halley helped Marilyn and me to get over this, at least on a personal level, by having us ask the other person to do something for him or her at least once every day. Now of course, I am asked for a neck and foot rub every day. It worked wonders for our relationship and lowered the anxiety level that I felt in dealing with other people. I still have trouble with not being able to ask for things for me, and it has thwarted my efforts to realize any of the good ideas I have had in business. I made it a method because it is a simple technique that we can employ in a relationship or at work.

This method can be altered to fit any recurring problem that you may have. The problem I had was that asking for something for myself didn't have any value system attached to it. Asking for a spoonful of cake icing had the same value as asking for a new car. You have to start out with the small things—a glass of water, a kiss good night, a back scratch in one little spot, and so forth—to get in the habit. You will soon be able to discriminate between small and big things, and when it comes time to ask for the big thing, like a raise, it will be easier.

I did so well with Dr. Halley that I decided to attempt at starting my own business. I took a booth at a trade show in the shipping business, and with the help of my brother, I was able to make a good appearance. The concept I had did not really work that well, and I did not get enough clients to really start the business. I did get a few job offers, however. I worked for several companies marketing their wares and did relatively well. I was working in Connecticut and New York and commuting back to Cambridge on the weekends. I began to again see Dr. Henry, the visualization guru who was now living in Connecticut near the parkway

I drove back and forth on. I found that I was spending more time trying to make my relationship with Marilyn work out than I was trying to solve my work problems. I was determined not to repeat my old mistakes in dealing with people at work.

Somewhere along the line, I lost the edge that had made me desirable as a businessperson. Anxiety, impatience, anger, and fear of failure, all of that stuff really works when you are a trader. I was moving back to my center and toward stability. Everyone thought that this was great. The only problem was that I was having a hard time making a living. My attempt at reentry into the shipping business failed after two years. I moved back to Cambridge. After having made the decision to change several years before, I was beginning to sever my ties to the trappings of my former self. I would lose a few good friends in the process, but a few of them weren't really friends to begin with. Finally, when I permanently relocated to Cambridge after seventeen years in the shipping and oil business, I got only two phone calls from anyone I had known in business and one call from a social friend. Three people were interested in what had happened to me. There was a top-ten song back then by Janet Jackson that was apropos, "What Have You Done for Me Lately." This taught me that we are not as important as we sometimes think when we are in a position of power or a job.

During this time of commuting back and forth to Cambridge, I joined a health club in Larchmont, New York. On the days I didn't go to the club, I would go out for strenuous walks. When I was in my thirties, I used to jog and run on a regular basis, usually for a mile or two, but as mentioned before, this can take a toll on the joints. I had a slight problem with my right knee that derived from an ice skating accident. I bought a pair of racing skates when I was a teenager. You can just glide along on these for hours. I was gliding along at about age forty-two on the Mianus River in Greenwich when I saw a patch of what they call "black ice." This is the smooth stuff. Smooth ice is like powder in skiing.

It was somewhat off to the side near some bushes, but I thought I would make a go at it anyhow. I circled around and started crossing over, crossing one skate over the other, to gain speed. When I hit the black ice, the skates really dug in, and the acceleration was thrilling. I made a few more passes. On the last pass, I saw a tiny twig right where I was going to step with the skate. I tried to extend my skate over it but landed right on it. My leg went out to the right, and I crashed on my knee. I slid to a stop near some young girls, and they asked me if I was all right.

"No, I'm not all right. I just like to lie on the ice and groan."

I had to go to London the next day for an oil conference. London is a place where you have the choice of walking to your destination a lot of times rather than taking a taxi. After about four blocks, I would get this pain in my knee, like someone was sticking an ice pick into it. I was even having horrible thoughts about losing the leg. The short form of this is that I know there is a problem with the knee and I don't jog or run for long distances.

# METHOD—Power Walking

I started out power walking. This is basically what you do on the treadmill. In jogging and walking, if you want to get the full benefit of the exercise, you have to concentrate on getting your whole body moving. I usually start by concentrating on my breath. I start breathing in a slow rhythmic, Yogic way. I then concentrate on the hips and legs. I lengthen my stride and make sure that my hips are rotating fully by consciously exaggerating the rotation. When I am extending my right leg, I rotate my right hip forward as well consciously. You can walk without rotating your hips much, but I am talking about an exaggerated rotation. ("Exercise" is a systematic exaggeration of daily movement after all.) In order to do this properly, your pelvis should be rotated forward by thrusting your pubic bone forward, an anterior pelvic tilt. After a few minutes of this, I start thinking about the swinging of my arms and the counter rotation of my hips and shoulders. Think of swinging your elbows, and you will be swinging your arms properly. The right shoulder is ahead while the left hip is ahead. This is the usual way of walking, but the arm swing adds the slight exaggeration that you want. I then think of my feet and consciously push off with my toes in back. This usually lengthens my stride a bit more. Lengthening your stride slows the number of steps you are making each minute. I keep my head held high but my chin down to keep my neck from getting tight. I use the same movement as described in the Alexander technique. I visualize Lee Marvin walking down the corridor in the Pentagon. If you reach your optimum stride, just before you are straining or before you have to run if you are on a treadmill, the motion is like running in slow motion. You are almost floating. I love the feeling. Because I am concentrating on each movement and it is repetitive, my mind breaks free from any anxiety, and my thoughts quiet. I concentrate on the different parts of the body in sequence to keep the movement going. Breathe, rotate hips, push pelvis forward, lengthen stride in front, swing arms, counter rotate hips and shoulders, push off with toes, keep head forward and up, and visualize. I do this over and over. You can change the order to suit yourself. You can start from the top of your head and work down or vice versa. On a treadmill, it takes ten to fifteen minutes for me to really get things working together. It is truly amazing how much territory you can cover while walking this way. I have had joggers pass me on the street, and they really weren't going that much faster. You can also wear yourself out in about twenty minutes. By that, I mean you can fatigue your muscles in that period of time. For me, that is about two miles. This method builds up your cardio strength, burns calories for weight loss, strengthens your muscles, increases flexibility, and reduces anxiety.

When you start seeing a shrink on a regular basis, you have this thought process about moving over to another sector of the population. You think you are suddenly a minority. I have been in a lot of situations where I am the ethnic minority, but this is different. This is the minority that is halfway between normal people and the nuthouse. I didn't see any point in concealing the fact that I was seeing a shrink. I found that many people were seeing one or had in the past. It was curious that the people I thought should be seeing one didn't believe in it (psychotherapy).

I asked a few of them, "Don't believe in what?"

A few didn't even know enough about it to even give me an answer. If I were able to probe, I usually came to the point with these nonbelievers. They simply didn't want to talk to another person about their problems. It wasn't that they didn't have any problems or knew enough about modern psychology to believe in it or not. Some didn't want to spend the money. I'm sure I could have found plenty of things to spend the $40,000 or so I have gone through with shrinks: a new car, half a bungalow on Cape Cod, or a burial plot at Fair Lawn overlooking the Hollywood Hills. I mentioned I was seeing a shrink to one of my business friends, someone I had known for twenty years, Bob.

He asked, "What do you need that for?"

I said, "Because I don't seem to be able to have things that you have: a wife, kids, a dog, a house, a job, and self-respect. You know you are really my hero."

I think he was shocked, but I had explained it to both of us.

I stopped seeing Dr. Henry because of the distance and asked if he could recommend someone in the Boston area who specialized in group therapy. I thought this was the best approach. He recommended Dr.

Norman, a former Harvard professor that Dr. Henry had studied under. Dr. Norman met with me and announced I was not yet ready for group therapy. I thought I was doing great, but I guess that can still had a lot of worms in it.

# METHOD—Only Try to Control What You Are Doing Right Now

If there were such a thing as a mother-in-law school, the phrase "only try to control what you are doing right now" would be a fine phrase to carve in granite over the entrance, don't you think?

Before I leave Dr. Henry, I want to mention an important method that he taught me. I am constantly repeating a litany of things I want to do to change myself. They usually involve things I am trying to improve on or bad habits I am trying to change. When I was smoking cigarettes, I gave it up every night. I still drink alcohol so I am constantly saying stuff like, "I'm not going to have a drink for two weeks." Or I tell myself, "I'm going to read all those magazines piling up in my office and throw them all out" or "I'm going to spend more time at the gym." The list is endless.

I was explaining all of this to Dr. Henry, and he told me flatly, "That is just not going to work."

I was disappointed because I have enough self-discipline to change things if I want to, even addictive habits. He explained that was not the point. I had the right idea, but my method was off. The past is fixed even though we have invented "I'm sorry" to alter that or "try to." (I try to limit my use of "I'm sorry" because it doesn't correct anything and it too easy). The future is completely unknown as long as there is a city bus with your name on it rolling around somewhere, so you can't really do anything about the future. You can plan, but you can't do anything about it. That leaves the present. Henry's point is that what you are doing right now, lighting that cigarette or walking in the liquor store, is the only—repeat only—thing that you have any control over whatsoever. This is one of those ideas that I accepted immediately.

I said something to the effect of, "Couldn't you have at least built up to that a little bit? I mean, my whole system of mental Post-it notes is now in a shambles. Dead. Gone."

The method doesn't need any more explanation than that.

Dr. Norman was at Harvard during the same time that Timothy Leary was there. The chair I sat in was the same one he sat in when he visited Dr.

Norman. I wasn't a great fan of Leary, but I still wanted to send all of my old freak friends postcards and tell them, but true to nature, they had all moved and not left forwarding addresses.

Dr. Norman is a brilliant guy, and I was lucky to find him. I felt like I walked away with something to think about every week. I find it is important to have some new idea floating around, something to experiment with, and shrinks can provide this. This, in itself, helps keep the anxiety at bay. If you are trying, then you are advancing. I call this the inchworm approach. Move a little bit at a time, but keep moving and keep moving forward. One movement a day in the right direction is good enough. I am usually in a big hurry to get things done. The best way to get things done, big things, that is, is to chip away at them every day. Do something about them every day. Think of the inchworm climbing a big maple tree. Anxiety is a big thing. I needed to chip away at it.

Dr. Norman was very pragmatic. He would say things like, "Your parents are joined at the forehead. You will never get them to change the way they behave toward each other, but you can change the way that they behave toward you."

Wow! All my life, I was trying to get them to change their behavior toward each other because of the effect it had on me. In one sentence, he gave me the solution that I could have used forty-five years before to relieve my anxiety.

# METHOD—Develop an Alternate Personality for Tough Meetings

During this time, I was once again looking for work. Jobs, as I had come to know them, where you get paid for doing something, were changing dramatically. Everything was turning toward jobs where you did something and then got paid for it, mostly commission work. There are many jobs that you can get that don't pay anything, even in a bad economy. I was trying to avoid that. I was having several interviews. I was having major anxiety problems with the interviews. They involve all of the worst things to feed my anxiety. My brother, who was still mentoring me, suggested a technique that he used when faced with a difficult interview or meeting. He would pick a movie star whose screen persona had a positive connotation for most people and who exuded confidence and strength. He chose Gary Cooper.

Before the meeting, he would sit for a minute in the parking lot and pretend he was Gary Cooper going to the meeting. He would then jump out of the car, stride across the parking lot, remove his ten-gallon hat when entering the office, flirt with the receptionist, and knock the guy's socks off in the meeting. I chose Lee Marvin, another one of my heroes. He is actually the one who taught me how to walk on the treadmill. I saw him in a movie in 1967, *Point Blank*. Maybe it was the *Dirty Dozen*. At one point, he is walking down a hallway in the Pentagon. He has shoes on that clicked loudly on the polished floor, and he is a man with a purpose. His walk said it all. The person where he was going was going to get it, big time. The confidence he had was fantastic.

So I sit in the car and make believe that I am Lee Marvin going in for a meeting. I jump out of the car, click my shoes across the parking lot, matter-of-factly announce myself to the receptionist, never sit down to wait even if invited, and totally intimidate the person I am meeting. People react differently when they are interviewing Lee Marvin rather than me. I have a poster of Lee and Paul Newman that I had hanging in my office. Every time I was going to make a business telephone call, I would look at that poster first. It worked wonders. This method is a good way to reduce anxiety and have a bit of fun.

# METHOD—Take an Acting Class

I saw an ad for acting lesions in Boston. I thought I would check it out. I went to two open houses at different acting schools. I brought Marilyn with me. She is my reality check on stuff like this. I tend to get excited about each new thing, each new possibility. "Maybe this will be the thing that I am looking for." The first school had a nice reception with wine and hors d'oeuvres.

The head of the school, who looked like Burl Ives to me, walked over to me and announced that I should take the entire advanced complete total acting course, which took two years. I was a natural. I asked how he could tell that I was a natural without even talking to me. He was so enthusiastic. I looked at Marilyn, who motioned at the door. The reality check had worked. I decided to take some courses at the other school. They were given at night in an old mansion on Commonwealth Avenue that had been converted to a boy's school. It was a shoestring operation by serious people. The first course was basic acting, required before any other courses. This was interesting because it was not about acting at all or what you would think is acting. It was more about perceptions, feelings, and what is going on inside you. I really enjoyed this. There was a lot of body movement involved in this class but no recitation.

The second course I took was voice. The power of the voice had always fascinated me. I had loved to listen to people like Richard Burton. I was in Oxford, England, once on business, and I was looking for some spoken word tapes by him. I was afraid to ask the British person I was with to recommend a place to find one because the British are often strange about things. I thought they might think that Richard Burton was déclassé because of his defect to Hollywood. I finally asked, and much to my surprise, they loved him. We were just passing by the theater that he had restored, and they thought he was the best. Blah, blah, blah.

There are different voices that can be used for different things. Politicians always give speeches at just below a yell. They are trying to get you excited. Leaders like Hitler actually shouted to get the blood boiling. When I was cooking in Lake Tahoe, I developed a very low voice to call the waiters when their dinners were ready. I wanted to make sure that the food arrived at the table hot. I would open the kitchen door, look at the waiter, and shout his name at a very low frequency and for a very short duration. After a bit of practice, each waiter could recognize this shout. Because of the din of the diners, the waiter would be the only one to hear his name being called. They could be forty feet away and still hear me.

Speakers who are the most convincing are the ones that moderate the voice between a shout and a whisper. A good example is Rush Limbaugh. It doesn't really matter what these people are saying, and in most cases, what they are saying are meaningless half-truths or bitching about people who don't like them. They are trying to convince you that one side is better than the other, and they are using the voice to convince you, not the words. You can convince many people of anything using these techniques. I believe this technique is now called audio-aural.

I wanted to learn more about this. I have always tried to imitate sounds of all sorts, mainly out of boredom. I can get some birds to sit on a nearby branch, trying to figure out what I am, like chickadees. Sometimes I can even rev them up into whole songs, especially catbirds and mockingbirds. The voice course was not what I had expected. I thought we would learn and practice voice exercises. We spent a lot of time doing massage, imagining things, and rolling around on the floor. The class commented on each other during the last class. They all agreed that I had to learn to open up. They thought I had some interesting things to say, but I was holding it all inside. They wanted to hear my real voice.

# METHOD—The Alexander Technique

The most interesting acting class I took was a class on the Alexander technique taught by Ms. Grody, an instructor certified in the technique. Alexander was a famous actor and teacher in the early part of the twentieth century. He had recurring problems with hoarseness and often lost his voice altogether. He consulted with medical doctors and voice teachers who recommended rest. This did not work. With his career at stake, he rented a mirrored ballet recital room with mirrors all around and began to observe himself reciting prose from different angles. He noticed that the larynx was constricted in two positions, when the chin was against the chest and when the face was looking up toward the ceiling.

To understand what I am talking about, first lower the chin to the chest, make a continuous sound with your mouth open, and slowly rotate the head upward. You will notice that the only time the voice comes out freely is in the middle position. He added an additional factor of consciously expanding the neck so you are moving up and out. He developed an entire technique based on this movement. It is a great way to learn about your body and to alter some of the body movements that contribute to anxiety.

The entire technique is too comprehensive for this book, but I highly recommend it. We were required to spend ten to fifteen minutes a day lying on our back on the floor with a book under the back of our skull near the top of the neck. The effect of this was to relax the muscles that attach to the skull and to other parts of the vertebrae, the muscles you use to nod yes. If you have the time, this is a great way to spend fifteen minutes listening to the weather and traffic reports or some music.

One of the positions I use from the Alexander technique to relax my body in a standing position is what they call "the monkey." This is aptly named because you look like a standing monkey. Monkeys do not have the same developed muscle structure that we have in our back and get fatigued quickly if they stand on two feet so they somewhat drape themselves forward with arms and head hanging. If I do this for thirty seconds or so, a lot of stress is removed from my body, especially the back. I find that, when I am in a stressful situation, I tend to roll my head back as if I were a turtle trying to get back into my shell. I contract the muscles at the base of the skull. This does create a change in the voice that diminishes my ability to be heard and understood, and I have to clear my throat a lot. This is compounded by my tendency to mumble.

To counteract this, I roll my head up and forward before I get into trouble and relax the muscles that Alexander discovered were the ones constricting his ability to speak. Imagine Jerry Lewis in some of his early movies. He talked with a high-pitched squeaky voice and rolled his head back in a submissive posture. Now think of Charlton Heston, erect with his head up and forward, speaking down in robust, forceful tones. Both of these people have developed signature postures and voices to get the desired image across.

I try to think of my entire posture on a regular basis, and correcting this small bad habit and your entire visage can be accomplished by opening the area where your spine meets your skull, relaxing those muscles that you contract in difficult situations and moving up and out. I practice this as though it were like looking in the rearview mirror while driving, something that is learned but becomes automatic. Look out. Here comes Lee Marvin again.

Thus, by relaxing and concentrating on the voice, we reduce stress. The way you hold your body has an effect on the quality of your voice, and the resulting posture controls the meaning of what you say. In Tai Chi, they accomplish the same thing by imagining that the top of your head is connected to a string and you are suspended from the ceiling. If this were true, it would have to be a large string, but more importantly, your head would not be either back or forward, but your eye sockets would be just a notch down from looking straight ahead.

I can't say how the acting classes can benefit except on a general basis. You are forced to look at yourself in a different way and to get out of your normal skin. They use many varying exercises to accomplish this, which have been developed over many years. Because these exercises are tried and true, it is difficult not to get the desired feeling when you try them. Acting classes can offer different things to different people, and this is why I recommend them. The one thing you should know about acting is that it is up close and personal. If you have a problem being extremely close to others and being touched or touching, then this is not for you. Or then again, maybe it is.

# METHOD—Avoid Violence of Any Kind

Violence is both something that creates anxiety and is created by anxiety. This is a double-bind situation, a lose-lose. My experience with violence has been intense. Prior to taking my medication, I had the unfortunate mental process where every thought ended with some disaster, usually very violent. One of the few exceptions was when I was painting houses. I had to keep switching my thoughts to stop this violence from happening. Violence filled my dreams. In my teens, my friends would ask me to go to the latest horror film. I stopped going after I saw a Bette Davis horror film where she was an axe murderer. I slept with a knife under my pillow for six months.

I remember telling people, "I have enough violence between these two ears that I don't have to go and pay someone to give me more."

Because of my proclivity for it, I avoided violence whenever I could. I have never been in a fight, slapped around any women, or intentionally killed anything except for flies, mosquitoes, horseflies, or ants when I was young. I have a catch-and-release policy in my house for insects. On the boat, where you can't catch and release, we just leave them alone. Maybe they are resting after a long flight across the water. Spiders get bagged in Ziploc sandwich bags until I can release them on shore. The insects they eat on shore will probably be waiting for me on the other side.

I went to a professional wrestling match once in my early teens and was horrified even though it was mostly acting. This is the violence causing the anxiety part, which for the most part is avoidable. The anxiety-causing violence part, the reverse, I have been able to contain to a certain extent by releasing violence on inanimate objects like wastebaskets, myself, and sport items like golf balls. I feel it is important for me to avoid anything that has gratuitous violence in it.

Take movies, for instance. If you study film, one of the first things you learn is that everything is important. You will not see anything in a film that is not important because, first of all, everything costs money, but more importantly, there is such a short time to tell a story. Violence is a trick, in my opinion, to shorten the amount of time needed to tell a story, and it shows a lack of creativity on the part of the people making the movie to have to include it, unless of course the subject is violence. There is always another way to get the same idea across. I avoid movies with a "high body count," as my brother puts it. When people recommend a movie or book, I always ask about the gratuitous violence. Why go and see that when you can spend the amount of time at the ballet or a symphony? I do like action-adventure movies. Usually there is a hero, which means the plot is fairly mundane and a lot of special effects and the gore is kept to a minimum or presented in a fantasy sequence. In *Star Wars*, only the robots and monsters got killed on screen.

I also avoid rednecks, especially when alcohol is mixed into the equation. The reason is that they love me. I'm just like a squirrel sitting on a tree stump, and they are the slingshot. One time I was floating down the Verde River in Arizona in a large truck inner tube. I floated past a group of rednecks. I was moving at about two miles per hour. I had long hair. One of them pulled out a .357 Magnum pistol and aimed it at me.

"You all think I ought to blow this hippie out of the water?" he asked his friends.

No, I did not give them the finger. I think they get as much fun out of the threat of violence as they would the violence itself.

The avoidance of violence in general may be an avoidance of reality. People, because of their physiology and the strong mental ties to the not-so-distant past of being hunter-gatherers, have hair triggers and are prone to almost instant violence. If you want to test this, just bang your head getting into a car. Wham! You are ready to kill. I live in one of the most violent cultures on earth where violence is worshipped in the form of wrestling and football. Even finesse sports like basketball have become more violent to become successful. In the 1980s, professional basketball was losing money until the rules were relaxed to allow more contact. Hockey would not even exist without checking, the process of crashing into another person to stop his advance or to punish him for the advance he has already made. Even our native sport of lacrosse allows for beating the ball carrier on the back with your stick if he fails to relinquish or pass the ball.

It often seems that we have lost the ability to discern between reality and fantasy when we hear news of the latest fast-food massacre or high school shootout. I must admit that I fantasized about bringing an automatic weapon to high school and using it on select members of the faculty, administration, and student body, but there was a dividing line back then. It wasn't reality, even for sick people. The dividing line was between the fantasy and the reality. Violence seems to have become much more public. Maybe that is the difference. It used to be hidden and not talked about.

In my travels, I have seen some of the most violent behavior imaginable. Mob justice is swift in the Third World. If you are caught stealing, the mob beats you to death on the spot, and your body is left there for days. If you kill someone, even if by accident with your car, you can find yourself with a tire around your neck filled with burning gasoline. In Africa, they call this "the necklace." The result is so grotesque that the results have to be seen to be believed. In Africa, we called getting shot "instant lead poisoning." Violence is part of the reason I am not still living in Africa, one of the most beautiful and unique places on earth. Avoid violence in person, on TV, or at the movies, and reduce your angst. Get your adrenaline some other way, like jumping out of an airplane with a parachute on.

My wife Marilyn grew up in Napa, California. I had spent a few years in northern California. Over our lives, we had spent about the same amount in time in San Francisco and dearly love the place. There are three places that, if I spend even part of a day there, I have had a good day. They are Cape Cod, Austria, and San Francisco. We had a wedding to go to in Lake Tahoe and decided to spend a few days in "the city," as it is called. There is only one "the city." Don't email me and tell me that you also call Des Moines "the city." We decided not to tell anyone that we were going to be in the city because, if you do that, he or she spends all of his or her time trying to keep you away from the fun stuff.

Actually we wanted to be tourists. We stayed near Fisherman's Wharf and had seafood in one of the tourist traps. We went up to Coit Tower, the namesake of Tower Records; rented bikes and rode in Golden Gate Park; went to the tea garden there and actually had tea; toured the aquarium; ate breakfast at the Cliff House; drank a cocktail at the Top of The Mark; and watched the sea lions that had taken over one of the local marinas (Unhappy marina owner). San Francisco is not a place to just aimlessly walk around in.

As a case in point, Marilyn was in charge of the map one day and decided we would walk about ten blocks to have breakfast at a little nook she knew about. Four blocks later, we were puffing up this almost vertical street where the first floor of buildings are about two stories lower on one side than they are on the other. Five blocks up, and five blocks down. After breakfast, we took a taxi back to the hotel.

# METHOD—Chinese Health Balls

One night, we decided to have dinner in Chinatown, which is really the point of all of this. We spent some time poking around in the shops. I noticed a young girl selling what I call Chinese balls on a table on the sidewalk. They are called "Chinese health balls" on the Internet. These balls come in pairs in an elaborate satin-covered box, and they have their own wooden cup stands. The surface is cloisonné, which has intricate designs outlined in brass, which are filled with brightly colored ceramic. They have a chime on the inside, which is activated by moving the balls around.

I started quizzing her about the balls, and she demonstrated how to roll them around in her hand. I picked up a few balls and duplicated what she seemed to be doing. She laughed. She explained that, with my large hands, I should be using large balls. Second, when I rolled them around in my hand, I had to do it in such a manner that they would not touch each other. I went from seeming expert to rank amateur. They were cheaper than they looked, about six dollars, so I bought a pair.

For the next few months, I spent about twenty minutes a day trying to master the balls. My hands would tire after about ten minutes each. In between sessions, the balls sit on my desk, looking handsome. They are quite sturdy. I have dropped them hundreds of times, even on wood floors, and they are still intact. After learning how to use them, you just find your hand moving over occasionally to pick them up and play with them. You don't have to watch them in your hand to get the desired effect.

The young Chinese girl had told me that they were to exercise your hands. I would add that they are an exercise in coordination of muscles that are not normally used in daily hand affairs, like my Johnny Carson/ John Wayne toe movement. This does something in the brain. You are also rolling a relatively heavy object around on arguably the most sensitive appendage on the body. All of those millions of nerve endings are getting rolled on. This has an effect on me that is not unlike knuckle pressure on a tight muscle. The sound of the chimes is a calmative. The motion is repetitive. They feel nice. They are another example of the great things the Chinese society has developed over thousands of years to improve life.

# METHOD—Watching

I have a category I can't fit some things in. I feel they have a good benefit in that they get you outside of yourself and at least suppress the anxiety. I will group them together as watching. This is sort of like what I did as a kid with the ants, but these are adult activities such as astronomy and bird-watching. I use these examples because they are what I am familiar with. I don't practice astronomy, although I have a good telescope. I don't have the patience, and things move quickly across the sky and must be followed. I like to lie outside at night and look for meteors. You have to let your eyes gaze over the heavens in a random fashion, and if you are lucky, you will see them. Because images that pass through our eyes remain in our brain or retina momentarily, the streak made by the burning meteor will last for a brief time but long enough for you to concentrate on it, even if you were not looking exactly where the meteor was. (This is why moving pictures made up of individual images seem like a continuous … well … movie). Looking generally in the southeast quadrant of the sky in the Northern Hemisphere also helps because that is where a lot of meteors enter our atmosphere. On the average night, you will see eight to ten per hour. During a meteor shower, like the Perseid meteor shower in late August, you can see up to one per second in the Northern Hemisphere. Even more impressive than what happens when you see a meteor streak across the sky is what your mind does when it is peering into the abyss. This is probably one of those antique things we have from our ancestors from fifty thousand years ago.

I begin to ask the big questions: Where did we come from? What is this all about? I wish I had more time to do this. I have one caution. Make sure you don't have any friendly raccoons or skunks, like my old buddies Ralph or Blossom, around because they will lope over and check you out if you are lying on the ground.

Bird-watching falls into this category. Both bird-watching and astronomy have a high nerd factor. You will run into some people who seem to devote their life to these things. They are usually helpful. They love to talk about their passion. If the members of my high school hoodlum car club find out about me birding, they may order a hit. This would be for my own good, of course. My wife is a bird nut. I like to feed them in the backyard. It keeps my indoor cats busy. Marilyn, on the other hand, likes to go out in the field and watch them in their native habitat.

When we first started dating, we had a pair of binoculars in the trunk of the car at all times. She was even birding one day on Plum Island in Newburyport, Massachusetts, and Roger Tory Peterson showed up. In birding terminology, Roger Tory Peterson was "on the line." He is like the biggest bird nut on the planet. You get birding creds for just being in the vicinity. I have been out with her birding a few times, and I must admit that I am getting interested in this. I won't get into the details of the thrill of watching cedar waxwings passing cedar berries to each other, but let it suffice to say that birding is a great way to "watch."

One Christmas, I "gave" her an osprey nest. What I gave her was a partly completed building permit and a signed book on ospreys by the biggest osprey expert in the business, Dr. Poole. Ospreys are birds of prey with a huge wingspan. They dive feet first into the water to catch fish. They are also not bothered by people so you can get pretty close to them. We got the permit and built the platform with a pallet for the Cape Cod nest in our condo in Cambridge. One day we drove to the Cape with the platform on the roof of the T-Bird and tromped out into the marsh behind my parents' summer house and erected it. Marilyn bought me a nice telescope so we could watch the nesting activities. It was the most fascinating thing of this type that I have ever done. We could see right into the nest. So far, as of 2012, we have had about sixty-two fledglings from this nest. It is a great accomplishment. If you are watching something else, you usually release your watch on yourself.

Two weeks ago, we were out walking in the woods in here in New Jersey. I saw a strange shape. It looked like a bird trying to lure us away from her nest, a common behavior. They may even pretend that they are injured to get you to chase them. Of course, they fly away and start the broken wing thing all over. This bird was a pileated woodpecker, about the size of a crow. It's very rare. I have only seen two in my entire life. Woody the Woodpecker was a pileated woodpecker.

Some good examples of "not watching" include demolition derbies, NASCAR races, ultimate mixed martial arts cage fighting, and NFL football. Keep it quiet. Keep the adrenaline under control. You are getting the idea.

# METHOD—Make Sure You Are Getting Enough Full Spectrum Light Every Day

Marilyn has a seasonal disorder that is related to the length of the days or, more particularly, the amount of light she gets in any given day. In the winter, when the days are shorter and we spend more time inside, she tends to get a bit depressed and grumpy. She takes medication for it. This disorder is common and well documented. I have read that the suicide rate in Finland goes up some 800 percent during the winter months when they have as little as four hours of light a day, and that is in the southern part of the country. I remember reading in the *Science Times* that this was related to the production of vitamin D in the body. A receptor in the back of the human eye is struck by light at a certain angle, mostly around sunrise and sunset. When light hits this receptor, vitamin D is produced and released into the bloodstream. Maybe this is why we all like to watch sunsets.

Knowing that this had something to do with sunlight, I set about to design a house with huge windows and ceiling lights with full-spectrum halogen bulbs. I also built her a wooden stand with a fluorescent light fixture attached to it. I installed full spectrum bulbs in that fixture. Now in the morning, she wakes up in the dark and switches on the sun in the bathroom. At night she can sit in front of the stand I built and do bills or read the paper. She says she feels warm all over when sitting in front of that light, even though it gives off no heat. If you are depressed, you are going to get anxious. This is worth a try.

# METHOD—Devise Positive
# Ways to Deal with the Pressure People

An important thing to learn about is how to deal with pressure from other people. My brother has helped me a lot with this one. He has a way of categorizing people that obviously has come from a lot of thinking and battling it out with others. He can pretty much hit the nail on the head with ease. He sees a lot more people in day-to-day activities than I do. We will be looking at the same thing, a big fancy boat, for example, and I will be thinking about the boat. He will see the big show-off owner trying to show everyone how much money he has.

I wonder, *Why didn't I think of that?*

When I get in trouble with people, I ask my brother for help. There seems to be many manipulative people out there. By that, I mean people who are trying to get you to do what they want you to do rather than what you want to do. They really have no concern about your welfare even though they may tell you that they do. These people can exist in a family, business, friendships, or anywhere. You have to discover their true motive, which is not easy unless you are thinking about it.

I once met some women at a wedding in Vermont. My friend Guiermo was really interested in one of them, and apparently one of them was interested in me. Guiermo spent an entire week trying to convince me to drive to Vermont to spend a weekend with these women. I just didn't want to go. One sign of encroaching old age is when you won't drive five hours just to get laid. He told me about all of the fun we were going to have, what this woman was going to do for me. He really spun a great yarn.

In the end, when he finally realized that I was not going to go, he said, "Well then, how am I going to get there?"

He didn't have a car. He had exposed his true motive in wanting me to go.

Manipulative people use what I call "time pressure" to get you to make a decision that is in their favor. They want an answer right away. My brother has me repeat over and over "I'd like to think about that" or "I would like to think about that overnight and get back to you." Your delay almost never has a bearing on the outcome and may shift some of the authority back to you.

If I tell my parents that I am going to visit them, they want to know when I am arriving and leaving. If I tell them three months in advance, they still want to know the exact times. After dealing with this for years, I now tell them that I'm thinking of visiting, but I'm not sure. This gives them some advance warning, but I don't have to give the exact times until I finally decide to visit. I usually decide about three days before the actual visit. It works for everyone. It is easier to change your mind if you have not announced your decision.

Another annoying personality is the person who suggests to you what you should be doing. I had one person bugging me for years to join a writing group she belonged to. She had read some of my writings from when I was living in Africa. She was a great writer, and the group was comprised of serious writers, some of whom had published books. After five to ten years of listening to the suggestion over and over, I finally told her that I was interested in joining her group. She said she would take care of that. I never heard another word about it. I was disappointed. I wrote down in a list the other times in my life that this had happened to me, and to my surprise, it was rather frequent. I guess, in their mind, the person making the repeated suggestion is putting himself or herself somewhere above you. I don't understand this kind of behavior, but I have developed a habit of agreeing right away to see if the person is serious.

A particularly obnoxious pressure type individual is one who thinks that your body is fair game for his or her derisive comments. Everyone has something that these people can find to comment on. I had a friend who was so thin that people would make comments behind his back, nasty comments that don't bear repeating. I am sure that he had heard some of them in his life. You would think that a person in this position would be sensitive to criticism of other's physical appearance. I have weight swings of five to ten pounds on a regular basis. Whenever he would see me at the top of a swing, he would say, "Hey, Cliff, you're really getting fat." One time he yelled this across a restaurant.

I feel that people who fall into this general category, the pressure category, look for vulnerabilities in other people. They may not be doing this intentionally or in a mean way, but they are seeking an advantage. I try to identify this when I see it and steer clear of them. If you are trapped into dealing with them through social contact or work, you have a bigger problem. I don't like to always have to be prepared for these people because I feel it is a negative way of dealing with life, but sometimes it is necessary. Have a conversation in your mind with the person, and have a couple of choice lines ready. The one I used on the "Hey, Cliff, you're really getting fat" guy was, "It must have been something I ate," along with a dirty look.

In grammar school, we were all plagued by one bully who would goose everyone in the room where we hung up our sneakers. This was really intimidating to some of the smaller guys, but no one would stand up to him. One day I got angry and gave him a goose that would have knocked down a cape buffalo. I thought I was going to get the beating of my life after school. Nothing was said. After being challenged, he had backed off and didn't bother anyone after that, at least not when I was around.

Because I have had to prepare so often for these insensitive pressure people, I have actually gained a minor reputation for great one-liners. I don't dislike any of these people by the way. I have just developed ways of dealing with them so it is a little harder to back me into a corner.

Bullying and being bullied is something that surely creates anxiety. It is something that I have not had that much experience with, or perhaps I have not labeled some behavior the right way. Not being bullied may have something to do with size. I am six-foot-two. But there is always someone bigger with a need to get it over on someone else. It is becoming a popular topic these days. I have to think about that and maybe update my book sometime in the future.

# METHOD—Don't Take Yourself Too Seriously; Have a Few Laughs

Humor is a great way to deal with anxiety. I'm not talking about *Saturday Night Live* or Three Stooges movies, which is contrived humor, but the humor that is all around us. When I get anxious, I tend to get moribund. Everything seems to get entangled and goes sliding off in a ball. I find that a good shot of humor will often disentangle this ball and get me back on track. The easiest way to do this is to get in a habit of not taking yourself too seriously. Most famous people are admired for a self-depreciating sense of humor. One of the best examples I found was in Secretary Robert Reich's book, *Locked in the Cabinet*, about his time as the secretary of labor in President Clinton's cabinet. He locked himself out of his house and tried to climb back in through a door he had installed for his dog. He only attempted this because of his size. He is probably less than five feet tall due to a debilitating childhood disease that stunted his growth. He managed to get himself stuck halfway in and halfway out. He described his thought process. His family was back in Boston, and he was thinking how long it would take for him to be missed by what was now the outside world and what condition he would be in when they found him. He had me in hysterics. If he can make fun of something like that, then it should be at least a possibility for the rest of us.

If you make the odd comment about the humorous side of some of the problems you have, you are going to find that other people will respond in kind. I have had relationships with people who consisted mainly of humorous vignettes from our lives. Everyone has locked himself or herself out of the car or his or her apartment, and everyone has gotten back in. You will be surprised at how ready people are to exchange stories just to have a few laughs.

I can't remember jokes for more than five minutes so I just deal with situation comedy, things that happen naturally. There is a lot of printed matter that contains hilarious material. I covered that under the METHOD—Reading Selectively. I find that people who laugh a lot are usually the healthiest.

I am really tight with a guy I met while in the shipping business, Bob. We met over thirty years ago. We had similar upbringings. Our fathers worked for the same company in shipping. We communicate almost telepathically. He sends me a mental message to call, and I do if I am not absorbed in something else or traveling. I call when I get back, and he knows I was absorbed for two days or whatever. He is a builder. For some reason, anything he does causes a very complicated result. When I - or he - get down, we talk or have lunch. We have no defenses with each other, and the conversations usually wind up with us both in hysterics. Somehow that humor just clears the air, and we both decide to keep moving on. I hope you have a relationship with someone like Bob.

One Christmas during my third of fourth year in the Boston area, I had occasion to deal with the Veteran's Administration. I had broken my finger, chipped a bone, on Christmas Day. I didn't want to go to a doctor so my wife suggested I go into the VA clinic. Some of the vets in her office went there on a regular basis. I had only dealt with the VA once after I got out of the army. Everyone honorably discharged is entitled to one visit to a private dentist, something that is not really advertised. I found out from another vet. It was a pleasant experience. I stayed away from the VA after that because I felt the guys who had fought in the wars and were rolling around in wheelchairs should get all of the attention. I showed up at the clinic with my chipped bone, and they put me through a screening process with a social worker. In the end result, they didn't do anything for my finger, but they offered to let me join a weekly discussion group for people having problems with drugs and alcohol. I didn't think I was having that bad of a problem, but I am always game for a learning experience. I was drinking about a bottle of wine a day at the time, more on weekends. I dearly love wine, with food or without at a party or alone. I was not ready for the group of people who I ran into in this discussion group. These were guys who would get so drunk that they would wake up under a bridge the next day about noon. If it were on Sunday when the liquor stores were closed, they would go into a convenience store and buy mouthwash to drink to kill the headache. They got rolled on a regular basis, usually by other alcoholics or drug addicts. The drug addicts themselves were even worse. The VA is doing a great thing in helping these people out.

I went to the meetings regularly and pitched in with suggestions. I was beginning to realize, at age forty-five, through these meetings, my visits with Dr. Halley, and a friendship with a friend who had a similar childhood that I was possessed by anxiety, that this was my main adversary. Everything I was doing had the sole purpose of fighting it. I didn't know if I were going to have as hard of a time fighting anxiety as those alcoholics and drug addicts were going to have with their problems, but I knew it was not going to be easy.

One thing the VA led me to was a vocational rehabilitation program. I was officially a dislocated worker with obsolete skills. I had the opportunity to retrain in any viable vocation. I looked into graphic arts and found a school in New York that I thought would do the trick. I looked at law school. My counselor was trying to convince me to go back and update my MBA (really an MIM). I really looked around and did a lot of research. I wound up joining a ten-month professional chef's program. I felt this would fit in well with my international experience. I knew a lot about sophisticated food from my upbringing and travels, and I thought this knowledge would blend well with some professional training. I had worked as the top cook in a restaurant in Lake Tahoe. My record was 167 meals single-handedly on one night so I knew about the work. I had worked in numerous kitchens. The school was great. We would "mise-en-place" various dishes, have them checked, cook them, and then have a great meal with wine at the end of the day. We studied Italian food, province by province, and then French food the same way and progressed through the year to American and Asian food, mentally stopping briefly in select countries to learn a dish or two.

In the second semester, I was an assistant instructor in the baking course. I cooked at benefits with the top chefs in Boston, assisting experts like Jasper White. I cooked and served a dish to Julia Child. I went to a culinary convention in Philadelphia that the top people in the business attended. In one seminar, I was involved in a discussion group with Jacques Pepin and Julia Child. I was mainly listening with my head bobbing back and forth like I was at a tennis match. They were about two feet away from me on either side, and I was in the middle. My brother and his wife gave me a trip to France over Easter break to take a school-sponsored course at École le Notre, where the French chefs go to update their skills.

By the end of the year, I was talking with the owners of the school about opening up a restaurant with them. It was an idyllic year. I was having a tough time studying for the final exam. I had passed everything so far but needed a sixty-five on the final to graduate. I was having a really hard time, and a lot of my methods were failing me big time. I was out of practice in keeping the anxiety at bay. I had the inevitable anxiety attack during the final and got a sixty. I crumbled. I could not face any of those people again and withdrew. I interviewed for a few cooking jobs on Cape Cod in very swanky restaurants. They all wanted to test my knife skills, which are excellent, and in some sauce preparations. I would call up before the test and cancel. I mowed lawns that summer.

I think that final exam was the end of the old me and the beginning of the new. I had crossed my own path. When you cross your own path, there is no return to the person you were before.

# METHOD—Mise en place

The important method I got from cooking school, apart from learning how to cook anything and a tremendous sense of seasoning and taste, was the "mise-en-place." This is a simple procedure of reading the recipe and preparing all of your ingredients before you even turn on the stove. The direct translation from French is "putting in place as in setup." You put all of the prepared ingredients into bowls or ramekins. The result is that your food preparation, the cooking part, takes place with ease and is really fun. Almost anything that goes wrong in food preparation can be fixed, but you have to have the ingredients and tools ready. It is just like the cooking that you see on TV. When the chef wants an ingredient, it is waiting for him or her in a ramekin. You can concentrate on the cooking and forget about the ingredients. This is really the way that food is prepared in great restaurants. Mis-en-place also takes all of the anxiety out of the food preparation. This method has led me to make similar preparations in many other areas from varnishing my boat to cleaning the gutters out in the spring. I still call it "mise-en-place."

I related my bad final exam experience to a couple psychologists who live near me on the Cape. We both knew that there were medications that you could take in such a situation. If I had some, I could have taken the pill, sat there for a half hour waiting for it to take effect, and then passed the test. I understand that senator and former presidential candidate Bob Dole used to take this type of medication on a regular basis when he had to give important speeches. The only problem with this medication is that you can't have any alcohol in your system. I didn't have any alcohol in my system when I took the test, but I could not get anyone to prescribe it to me if I drank at all because they didn't trust me. One lousy stinking pill.

Food is a complex subject and well beyond the scope of this book, but I think John Lennon of the Beatles probably put it the best, "You are what you eat." I do have a few ideas to squeeze in. When I was in my teens, I had bouts of gastrointestinal disturbances. I spent a lot of time at the doctor asking questions and listened to a lot of speculation. I learned that, in general, medical doctors and internists do not know a whole lot about nutrition. I was advised to stay away from gas-producing foods like cabbage. Gas was not the problem. I think that acid may have been the culprit. The big A caused the acid. (I am now diagnosed with acid reflux problems and take medication for that.) I was a voracious eater as a kid and ate about everything that was around. Later on in life, I tried all sorts of foods in my travels. There are only a few things I don't like, for example, shaved coconut, like you find on cakes; lychee nuts, which squeak on my teeth; tempeh, which is fermented soybeans; and authentic kimchee, a Korean concoction. The Koreans cook a lot of vegetables and then bury it in a jar or crock in the backyard to let if ferment. A few months later, when the concoction is good and ripe, they dig it up and eat it. It tastes and smells foul. The worst bad breath I have encountered in my travels is in Korea. I once held my breath in an elevator in an office building in Seoul for thirty-one stories with three stops to avoid barfing. There are things I would not try unless someone had a sword over my head, like goat's eyeballs, monkey brains, and durian, but that is another story.

I consider myself a liberal eater. I know a few vegetarians, several whom I have known when they were meat eaters, and I know they find great benefit in the vegetarian diet. I would love to be a vegetarian, but like drinking and drugs, meat eaters usually find themselves hanging around with other meat eaters. If you are a meat eater, it is very difficult to find and stick to a vegetarian diet. It may be a bit easier in a major city but is difficult nonetheless. I do 95 percent of the cooking at home and make about 25 percent vegetarian meals, mostly pasta sauces. I can remember a time when 100 percent of my meals had meat. I have also made a shift to lighter meats and fish. I eat more than the five helpings of fruits and vegetables recommended daily. I drink a lot of (fermented) grape juice. There has been a noticeable change in my overall, for lack of a better phrase, lightness of being because of these changes in diet.

# METHOD—Learn about Natural Herbs and Foods

About eight years ago, I was introduced to a person who became a good friend, Steinfield. We had a lot in common and similar anxiety problems. He explained what had happened to him. He had been raised in an atmosphere where there was lots of verbal abuse. Let's leave it at that. The result was that his body became accustomed to secreting copious amounts of adrenaline and other chemicals in a reaction to this constant barrage of abuse. As he matured, this flood of chemicals continued even at minor provocations. His body was out of control. It is relatively easy to temper this with man-made drugs, but the human body and mind are so complex that it is rare when a true balance is reached with drugs. He wound up being so dependent on so many drugs that he was advised that he would have to be hospitalized to get off the drugs he was on and on to some new combinations. He was told that there would probably be major withdrawal issues, like convulsions and maybe even a seizure or two. He was so fearful of this that he finally started researching herbal and related substitutes. He was able to withdraw from the prescription drugs using substances like DHEA, St. John's wort, and raw adrenals. I tried them for a while, but the combination was too strong for me.

The short form is that his explanation of what had happened to him and how it had unbalanced his chemistry sounded exactly like what I was going through. Unsupervised use of these chemicals and herbs can be harmful and even fatal. Steinfield had done a lot of research and had consulted informally with trained medical personnel before using them.

St. John's wort is the most popular remedy for anxiety and stress in Germany. Unlike the United States, Germany and Switzerland regulate the production of herbal remedies and produce pure extracts. In the States, because of the lack of regulation, companies may produce products with the same names but with different strengths. Products with the same names can be produced from completely different raw materials that the body uses differently. They are often imported from places around the globe, which do not have to—and often don't—use high standards to produce their products. Some herbs cannot be taken in combination with certain prescription drugs. Many medical doctors do not know anything about herbs because they don't study them in medical school and have no interest or time to learn about them. There are many issues with herbs, and it is up to you to learn about these to protect yourself. The study of herbs is ancient and should become a serious hobby for anyone who is going to start taking them on a regular basis.

There is also a number of people out there who make their career promoting stuff they believe is the answer to any given problem. The only problem with this is that they really believe what they are saying. I read one book on extending life expectancy. They suggested using DMSO, a horse liniment, on injuries, as it contained antioxidants that would "scavenge free radicals," presumably the oxygen compounds that receive much attention in the medical press. I severely injured my ankle once playing (My version of) racquetball and used DMSO on it. I thought the ankle healed quite nicely and quickly, and I was pleased. My doctor was not so pleased when I told her about it and practically strangled me in her office. Snake oil is alive and well, folks.

I have taken things like spirulina, ginseng extract, and refined garlic in the past, and I have not noticed any difference whatsoever. Now I take an aspirin a day, a multivitamin tablet, a fish oil capsule, and a tablet that does have antioxidants to promote the health of my eyes.

# METHOD—Learn about Organic Foods

Last summer I went to a vegetarian cooking demonstration put on by a chef who concentrated on organic foods. I was amazed that, with all of the different foods I have tried, studied, and cooked, I really didn't know what organic meant. It is a government standard that requires that the growing medium, soil, hydroponics, or whatever has to be free of herbicides, pesticides, synthetic fertilizers, antibiotics, and parasiticides for at least three years. Now I don't think that there would be any argument from anyone that, the less pesticides you have in your system, the better off you are going to be. Even the hardened varmint-killing, redwood-logging, kill-it-and-grill-it, shotgun-toting kinda person would have to agree. Organic is different from natural and vegetarian.

I told my current medical doctor that I cooked with all natural ingredients. She reminded me that cyanide and nicotine were natural ingredients. Vegetarian in the Hindu sense means that there is no killing involved in the ingredients. Organic is free of herbicides, pesticides, synthetic fertilizers, antibiotics, and parasiticides to the extent that even fertilizer and feed must be organic. If the cow that makes the manure is eating pesticide-laced grain, then its manure is not organic. The plants grown in that manure are not organic. Sales of organic foods are growing at a rate of 20 percent per year.

Lately when I am alone, I eat breakfast and lunch using organic ingredients and dinner of "normal" ingredients, meaning they don't have to be certified organic. I slip occasionally, like today, and go to the diner for some grease and glop. I can't say that I feel any better because of eating organic foods, but the theory I will be healthier is bulletproof. If you are healthier, then you will be less anxious. I am making this a separate method from learning about natural foods and herbs because it came to me at a different time in my life, when I had a different understandings of things.

I will leave food with a funny self-deprecating story about my cooking. While I was in cooking school, my wife was working in Washington DC and would return to Boston on Friday night for the weekend. I would have this great gourmet meal ready for her. One Friday I had prepared Steak Diane. The great thing about this preparation, apart from the sauce, is that you get to flambé the steak, that is, set it on fire with brandy. I closed all the doors to avoid draft, shut off the fan, poured in the brandy, and very professionally lit the alcohol. The flames leapt up reaching for the ceiling and my hair. It was a big ball of flame.

I soon had this under control, and when I had plated the steaks, I asked my wife, "What did you think of that?"

She replied, "If you are going to do that again, I think we should buy a fire extinguisher!"

# METHOD—Stay Healthy

It sounds like a preposterous idea. Most people think they have nothing to do with getting colds or the flu. I have noticed that most people who work in large offices or have kids in school get the most colds. They must be getting these colds from other people. Through my readings in the *Science Times*, I have found that most of what are called the "common cold" are rhinoviruses. The virus enters your body through your nose, establishes itself, and then spreads to the rest of your body. The rhinovirus usually gets into your nose from your hands and fingers. It usually gets on your hands from touching other people's hands or stuff they have touched.

I have a strong immune system, but when I started doing business in Africa, I had good reason to take care of my health. Where I was, access to good health care was difficult to find. I bought a dozen handkerchiefs and swore I would never touch my nose, eyes, or ears with my hands unless I had just washed them. Whenever I had an itch or had to take care of some personal hygiene, I would pull out the handkerchief first. What a pain in the ass this was, but it worked. The four years I used the handkerchief, I didn't have as much as a sore throat, unusual even for me. Using a handkerchief was the first good habit I dropped when I moved back to the States, but I am still conscious of keeping my hands clean when out in public or in the gym.

Since the common cold accounts for a large part of sickness, not getting them can lower your angst. Also get a flu shot every year. I hate needles, but these are so small that even I don't mind. Serious scientists comb the densely-populated cities in the world every year, collecting samples of the flu strains that are prevalent. They are able to predict what flu will be a hit in the United States the following year and prepare a concoction to fight it. This is what the flu shot consists of. I am glad these dedicated people are doing this rather than trying to guess what the stock market is going to do.

Now I even get a pneumonia shot every year, and I've been immunized against hepatitis A and B, bad diseases you can pick up in a restaurant, any restaurant. And make sure your whooping cough vaccine shots are up to date. This disease is making a comeback. It probably won't kill you, but you will cough for about six weeks, more or less, continuously. People have been known to break ribs because of the coughing.

I know someone who had lost a lot of weight over a period of about four months and wound up in the hospital with appendicitis at age forty-three. The doctor told me that chronic appendicitis is rare, and her weight loss was probably due to something else. I say BS because I witnessed it.

She was so angry at herself that she told me, "I take better care of my car than I do my body."

Last week a neighbor and friend had appendicitis at age seventy-nine. He had hernia surgery last winter, and they could have snipped his appendix right there, but they didn't because appendicitis is rare in older people. If you have trouble challenging authority because of your anxiety, you may wind up in big trouble if you get sick because you will not speak up for yourself. You need an advocate, someone who will fight for you in the hospital. I don't know much about the laws for someone advocating for you. I know a spouse or parent can, but a friend or a gay lover may be barred from even talking to the doctor. I just don't know. This can lead to tragedy. Look into it. I will and update this book when I find out about it.

# METHOD—Self-Help Books (Revisited)

There are many self-help books out there. I have read a lot of them. I started with the Dale Carnegie books like *How to Win Friends and Influence People* and progressed from there. I felt that I was so clueless that I could turn to books for the answer. This type of self-help book may be great for some people, but I don't think that the general self-help book holds much for someone with any disorder, no less anxiety. If you can't talk to people without getting strung out, then how are you going to win them over and influence them? I did get a lift from these books, but it was usually short-lived and ended the next time I got sand kicked in my face.

Perhaps the greatest gift from these books is their role as a starting place. If you are going to get on a path to recovery or control anxiety, you need an initial kick. If you get into the habit of reading self-help books, you will pick up a vocabulary that will help you recognize newspaper articles and conversations about the subject. If you don't know what, for instance, codependency means, then it will be difficult for you to determine if you fit into that category even if you are codependent and don't know it. You just know that something is wrong.

When I picked up the first Dale Carnegie book, I probably was looking for something but didn't know where to look. I had social problems and thought he might provide the answer. The social problems stemmed from the anxiety, but I didn't even know that I was anxious. I heard on the radio that there are thirty-five hundred self-help books published every year.

The more useful class of self-help books are those that are about something, written by people who are in that particular soup. I hope this book is in this class. This gives specific ideas of what to do about the problem. If I didn't have anxiety problems, I might have the problems that are addressed in the other self-help books. If the specific suggestions and methods in the book do not work, then you are at least reading a story about someone who has the same problem that you do. I used to feel so alone in my youth when I was being criticized for my behavior. I felt like I was the only one who had problems. I wanted to kill myself to rid the world of this pestilence. I believe that these feelings led me to decide in my late teens that I would not have children. I didn't.

I have to put in an aside here. I was watching a piece on *Oprah* the other day, and Tyra Banks was on the show. She is an African American model, a real sweetheart. I figure that, after God finished making the world, man, and all that and took a day off, he decided he was going to have some fun and create the perfect woman. The result was Tyra Banks. Here she was on *Oprah*, describing how she used to lock herself in her bedroom as a kid so no one would see her. She was so skinny that she was ashamed. Sophia Loren had the same problem as a kid. Now you know what I mean by feeling alone.

Another class of books and magazines are ones about psychology in general. *Psychology Today* was a great lay magazine about what was going on in the field. Psychology is a fascinating topic. There are hundreds of books worth reading that will give you a better understanding of the human condition and where you fit into it.

I'm going to include self-help books as a method because there may be good tidbits there for others, and after all, this is where I got my start in understanding what was going on.

# METHOD—Formal Stretching

About three months ago I decided to get back into yoga. This was after I had restarted Tai Chi over a year ago, so this is putting the cart before the horse chronologically, but I want Tai Chi at the end for a reason. Actually, this section is not about yoga either. One day my yoga instructor failed to show up at class, and one of the regular trainers from the club offered to give us a class in stretching. Yoga is basically stretching with a philosophy. I never thought that ordinary stretching was very highly developed. I had been stretching since high school. I made a brief stab at hurdling, which requires a lot of leg, especially hamstring, stretching beforehand if you want to avoid just running down the track kicking over the hurdles. I had also developed a stretch, actually learned from my cat George, where you try to reach as high as you can, stretching every muscle in your body. You just keep trying to reach higher. Cats do this almost every time they get up. When you relax after thirty seconds or so of reaching for the sky, everything seems to fall back into the right place. George also taught me how to yawn. I noticed that he would have a normal yawn like any mammal, but at the end, before relaxing, he would add a conscious pull back of all of his face and mouth muscles, resulting in a giant yawn. I tried it the next time that I yawned. Boy, did that ever feel great. Try it.

I have to digress on yawning. We all know it is contagious. That is why you are going to be yawning uncontrollably for the next fifteen minutes. When I was still going to church, I was bored to tears during the mass. As a diversion, I would try to see how many people I could get to yawn in the hour or so. I averaged about nine. Somebody is always looking around instead of paying attention, and they are pretty easy to snag.

Another good way to pass the time in church is to pay attention to children who are more bored than you are. They start to misbehave immediately. Their parents discipline them in hushed tones, and then the kid gives you the look, which means that both of you know something that the parents don't know. After all, weren't we all trained not to pay attention to kids to get them to calm down? Marilyn regularly calls me a monster. Now I know why.

Okay, okay, back to stretching. The first thing I learned in class was that, for a good stretch to be effective, you have to hold it for twenty seconds. I used to think that a stretch was successful if you achieved the objective, like touching your forehead to your knee. You also have to keep breathing while holding the stretch. I use the outgoing breath to let my muscles relax a bit more with every breath. Note that I said relax rather than pull or stretch. The difference is that there are stretches where you get into position by using your hands or some other part of your body to pull or push the muscle to be stretched, or you use the weight of your body and gravity to exert stretching pressure on the muscles.

After the initial stretch using these techniques, you can gain additional stretching of the muscle by just thinking about it (I use breaths) or because time passes and the muscle just relaxes. You don't have to put additional pressure on it. One should never bounce to stretch a muscle, as this can cause major damage to the connective tissue, which can take years to heal. Some of the stretching positions in class are different and more effective than the ones I was using. I try to go once a week now. I feel it is a complement to the yoga asanas (positions) rather than a conflict. Formal stretching is more aimed at everyday life with a particular freedom of movement in the hips and an ease and enjoyment in walking after a session.

Because I feel that you should begin with a formal class in stretching, I have named this method as "formal stretching." Any kind of stretching is beneficial, but having a trained instructor will help you to learn more and to avoid stretches that can result in injury.

I have one refinement. Any exercise that is aimed at improved everyday life is called a functional exercise in the vernacular of personal trainers, which I am - at level five. It is a good term to look for as an objective of an exercise program and to use when talking to people in the gym, professionals or not. When I explain to people that I am lifting eight-pound weights rather than eighty-pound weights, it is because I am doing functional training.

I once read, I believe in one of Dr. Lilly's books, that the unconscious brain regulates the muscles that support the skeleton. The reason for this is that, without a certain amount of tension, the skeleton and especially the spine could easily be damaged in a relaxed state. This system evolved to work even when we are in a totally unconscious state or asleep. Muscles are what hold us in an erect posture. If they stopped working, then the spine would bend to a point where the nerves controlling heartbeat and breathing would be severed or pinched, and we would die. I found this to be a great explanation for tension in the muscles. What stretching does in this context is to reeducate that unconscious brain to accept greater flexibility as normal. This is accomplished by stretching muscles using a greater range of motion than we would in day-to-day life. After basic health, I feel that flexibility, the ability to use your body, is the key to enjoyable older age.

Several times in my life, beginning in high school, I have been drawn to karate. I think I was drawn to the discipline. I actually took a few classes here and there and learned just enough to really piss off my attacker if I tried using it. The last time I went to a dojo, the female instructor kept telling me to relax, that I didn't have to kill anyone that night. I didn't get it. I thought you had to be tense to be ready to fight, which is what karate is all about, or so I thought. Karate is much more complex than fighting. It is a life discipline that teaches the avoidance of conflict that would lead to a fight, as is my understanding. Now that I have studied martial arts a bit more, I think of the cat staring at a mouse hole for an hour. The cat looks tense but is perfectly relaxed, ready, and focused.

# METHOD—Tai Chi Chuan, the Highest Recommendation in this Book

Another martial art I was mainly encouraged to try by friends was Tai Chi Chuan. Calling it Tai Chi Chuan is like saying Hava-ii when you come back from Honolulu the first time, so I will refer to it by its common name from now on, Tai Chi. There seem to be many different ways to spell Tai Chi, usually with apostrophes. Because there are so many, I have decided to spell it Tai Chi.

Tai Chi, as I understand it, is an outgrowth of Taoism, a Chinese system of beliefs that is closely tied to the forces of nature and its cycles. The familiar circular yin and yang symbol is based on the belief that opposites are mutually inclusive. Everything in Taoism is either yin or yang. Examples would be fire and water. There are energy flows moving throughout the universe, the earth, and the body. These energy flows, life forces, are called Chi and are either yin or yang. Tai Chi, a martial art, was developed sometime in the thirteenth century. It is based on fluid movements, unlike the striking movements of kung-fu and karate, but like them, the root of power is in the earth and flows through the body into the hands. Tai Chi has been described as moving meditation. Indeed that is the first definition I had of it before I knew anything more. You follow a set of linked movements called "the form." The form I practice is called the Yang short form.

While you are performing the movements, you concentrate on visualizing different ideas that relate to the movements, and you practice balance, relaxation, and breath control. There are numerous claims of the benefits of Tai Chi including health, flexibility, strength, and balance, especially important for older people, vitality, inner awareness, spiritual growth, and so forth. The self-defense aspect relies on having the knowledge and ability to diffuse a tense situation before the situation reaches critical mass. This would usually lead to physical combat. The blend of training the mind and body leads to a result far greater than the training of either individually and is a natural process. Tai Chi is taught in many places. If you cannot find a dojo near where you live, there is an excellent beginning video by Terry Dunn named *Tai Chi for Health*.

There was a period of about twenty years from when Tai Chi was first recommended to me and the first time I took a class. The first classes I attended were in Scarsdale, New York. The master was an American, and he was a great teacher. Unfortunately, I moved back to the Boston area shortly after starting, and I had to discontinue the classes. He concentrated on the Yang short form. There was little or no warm-up that I can remember. The teacher would immediately start on the movements of the form. He did not really concentrate on the philosophy, but I was in a beginning class, and the philosophy usually follows learning the first form.

Several years passed before I was again able to take a class. I was working in Cambridge, and I signed up for an ongoing class at the Chinese School of Martial Arts. An old Chinese master and his daughter taught the course. He did not speak English, and she had to interpret what he said. We had to wear these uniforms that were made up of lots of gathered material, a sash to hold it all up, and stylistic leather boots with rubber soles. The dressing room was in the basement that also contained huge bags of herbs, so I guess he was an herbalist as well. This is not surprising considering that the Chinese health care practices are a combination of things including folk medicine, herbs, and Western-type medical practices. It's the same thing in Africa.

Loose clothing is important in Tai Chi. This master strictly adhered to the practice of the form. I have a feeling that this is the way that he learned in China. We practiced each movement over and over until we got that particular movement down pat. He would move around the room and adjust the student's positions and movements. For some reason, he would not even come near me, no less adjust my positions and movement.

I asked his daughter about that. She told me that he found my Chi too strong. There's nothing like dumping some information on someone that he could not possibly understand. Perhaps he was reading my anxiety.

The Tai Chi forms rely on a constant fluid movement through each position. I found myself trapped in awkward positions repeating the same movement over and over again. I'm not that great at exact repetition of movements of any kind due to a lack of coordination. It was very painful for me at times. One night in a rainstorm, I found myself hanging onto a street sign on the way home to avert a muscle spasm in my lower back. I figured that Tai Chi was not for me. I stopped the classes and attended my professional chef's program for ten months. Soon thereafter we were making plans to move to New Jersey. Moving and the subsequent two years of building and finishing a house precluded most outside activities.

While having dinner with one of our neighbors, the conversation turned to Tai Chi. Our female host, Junco, is of Japanese origin and has been studying Tai Chi for some time. She invited me to join her class. The following week I tried it out and was surprised at the lack of rigidity and adherence to learning the form followed by our master, Master Joe. He spent a lot of time practicing individual movements and doing meditative movement exercises. (It turns out these were Quigong exercises, the next method.) He also taught breathing and thought processes like projecting Chi and visualizing the Chi, or life energy, flowing from the universe and the earth and through the body. We would go through the form movements only once in each hour. It was a liberating experience. I invited my wife to join me on Saturday mornings, and we have been going for almost two years now.

This method of learning the form slowly and interspersing the training with philosophy and meditative movements is a very important thing for the neophyte to consider. If you are looking for something that you can use for the rest of your life to combat anxiety in a natural way, then why is there such a hurry to learn the form? Without the thought process, the form, while not boring, is mechanical. I would suggest interviewing the school director about the training philosophy before beginning or ask to sit in on a class without participating. Actually, this is a good practice before starting anything, but it is sometimes difficult to know what to ask. Being a naturally anxious person, I usually want to jump into something and learn it all at once.

If there is a hidden theme in this book, then it one that suggests that just jumping in is a fruitless endeavor. Many schools teach Tai Chi. Master Kim Song, a Korean martial arts master and teacher, runs the school I am studying with now. They also teach Tae Kwon Do, a version of karate. I'll probably get slammed for comparing the two. Adherents of martial arts styles all have their opinions of other styles.

I have tried several versions of Tai Chi, but I like the Yang family style the best, and it is popular so it should be easy to find a master. There are long forms, short forms, very short forms, and so forth. Don't worry about any of that. Just start. You can change to a different method later when you learn more about it. One interesting form I worked with at the local Y and that is worth mentioning is named Tai Chi for Arthritis. Apparently, someone who knew Tai Chi and the effects of movement on arthritis went through all of the forms and picked out the ones that would benefit someone with arthritis without aggravating the disease. If you live to be sixty or sixty-five and you do not come from some yogurt-eating ethnic group living in Yurts in Outer Mongolia, you are going to get arthritis.

This class was fun and relaxing, but a new director of the Y was appointed and, of course, had to shake things up. He decided that our class was too small for their resources and ended it. We got a new teacher who did not follow the form at all. He had us rolling around on balls and doing balancing drills. That was okay, but there was a talker in the class, and the teacher would interact with the talker. I'll leave out the gender of the talker. Talkers will join a meditative-oriented class like Tai Chi and talk incessantly. I quit the Y and left a sharp note for the new director. Talkers are everywhere, and they are male and female, young and old. If they bother you like they bother me, just move on.

One good thing about Tai Chi is that you are always supervised, either by the master or a more advanced student. If you become proficient, you will be asked to work with less proficient students. This is how the learning progression works. If you ever get to the master level, you will know it. Nobody has to tell you, and there are no tests that I know of.

Tai Chi is such a spectacular mental and physical endeavor that I recommend it above anything else in this book. Perhaps I have been able to gain so much from Tai Chi in such a short period of time because of all of the other things I have tried. I think this is the one I am going to stick with. Perhaps I will be a Tai Chi master in ten years or so. If you don't try anything else in this book, try this.

# METHOD—Qigong (Pronounced Chee-gong)

(This section was actually written about two years after I finished the main body of work.) Shortly after I finished the section on Tai Chi, my teacher, Master Joe, decided to retire and move to Maryland, a four-hour drive from where I live. He tried to maintain his Tai Chi classes by driving up every week but finally gave up. The alternate teacher, Master Al, took over for a while and began to introduce us to some variations in the Yang style method of Tai Chi. The variations were what he described as "coiling" and "expanding." They were borrowed from an entirely different method of Tai Chi taught by Richard Lund in Woodbridge, New Jersey. Richard was a follower of Master William Ting, who resides in Cherry Hill, New Jersey, near Philly. Master Ting, I believe, is the originator of the coiling and expansion that Master Al was teaching us. Master Al decided to drop the classes I was in, probably because I was the only one showing up, and suggested I join him in Richard Lund's classes. I did. I went with my wife for a while, but she lost interest because the method was too stylized. I didn't understand this at first but soon would.

Richard began each session with several movements repeated over and over with wonderful names like "circle heaven and earth" and "push the water." These lasted for about ten minutes, and he then spent the remaining forty-five minutes concentrating on the form and the perfection of each individual movement. The first ten minutes, which he called Qigong, were very similar to the meditative movements that Master Joe had spent so much time on. I really enjoyed these movements, as did my wife. It took me quite a while to realize that what Master Joe was doing for most of his hour was actually Qigong. (There is actually a point in this entire diatribe, so stick with me.)

My take on Qigong is that it is individual movements or forms, some of which are part of the Tai Chi form and some of which are stand-alone movements. The Yang family short form is a number of individual forms linked together to form one continuous form. I guess the word form has two meanings. (Ahhhh sooooo, as they say in the old country.)

Quigong has not really become popular in the United States. I don't know why because its power is unmistakable, even for the beginner, and you don't have to learn a linked Tai Chi form (movement) and remember any sequence to enjoy it or to gain the benefit from it. Because of its relative obscurity, Qigong exercises may be hard to find. There are many listings for Qigong on the Internet, but I can't recommend any of them. Master William Ting has an excellent video out, *Qigong*. His site can be found at www.silvertigertaichi.com. Look under Tai Chi gear for the tape. As mentioned before, his form of Tai Chi, Wu Ji Jing Gong, is very different from the more popular Yang family form, so be careful to do your homework before buying any Tai Chi tapes.

For some reason, I began to think of the possibilities of linking all of the ideas in this book together and developing a method, a sort of à la carte menu of possibilities for people with anxiety, where they could customize a method that would best suit their level of anxiety and lifestyle. My mind started its usual uncontrollable fantasizing about what it would be like to be able to offer this to the public. I approached Richard Lund with the idea, and he was very positive in his response.

About the same time, my wife and I decided to change health clubs because some of the men in the club where we belonged were rude and obnoxious, and it was starting to bug her. The male equivalent of hamsters is "meatheads," it turns out. At 220 pounds, I mainly ignored them. At 105 pounds, it was a little harder, and she was on the verge of punching one of them out, a definite possibility, believe it or not. If you want to push around 105 pounds of someone, don't pick on Marilyn.

I started a research project on clubs in the area. I told everyone that I wanted to change from XYZ club because of the behavior of some of the members in the club where I belonged. I finally found a good one. It was new and clean. Their windows looked outside, and skylights were in the ceilings. The staff was friendly. (I actually learned the term "meathead" from the woman who gave me a tour of the new club.) The clients actually had clothes on rather than torn sweatshirts. One of the benefits they had was four sessions with a personal trainer in the first month.

My wife loved it when I took her over, and we signed up. We went back to the same old routine, moving from machine to machine and treadmills on alternating days. I worked my upper body one day and my lower body on the next visit. I signed up for our personal trainer. I had asked around about who the best trainer was, and several people mentioned Rodney.

Rodney deserves his own paragraph. He was so impressive that we signed up for a weekly session with him for twelve weeks. He explained how to do each exercise, why we were doing them in the sequence, and why repetitive work on machines using the same routine week after week does not work. He talked about diet, eating before and after exercise, and so on. He weaned me off my macho (and ignorant) habit of setting machines at 160 to 180 pounds and moved me to 40 pounds on a different machine or with free weights. And by doing the exercise the proper way, he showed me how I would benefit more with less. Boy, that is a new concept in exercise, more with less. I was amazed that, after twenty years of belonging to health clubs, I found out that I was a hairsbreadth away from causing serious permanent damage to my body.

After about four weeks of working with Rodney, I found a flyer in the gym about a six-week course at the local community college to become a certified personal trainer. I sat and read it in the car. Click! The light went on. I was doomed. Richard Lund had mentioned that he had begun his career in teaching Tai Chi by becoming certified as a personal trainer and teaching water aerobics at the local Y, something he still does. I signed up.

In the meantime, Rodney started his own studio, Chisel, LLC. We followed him over. Working with Rodney, I began to understand more about core strength (as the core muscles are the ones deep in your body that you don't generally see on the surface), balance, and movement. There is a right and wrong way to do everything. After a year, I really feel a lot of relief in my body, both from the correctness of my movement and the increase in strength in my core muscles. I got my certification from the World Instructor Training Schools, both as a certified personal trainer and as a senior fitness instructor. I figured that, because I am almost a senior, I should learn something about that. At the time that I wrote this, I was fifty-eight and three-quarters. I am now sixty-eight. It's funny. The two times you measure your age in quarters is before you are a teenager and as you approach sixty.

The most important thing I am beginning to realize—and I am amazed that I am still beginning to realize things about anxiety—is that there is a connection between mental and physical methods that is very important to the control of anxiety. The intertwining of various methods will make each of these methods stronger, but there must be a mixture of the physical and the mental. As you gain strength and flexibility, you will become more whole. Taking any method into your life will change part of your life. It is up to you to decide which of these and many other methods you will combine to get control over your anxiety. You will realize that these methods must become a part of your life and be used all the time for you to really gain control over your anxiety. Perhaps we are blessed by our challenge for we will become stronger for having to overcome it. As for me, I'm going to continue to explore the relationships between the physical and mental, the yin and yang of anxiety. Stay tuned.

At the time of this last review, I am a level five personal trainer and have an additional twelve certifications including being a Katherine Roberts Yoga for Golfers instructor. I have never trained anyone, but I like it. I am the most certified trainer that has never trained anyone on the planet. I have mentioned that I just jump in—I should have added—with both feet.

# METHOD—Pressure

I realize that this word probably does not belong in this book without explanation, so here we go. There are two kinds of pressure. The mental kind causes anxiety. The physical kind can help. When I was quite young, I asked my father why cars driving on a road melted the snow or ice.

He, being an engineer, had the answer, "Pressure creates heat."

I was so amazed that I remember that about sixty years later as though it was yesterday. That conversation has nothing to do with anxiety, but it shows that something we take for granted, like gravity, can have a detrimental or beneficial effect on us depending on our situation. Gravity helps us to stick to the earth and walk around rather than floating around like astronauts. We would probably look like amoebas without gravity. Gravity can be detrimental to your personal health if you have a noose around your neck and are hanging from a tank gun in Afghanistan, the Taliban's preferred way of getting rid of a traitor. The good side of pressure is the physical side known as weight in some instances, but it can also come from all sides. For example, the deeper you submerge yourself in water, the more pressure you will feel. I have used pressure from an early age to combat anxiety but only recently realized what I was unconsciously doing.

I have some background. I was visiting some friends of mine on Cape Cod, and I noticed that their dog, a really cool basset hound, Duke, the dog I used to massage, had this blanket-looking thing wrapped around him.

I asked, "What is that?"

I could not even make a funny guess at what it was. It was a "Thundershirt." They make them for both dogs and cats. It is a thick material vest sort of thing that wraps around the animal's chest and has holes for the forelegs. It is open on one side, and you secure it around the animal using Velcro. The inventor probably realized that pressure could abate the animal's anxiety. Some animals are fearful of loud noises like thunder, wind, and fireworks. The pressure, I am guessing, makes the animal feel more secure. I was amazed. Inventors who invent things like this amaze me because they can take a problem, understand it, and devise something that solves the problem. I applied for a patent in 1982. The thing I applied for a patent for was patented in 1934, so I am not that person.

Upon returning to New Jersey, I ordered a Thundershirt for an employee's dog, an Akita. Akitas were originally bred to hunt boar and bears and later unfortunately for dog fighting. Actually he was appropriately named Bear. They are friendly to people they know but are very territorial and great dogs for protection of the home. The one time I played with an Akita, I got my finger sliced open, and we were just roughhousing. Their teeth are like razor blades.

Bear was terrified of windstorms. We have a lot of them because we are so close to the water. Of course, Bear's owner did not wait for a windstorm but put the Thundershirt on him as soon as she got home. Bear was happy. When she tried to remove it the next day, Bear started growling and baring his teeth, a classic dog warning that, if you keep doing what you are doing, you are going to get it. This went on for almost four days before she could get the Thundershirt off.

I thought about this pressure/calmness reaction for some time. Then I realized that there were instances where I had employed pressure for the same effect. Think about this. When you go to the dentist and they put this heavy lead blanket on you to take x-rays, it feels good for some reason. It's comfy. When you bundle up to go out in a snowstorm or to go skiing, it feels comfy. When I snorkel or scuba dive, it feels comfy when I am about ten to thirty feet down and the pressure all around me presses on my body. If I had thought about pressure before I learned about the Thundershirt reaction, I would have guessed that pressure would have set off a reaction like claustrophobia. I can't even watch a show about spelunking (exploring caves) because the thought of being trapped. I like a little pressure, but not a whole cave collapsing on me. The German movie about U-boats during the Second World War, *Das Boot*, although a brilliant movie, was an absolute horror film for me. I only stayed because the movie was in German and I was studying the language.

I used various ways to feel pressure to feel secure. When I was young, my parents spent a lot of nights entertaining in New York City. I was left in this large house with pine trees all around, and I was sleeping in a room with windows on all sides except for the entry door. It had four sides of windows. It was like sleeping in a lighthouse. When the wind began to blow, the pine trees started moving and turned into all sorts of monsters. It's all imagination, of course. I even have a note that I wrote to my parents back then, complaining about the monsters. What I did to counteract this was to remake my twin bed so the sheets and covers were so tight that I had to do a jackknife maneuver just to get in. I did this for many years. I would even stick my feet down on the side of the mattress, I guess, for more pressure. I felt secure.

For several years, I slept on the twin bed with a male Dalmatian, Mister. I used to love to stick my feet under him. It was warm and secure. If I turned over too much and disturbed him, he would bite my leg through the blankets. It was a strange way to wake up. Nowadays I pile pillows at the foot of the bed for weight. If they fall off in the middle of the night, I feel exposed. By the way, I have already applied for a patent on this, so save your time and money.

# METHOD—Wish for It and It Will Come True; Build It and They Will Come

I don't go to the movies very often, about twice a year. I saw *Field of Dreams*. It's sort of what this method is about, things that can't be explained. It's also a great movie.

I could have used a lot more titles for this section. I don't even know if it is a method. I have had some interaction with people who really believe in things or convince themselves that they do and these things actually happen or manifest themselves from the unending flow of energy in the universe. I met a person caddying when I was fifteen that claimed he could have a drink of water and have it taste like anything he wanted. I had no luck with that one, but I gained the idea that you might be able to change things mentally. Everything begins with a thought, no?

Feelings may also qualify. I met a young woman in Sacramento, California, around 1973, who claimed she could get anything she wanted just by willing it. She was very convincing and had many stories, most of which her boyfriend corroborated. There are several books out there that touch on the subject of manifesting things. One I read in the 1970s was *Autobiography of a Yogi* by Paramahansa Yogananda, detailing his search for a spiritual leader. Several things in this book were strange to an uninitiated Western person. I remained interested in actually being able to have a spiritual effect on things but never had any realization of this interest until much later when I was living in Cambridge around 1996.

I met a woman quite by coincidence through a friend of my brother. Her name is Wendyne Limber. This is one of the few real names in this book, but I have her permission to use it and tell you about her. She runs Solutions Center for Personal Growth in Stuart, Florida. I joined her email list and received regular newsletters from her center. She had a course on one of the first newsletters I received that I have not seen on any newsletters since. That in itself is strange. It was a course entitled "My Money Grows on Trees." Basically, it teaches you to manifest money into your life from the infinite universe by teaching yourself a way of thinking, which includes meditating, interacting with strangers in a positive way,

234

keeping a diary (actually a manual), setting up an altar to money replete with candles (mine was in the second bathroom tub), picking up any money on the street (even pennies) that came my way and keeping it in a jar on the altar, giving anonymous gifts to people, sending small amounts of money in the mail, and pasting photos of things you wanted on cards and displaying them around the house. (For the last one, I had a helicopter, Ferrari, waterfront home in the Bahamas, and so forth). To be honest, I felt a little goofy doing all of this and a bit embarrassed when I gave poems to strangers about how they were going to get a gift of money and so forth, but I knew from my casual experiences with this realm that, if you didn't believe it, really believe it, you were really wasting your time. So I believed it.

Within a few weeks, I found myself in the book section at Costco, a huge warehouse-type store, and I came across a book entitled *The Secret* by Rhoda Byrne. I thought, *You know, if I am going to make this work, I should probably read up on it, meaning similar things to my money course.*

The book is all about the law of attraction. You can attract anything you want, including money, into your life. I then ran into a book entitled *Ask and It Is Given* by Esther and Jerry Hicks, which explores the teachings of a nonphysical entity Abraham and teaches you how to manifest your desires. The next book was *The Power of Intention* by Dr. Wayne Dyer. In this book, he "has researched intention as a force in the universe that allows the act of creation to take place." Why were these books seemingly coming into my life at this time?

I have a theory about why, which requires a digression back to Lake Tahoe in 1973. The short form is that whatever you are thinking about seriously suddenly stands out and everything else recedes into the background. It was always there, but the balance of your concentration has shifted. I was cooking in a restaurant (with my recently acquired master's degree in business), a steak and lobster place. It was the fall, and I needed to do something to make enough money to get a season's skiing pass at Heavenly Valley ski area, four hundred dollars. That would be about six days of skiing at today's prices. I also wanted to get in shape to ski my ass off all winter. I got together with a friend who had a pickup truck. We bought a big chainsaw and got permission to cut fallen trees on the giant downhill slope at Heavenly Valley. They wanted to get rid of the trees. We took them all back to his yard and rented a log-splitting machine. And voilà! We had cords and cords of firewood that we could sell. The point is, something amazing happened to my perception after we bought that chainsaw. Now that I was in the firewood business, everywhere I looked, I found fallen trees to cut up and sell. They were everywhere. It was driving me and everyone around me nuts.

It was a "Wow! Look at that tree!" type of thing. Lake Tahoe has many large trees like lodge pole pine, tamarack, and sugar pine. For some of them, both of us could not reach around because they were so big. We wrestled them into the truck and did actually get in shape. This change in perception stayed with me, and when I got into the shipping business, suddenly ships were everywhere.

In another instance, I used to go for walks in New York at lunch hour, mostly in Battery Park or on Nassau Street. I was single, and many cute girls were out on the street. The interesting thing was that every day it was something different with the girls. You would imagine that one would have nice legs, another had nice boobs, someone had a pretty face, and so forth, but no, it was not that simple. One day it was only nice legs. Another day it was only nice boobs, and the next day it was pretty faces. It had to have something to do with me. If you went out looking for something in particular, you would not find it. I have not yet figured this out, but it has something to do with what was going on in my life, something like wood and seeing firewood all over the place.

So I continued with Wendyne Limber's course, "My Money Grows on Trees." She would email me every week with some ideas. The last one after I finished the course, which took a long time, was that I had to wait. I kept meditating because it is enjoyable and centers me. I know that there are more skeptics out there than there are believers.

About six months after I finished the course, someone gave me a retirement-worthy amount of money, and it was not an inheritance. It was a flat-out unanticipated gift!

What's the moral to the story? It works for me.

# METHOD—Connected Other Stuff, the Self

A few things seem to be connected and would not be valid to investigate as individual topics. I bundle them all into the sense of the self. There are a couple things I have thought were good ideas, things that would lead to true enlightenment if I didn't have the anchor of anxiety pulling me down. Some of the more serious ways of reaching an enlightened state involve rigorous methods and do not fit with the world we live in, at least not for the family-oriented working stiff.

Some may ask, "Why enlightenment?"

I'll try to answer that in a roundabout way. First, many of the methods I have learned about and developed involve getting away from your day-to-day self. This is a coincidence that I have realized in retrospect. Getting away from yourself gives relief from who you are. The person meditating in a cave in the Himalayas may be trying to get away from the self to be closer to God. I try to get away from myself to get a break from the anxiety or possibility of anxiety. Some methods work temporarily; others have longer lasting results. Some work best in combinations or in sequence. The major similarity is that they do not work at all unless they become a part of your life. Temporary relief can be gained much easier than rolling around on the floor doing yoga or trying to learn golf. You have to be ready to give up some of who you are to find lasting peace using anything that has a philosophy attached to it. Many of the advanced stages of the meditative arts involve the destruction of the ego in one way or another. They all involve a responsibility that is above the self. I remember taking an oath at the Chinese School of Martial Arts in Cambridge that I would never do anything to bring dishonor on the school. I gave my word without hesitation. I was not learning a martial art to kick some bully's butt in a bar. I was learning it to reach a higher state as an individual. If this higher state relieved me of some anxiety, then so much the better.

The central idea in several of these methods is that the quest, the path, has a value in itself. You may not reach the top of the mountain, but any level you reach will have its own value and benefit. In college, I had a roommate, Chip, who was an avid weight lifter. He had a flawless, beautiful body. I used to spot for him, be ready to grab the weights if he dropped them, and often went through rounds of exercise myself. I remember him discussing weight lifting with some of our classmates. They all had the idea that you would turn to jelly if you stopped lifting, that you had to do it all the time. Chip's idea was that any amount of lifting you did, "Even the amount that Cliff does," was beneficial. You didn't have to spend a lifetime lifting weights once you start. You could go as far as you wanted.

Another principle you have to prepare for when dealing with when working within any philosophical art is balance, both physical or emotionally/intellectually. The concept of using your opponent's force against him or her may seem easy to grasp, but it may not be as easy to practice. You will be faced with balance in meditation or swimming. You may not be able to meditate effectively because of a negative circumstance in your life, but you still have to inch along that path. You may not be able to swim because of an injury, but that should not keep you out of the water. You may have bad habits that affect your balance, such as adherence to a double standard. You can't have it both ways if you are interested in true progress.

I had a double standard with women that I had to lose before I could really love a woman. Tolerance is also an important issue for people trying to make a change. It is much easier to be an extremist in anything than to be a middle-of-the-roader. Compromise is the way we move forward as a society. You will have to make compromises within your own system of beliefs, to yourself, to gain any kind of lasting freedom. This may sound like a laundry list of good virtues, but they are things I have banged my head against time and again in my personal quest.

More often than not, I have found that all of these methods deal with the concept of time in one way or another. I may never be able to explain this, but I will try. In order for me to gain any kind of control over anxiety, I had to get some control over my concept of time. I used to think that it was just tick-tock tick-tock and I had no control. If you think about the concept of a city block, you have an idea of how far it is in a measurable distance, a kilometer or a mile, soccer or football fields. If you go to Paris or La Paz and ask the locals how far something is from where you are, you soon learn that there are many concepts of what that distance is. You can spend an hour walking "three blocks." In Bulawayo, Zimbabwe, the main streets are wide enough to make a U-turn with a twenty-mule team and a wagon. They were designed for just that. This is wider than Park Avenue in New York, including the center divider and sidewalks.

Time is like that. It is different depending on where you are and how you are dealing with it. I used to wish that unpleasant things, like high school years, were over, so I could go to Cape Cod and enjoy myself. I wanted a lot of things to be over, weeks for weekends, marriages, loans, airplane flights, or just a lot of things. I wanted more things to be over than I wanted to not be over. This went on until I got a grasp on the concept of time and changed it. If I had kept wanting everything to be over, then I might already be dead. It might be over. I needed to get myself into the moment, and if I did not enjoy it, I could at least experience it.

Since I started working on this, my concept of time has stretched out. When people say, "It seems like the New Year was last week, and here we are Christmas shopping already!" I think to myself, "It seems to me like the New Year was ten years ago. So many things have happened." They say the vice president of the United States is only one heartbeat away from being president. I may be one heartbeat away from the whole thing being over, so I want to be there when it happens or when anything happens for that matter.

One of the books that had a profound influence on my concept of time and me was *One Hundred Years of Solitude* by Gabriel Garcia Márquez. It may not give you the same description of time to use that it did me, but it is worth reading anyhow.

# Katherine's Question—Not a Method

I took a novel writing course several years ago. I don't know why, but after all, the book you are reading started out to be the great American novel, so I must have been interested in writing novels even though I haven't read one since the sixties and haven't written one yet. If I do, it will be bizarre. I guarantee it. As I remember, there were many novels back in the 1960s that sort of broke the mold, the novel-writing norms of the time. My favorite expression about the 1960s is, "If you remember the sixties, you weren't there." If you didn't read any of these novels, you weren't there either. The title that comes to mind is *One Flew over the Cuckoo's Nest*.

One of the women in the novel-writing course was named Katherine. She is the only one from the class who wrote and published a novel, *Hippy Chick Reunion*. We became acquaintance friends. When I had her read the first few chapters of this book and we had a basis for a conversation about it, she told me I had to answer a question to make the book complete. "Was anxiety a driving force, a creative force in shaping who I was that eventually led to my success?" (These are my words but her thought.)

It would be easy to say, "Yes, of course. Everything has an effect on who you are." My wife's uncle put that best, "You are the sum of your experiences." But really, can a negative force produce a positive outcome from a developmental perspective? Did it?

There are many success stories out there where disadvantaged people overcome and become successful. First I have a word about the word "success" itself. It makes me think of something Sophia Loren said when she was asked if she were happy after success as an actress, an Academy Award, two lovely children, a loving marriage, and so on. Her answer was, "Happiness is a big word."

I may have used this quote before, but it is apropos in many situations. Success is a big word. You can be raised in a ghetto or an internment camp and grow up to win a Nobel Prize. People make a big deal about these stories, even bigger than if the individual comes from a privileged background like I did. I have the feeling that rags to riches is the exception in the great majority of cases. So just having a disadvantage doesn't necessarily propel one to succeed. It's probably more like the opposite. It is a stone around your neck.

So I will start out assuming that anxiety is a disadvantage in most cases. It sure was in mine. You never knew when it was going to appear, you can't predict it, and it is difficult to acknowledge it when it shows up. It's the proverbial skunk at the garden party. You are inches from your first real kiss, and suddenly you are drooling on yourself. It is not something you can plan around. Being a negative force, I tried to learn about it and fight it. Usually I didn't even realize I was doing that. Things were just happening as they tend to do, and I didn't realize that I was reacting to anxiety or the constantly looming possibility that it would appear. The negative genie would pop out of the bottle. If you messed with the cork, you automatically got nailed. As we learned from the movie *Alien*, "Just when you thought space was safe," genies are not necessarily nice. Unlike the delightful Barbara Bain, they don't like to be bothered.

Some of my interests and a lot of my learning processes were no doubt driven by these forces. The learning process itself was probably shaped by this. You can become addicted to almost anything. I became addicted to learning. I loved science and psychology. I didn't have the attributes or education to become a scientist or a psychologist, but I sure did spend a lot of time learning about these things. I still do. I am interested in almost everything. My wife calls me a polymath although I usually think of polymaths as wildly intelligent people. A synonym is a Renaissance man. I am trying to follow a thought here to find some sort of conclusion.

I guess, if you wind up having a life with many different experiences and you don't wind up dead or in the gutter, then it might have been worth it. I saw a woman walking down the street in Ubud, Indonesia, in the 1980s going the other way. Her T-shirt read, "Been there, done that." That sort of sums it up. If my addiction to learning, experience, and travel is the best learning experience there is and was caused by anxiety, then yes, a negative force has created a positive outcome. I never wanted a lot of possessions or money, but I could have had them. I'm sixty-eight, and I'm on my second new car. I have owned only one house, but I have been to some fifty countries. I have met all of the women my young self loved from afar: Sonja Henne, Teresa Brewer, Sophia Loren, and Shari Lewis. And I am still hoping for Kim Novak. I just wanted to know more than anyone else about a lot of stuff and to have a great part of it come from experience.

I have a wonderful family in my wife Marilyn and our cats, fish, and ospreys on Cape Cod. I have my brother on an island off Seattle and some loyal and longtime friends. I didn't get some things that I wanted, like being an architect or being able to play the guitar like Stephen Stills. I could have had kids, but that is okay. I also didn't wind up sitting behind a desk in Manhattan trading oil and commuting back and forth to the wife and kids in the suburbs, wondering what it might be like somewhere else. It didn't work out so bad for a kid who did not commit suicide only because he was curious how it would turn out. Overall I am pretty satisfied. I still wake up in the middle of the night and freak out. I say to myself, "Holy shit! I must be nuts. What am I doing?"

So be it. Put more simply, a negative force can lead to a positive outcome if you let it. Half of it is just letting it happen.

# POSTSCRIPT (PS)—
# Mindfulness and the Inchworm

I had to add something at the end. My quest for methods to fight and control anxiety has not stopped since I first published this book several years ago under a different title. The book remains pretty much the same, but many other things have changed, which is the way things go. And besides, I am usually disappointed when I finish a book. If you are too, here goes.

For the last two years, I have been trying to simplify my life, selling a house and dropping off many, many belongings at various places that will recycle them. Auctioning off belongings is much too complicated, so I take them to a place where people can pick them up for free and they can auction them, take them to a flea market, or use them.

I also stopped drinking alcohol. I have done a lot of alcohol drinking in my life. If you drink, let's say, every day, chances are, you use alcohol for everything: celebration, fun, sadness, entertainment, attempts to make TV sitcoms funny or airplane flights shorter, gifts, and so on. Offering someone who enters your dwelling a drink is as old as people have been dwelling inside. It is usually an insult if you don't offer someone a drink when he or she enters your dwelling and also an insult to refuse one. It's a bad way to start out or a good way to insult someone, depending on your intent. The other person may not ever register the insult consciously, but his or her "old brain" will, and he or she will forever be wary of you as a threat.

Besides losing thirty-five pounds because of a lowered sugar intake (as alcohol has a lot of sugar), it has made my doctor very happy. I have also gained something wonderful, time. When you are using alcohol for anxiety and can wait until 5:00 p.m. to start drinking, which I had no problem with, then from five until the time you go to bed, you are either OIU, "O" for "operating" or drunk. The following morning, if you were drunk the previous night, you are either still drunk or OUI. This is a no matter what thing - with no exceptions.

I found evidence of this when I went to Northern Ireland for a month to build a guitar. This was after I stopped. Contrary to popular myth, the

Irish, or, in this case, the English/Irish, are not drunk all the time. Here is the evidence though. The legal limit there for driving is 0.2 percent of alcohol in the bloodstream. This arbitrary limit for determining if someone is driving while intoxicated is significantly higher in most states. In the United States, 0.02 percent is a drink or a drink and a half, depending who is pouring. So what the cops do in Northern Ireland is pull people over in the morning to give breathalyzer tests. In the morning! They catch people when they are on their way to work. DWI. That's ten grand out the window. That is an expensive drive to work.

The short form is that I have a lot more time. That coupled with my desire to limit the number of things I am doing to limit my anxiety has led me in an interesting direction. I'm more goal-oriented. I feel I can see where I am going. It may be a "the light at the end of the tunnel may be the train coming toward you" sort of thing, but I am hopeful that there is some reality in what I see. Interesting things have found me and come my way. Many things (opportunities) pass by you all the time from all directions. If you are drawn into your shell because of anxiety or fear, you will not see many of them. The same is true of being drunk or stoned, which alter your reality because, after all, isn't that the reason you got that way to begin with? Very few people get drunk or stoned by accident despite the often-repeated thought or phrase, "I didn't mean to get that drunk." The common expression for psychotropic drugs is a long and emphatic "Wooooowww."

Opportunities flit by constantly, and the same or similar ones may flit by on a regular basis. When you are able to focus in on them, to see them, you can evaluate them and decide if they are for you or not, if you should let one of them penetrate your carefully constructed armor exoskeleton or outer shell or let them continue flitting. Letting a new untried idea like this inside when you are drunk or stoned is not a good idea. Everyone knows at least one person who has weird things happen to him or her, often on a regular basis. Look carefully at this person and think if he or she is evaluating stuff before he or she lets it in.

I have an example of a bad idea let in while drunk. Several years ago, I drove to the local marina to check on my sailboat. Eight-ton sailboats out of the water usually don't go anywhere, but we check anyway. I saw this really futuristic-looking boat in the parking lot with sponsorship stickers all over it. I approached without thinking about it and immediately struck up a conversation with one of the owners of the boat. He was Dutch, and I said enough Dutch words for him to know I knew where he was from. I asked him what they were doing with the boat.

"Rowing to Europe," was the reply.

I was curious about the origin of this adventure, and he told me, "It started in a bar in Amsterdam, and we were really, really drunk."

Enough said. Remember, I was in New Jersey. If I had been in England and found someone rowing to Europe, that would have been a dicey adventure, and it is only sixty miles. But from New Jersey?

When I moved to Africa back in the 1980s, I stopped using recreational drugs. I had smoked marijuana regularly for more than fifteen years. (I did tons of other stuff as well.) I stopped because African nations in general have harsh punishments for drug possession, and I was traveling all over Africa on business. Jails in some places consist of one room with eighty to a hundred people in it with an open oil barrel in the middle. That is the bathroom. I'm not that good at balancing my ass on the edge of an oil barrel. I never tried it, but I am sure. I have had plenty of experiences where natives stand around to see what the *mzungu* (white fellow in Swahili) is going to do, but this was not going to be one of those times.

Sobriety is a beacon for many users, but having an example is more often than not insufficient to cause a change. Wanting something is not enough. You have to do something, actually anything. My favorite expression about how an individual can aid our faltering environment is, "Anything you can do." Even the smallest action like picking up a paper on the street and putting it in a refuse container is something.

When I came back from Africa, I stopped smoking tobacco. Now I don't drink. Yes, it is boring. But you have more time, and you can focus on opportunities as they flit by or not. It's your choice. When you're drunk or stoned, a lot more things seem like a good idea. Most are not and take up a lot of time you could spend on productive beneficial activities.

To be honest, I am seeing a medical doctor, a psychopharmacologist who has prescribed and is monitoring some potent drugs that are aimed at my receptors for alcohol and other substances but also to stabilize my swings in anxiety and depression. I am also seeing both a cognitive behavioral therapist (CBT) and a dialectical behavioral therapist (DBT). This is all at great expense, and it is a great deal of effort, but I am improving. I can't recommend this type of treatment because I don't know enough about it and it would be illegal and irresponsible. So far, the combination of CBT and DBT plus the psychopharmacologist has done wonders for me. My primary care doctor referred me to my psychopharmacologist, who referred me to my CBT and DBT doctors. If you think it sounds interesting, ask your doctor about it.

When I told a good friend of fifty-eight years about this multipronged treatment, his comment was, "You're seventy years old. What can they fix now?"

I guess he meant, "at this late date" or "can't teach old dogs new tricks" sort of thing. My take on it is that it is never too late for self-improvement. (Now is always the best time). I told him about it because I am not ashamed. It is what it is, and I am who I am. I am mentally ill to an extent, and I am doing something about it. I'm proud of that. I also can't stand it when people are disingenuous and say they are fine all the time when they are not. I'm not fine. I'm working on it. When people ask me if I have been working out in a gym because I look better than when I was drinking and bloated, I say, "No, I stopped drinking."

I'm just me. I'm also not saying it in a way that I am better or stronger than they are. I just state the fact. I don't walk up to friends and say, "Yo, I stopped drinking, and you can't." Assholes do that.

It is wonderful to have an MD to relate to who specializes in addiction, especially one who started practicing recently. A lot of research has been done on the brain in recent years. The unfathomable depths are being plumbed, slowly perhaps but at a steady rate. A lot of this research is funded by the US government through the CDC and other organizations through grants. My doctor has studied and understands anxiety and depression because these afflictions lead so many people to become addicted to controlled substances.

Here is an example of how great it is to have a doctor who understands the problems we have. Previous to my submitting to his care, any thought I had, good or bad, would eventually end in violence, so I could not think about anything for very long without stopping the thought and forcing myself think about something else. It is something like enforced ADD on my part, using the layman's definition of not being able to concentrate on any one thing for very long. He said simply that my violent thoughts were "a symptom of anxiety." Just like that, something that had been bugging me and I didn't understand why for my entire life - explained.

Also lamps and wastebaskets, my former preferred items for destruction, are a lot safer around me, and I am a more pleasant person to live with, or so I am told. I have to fill my time, which otherwise would be totally boring, with interesting but limited-in-number things to do, learn, and accomplish. I am a polymath, which I describe as being interested in everything. (It has little to do with being intelligent, I feel, as I mentioned previously). My limitations include:

- Learning to read music notation.
- Playing one of my eight guitars. You can never have too many guitars, even in a one-bedroom apartment.
- Meditating. Check out Sharon Salzberg, my teacher, and her excellent book *Real Happiness: The Power of Meditation*. Meditation is one of my methods.
- Volunteering at the ASPCA as a cat and dog socializer. This means I play with them and take dogs for walks. All my dog - and cat-loving friends, which means all of my friends because I don't have any friends who don't like animals, are totally jealous.
- Studying languages I have spoken in at one time or another - and forgot. This includes Dutch, German, French, and English. There are several I have studied but never spoken, like Italian, Swahili, and Portuguese. I get one word a day via email in each language and a sentence in which it is used. I'm taking a formal course in French at the Y.
- Exercising at the gym. I do Ch'i Gung, Tai Chi, yoga, stretching, lengthen and strengthen, and various other classes for strength, flexibility, focus, and especially balance, which deteriorates as you grow older. I go for about thirteen hours a week. I think I have mentioned Terrence Dunn in this book. His DVDs on Tai Chi are absolutely brilliant.
- Writing stuff like this book and some songs.
- Doing voiceovers. Any spoken word you hear that doesn't have a face attached to it in the media is voiceover. I'm concentrating on

narration, like you would hear on a documentary and audiobooks. Getting paid for reading books and learning about science is outrageous. It involves pressure because time in a recording studio is expensive, but it is also a good creative outlet. I am also fortunate not to have to make a living from it. My voice over website is www.cliffwisevo.com. Help me get some work!

- Practicing mindfulness.
- Exploring New York City, including plays, music, opera, ballet, movies, walks, and tours, all of that good stuff.
- Cooking and baking. I didn't do much of when I was drinking and had a chef-designed kitchen and five thousand-dollar Italian stove and oven that was painted red in the Ferrari factory. (I'm not kidding.)
- Building guitars. Now I am reduced to assembly because I am in an apartment, but that is okay. I get to meet a lot of nice people who build the parts for me.
- Being happily married. That, I would qualify, is the view from my end. On the other end of the stick, things may be a bit more tenuous.

So I am not exactly bored.

## Mindfulness

This is the real reason why I wrote this postscript. You might think I am bragging about what I do to keep myself amused, but I am doing all of this mindfully. I have been studying mindfulness for about two years. It is one of those things that kept flitting by, and when I sobered up (and my body is still adjusting to sobriety and clarity of thinking after two and a half years), I allowed mindfulness to pass through my armor and into my mind and body. There is a lot written and spoken about mindfulness, so look it up and learn about it. (There are also a lot of old snake oil cures that have cloaked themselves in the mindfulness movement to make money.) Any degree of mindfulness you can do will help your anxiety and depression. Mindfulness is different for each individual. It is not formulaic, but each individual version involves the same things. For me, the commonality is intent. I try to do everything with a variation of the magnitude of intent but everything with some intent. It is the most wonderful sensation I have ever felt. Yes, it is love when applied to one you love. It's better than sex, as they say. It is fulfilling. You don't have to do anything well enough so others think it is good because, if they understand mindfulness, they understand that what you are doing has value. What you are doing mindfully does not have to be an important endeavor. It is the how, not the why. You have a feeling of accomplishment when you do something, actually anything, because you watched as you did it and felt it happen. Another commonality is to be non-judgmental which is a kind of freedom in disguise.

What mindfulness does is bring me back to myself, the person I have been running away from for so many years. Along with breathing, meditation, Tai Chi, and so on, mindfulness brings me back to the present, the conscious present. And when in the present, I am not spending energy on the unchangeable past and the totally unpredictable future. This state is not something that is interesting or safe for some people, but like I said, mindfulness is different for everyone.

It helps to have a guide of some sort. Guides are cool. One of mine was Little Cat, the guitar I built in Northern Ireland. Some of her DNA is in me; some of mine is in her. We worked together for four weeks, eight hours a day, to get her built. I asked her for guidance when I needed to shape the parts that would make the sound. I have received compliments on the sound and build from master luthiers. The build was the most relaxing thing I have ever done. I built Little Cat with intent. On a less ethereal plane, are my CBT and DBT therapists. Just playing music with intent is more satisfying.

Mindfulness doesn't cost anything. It is a freedom. It is portable. It is you at your best. I got the portable idea from Sharon Salzberg. She got it from someone else. You, your marvelous breath that controls your life and mindfulness, are portable.

### The Inchworm

I cleared this with one of my shrinks who said she would use it with some of her other patients. The inchworm is one of my favorite animals. In the spring in Larchmont, New York, in the suburbs of New York City, the inchworms would hatch and begin eating the oak leaves. Most caterpillars fall off the leaves at least once. They leave attachments on the leaves when they move about with the gland that emits the silk they use to produce their cocoon. When they fall from the leaf, the silk spins out of the gland to break the fall, much like spiders. The result is inchworms hanging about in the yard. They patiently wind themselves back up the silk until they are back on the leaf, tired probably.

I was into catching stuff when I was a kid (still do actually) and observing how they move about. I try to leave the animal in a better place than when I found it. I don't know if they agree. I have been stung and bitten a lot. The inchworm has to eat an amazing amount of food in a short period of time to make it to the next stage in life so it wastes no time in trying to get off me and onto something edible. Its way of moving around is unique, at least to me. It attaches the front part of its body to something and then brings the back part of the body up to meet it. It looks like a big upside down "U" when it is scrunched up. Its powerful back legs then attach to something, and the front part/head of the worm reaches out as far as it can, looking for something to attach to.

This form of locomotion seems to be very awkward, but the inchworm keeps moving one contraction, an extension at a time, until it gets to where it is going. I would let them crawl on my hand for a while and then put them on a nice, tasty oak leaf. Then I would pick another out of the air.

When I was outside, my mother gave up asking what I was doing when I was about twelve years old. She hated bugs. (I think newts, fiddler crabs, eels, snails, and all of that as well.) I used to come in for lunch and empty my pants pocket of whatever I was studying at the time so I wouldn't squash it when I sat down, usually earthworms. After lunch, I would scoop them up and put them back in the pocket, and off I would go, out into the wilds of the New York suburbs.

When I decide to do something that is difficult, I try to remember how the inchworm moves, how it reaches its objective. They have a goal of food. We have a goal, completion of a project without a meltdown. The anxious person is going to try to get to that goal as soon as possible to get it done. The anxious person amasses a huge amount of energy and focus and attacks the goal from as many directions as possible, at least I do. It has to get done quickly. This method is doomed to failure because each new endeavor is a learning experience and needs to be done in an orderly, step-by-step inchworm way.

If you paint eleven houses, which I did while in graduate school to pay the bills, the twelfth house is similar but at the same time, totally different. If you just load up the paint, ladders, brushes, drop cloths, and all of that and start painting the twelfth house, just like you did the eleventh, you are going to fall off the ladder and land in the bushes with paint all over you like I have done, or worse.

This type of accident is a disaster for the anxious person. You are an idiot and a worthless person who can't even paint a house. This may not be a good example, but the idea here is that you have to take things one step at a time. You are going to get there, but to avoid the anxiety, you are going to try to get there in a methodical way. Someone without problems, meaning a person without anxiety or depression, may be able to get there in what looks like a short amount of time with very little effort. The word "hubris" was invented for people like this. They look like they know what they are doing. They may even believe it. They may actually know, but mostly they don't have a clue. For us anxiety folks, the inchworm is our friend. The inchworm practices intent.

Think inchworm when you approach a complex task. When you accomplish a task in this way, it will be rewarding. You won't have to think about all the screw-ups you made in getting there. You will just "be there" and have a big boost in your self-esteem. You will look forward to the next complex task. You know you can do it. We need these kinds of experiences. We need good ones. The more anxiety and depression issues you have, the more difficult any task will be.

By the way, the person with no problems does not exist.

Just for the record, the octopus is another favorite animal. They have a beak like a parrot on the underside where all of those legs come together. It is the only hard part of their body. They bite really hard. They are very intelligent and have an eye structure that causes them to see the world just like we do, which is unusual in the animal kingdom. I would love to have one on me right now, crawling around and checking me out.

## Closing

I learned an expression in Tai Chi from my current Tai Chi teacher, Andy. Andy brings a lot of knowledge that he has learned by studying martial arts and Tai Chi since the 1960s. He shares it with us freely, which is the way it should be. I will paraphrase it. I condensed it for the cover of this book. The universe is chaos. The purpose of the form (as the chain of Tai Chi movements is called "the form") is to bring order to this chaos. I intend for these methods and many more to bring order to the chaos of my life and yours. Bring order to the chaos.

## The Future

I have started a website that I hope you will help me to develop. The purpose of this is to amass more methods that anxious people have found to be useful and to disseminate basic information about the disorder. We may be able to help a lot of people using the website. As I develop a unified practical method combining some of the methods in this book and others, I will use the website to give progress reports and gather information. The address is challengeangst.com. It will take a while to get this up and working.

Go well.

# APPENDIX 1—
# How I Know When I Am Getting Anxious

Being able to read the signs in your mind and body is very difficult. If you don't learn what they are and counteract them right away, you are building up to a panic attack. This is very easy to read once it happens. It is like dying. The signs are shallow breathing, sweaty palms, cold hands, a need to clear the throat, a feeling of sadness, pressure on the sides of the head, a change in hearing or a ringing in the ears, tunnel vision, excessive swallowing of saliva, and a want to" get out of there."

# APPENDIX 2—
# Finding and Hiring a Psychologist

I refer to them as shrinks in this book, but it is mostly in jest. I recently met up with an old friend at a reunion, and I hope to collaborate with her on one aspect of anxiety that I could not cover because of lack of knowledge. I want to have footnotes where you can read about something that is happening, like a panic attack, and then read a description of what actually happens mentally or physiologically. Understanding what is going on should help the individual to fight anxiety.

Interview different psychologists on the phone until you find one you feel comfortable with. This is sort of a Zen approach to finding one, but it works for me. I would suggest setting up a convenient time where both of you have fifteen to twenty minutes to talk. Beware the person who just wants you to come in and talk about it. I look at this as a sales approach. The person gets you in there, and then you are embarrassed not to sign up for a few sessions. You should ask the person about his or her background and qualifications and describe your background and what you are trying to accomplish.

If the person expresses the idea that life is a whole ball of wax and that you can't just concentrate on anxiety or even the task of finding out if anxiety is your big issue, then move on. You want results. If the psychologist states that he or she thinks he or she can help you, then go in for an appointment or two. If, after meeting the psychologist, instinct tells you that you don't relate, then find another. You wouldn't take your car to any mechanic, so why take in your brain without doing some research?

# APPENDIX 3—
# If You Have a Good Friend, Lover, Spouse, and So Forth with Anxiety and You Want to Be Able to Better Deal with the Problem

Consult with a psychologist about the person you are concerned with. Psychologists are used to concentrating on the problems of the person with whom they are dealing with, not with second parties. You will have to stress that it is the anxious person you are trying to deal with that you are interested in helping and not yourself that you want guidance in dealing with. You need to have quick reads on the recommendation of using different methods.

Don't buy a copy of this book and give it to the anxious person! You might as well hand him or her a live hand grenade with the pin pulled. Read the book, and tell the person about how interesting or dumb you thought it was. When I was in college, someone sent me a book, *Up from Depression*, in a plain brown wrapper with no note. I don't remember the author's name, and I didn't read the book. I didn't think to look at the postmark to see where it came from. I wondered for weeks who had sent me that book. I was furious that someone would give me a book about depression. Me, depressed?

When I finally found out it was my mother and confronted her, she admitted sending the book. She had not read it or even looked at it. I'm still pissed about this lack of sensitivity forty-six years later. That was almost as bad as the time she tried to give me a pill by putting it in a jelly donut. I was about five. When I crunched onto the pill and realized what was going on, I accused her of putting me on the same level as the dog.

If you don't have anxiety problems yourself, try to learn something about them. Everyone is different, so this book is not really a definitive guide. There are probably hundreds of methods that I have not found or learned. It is important to judge how old the anxious person is and how severe the anxiety is. You could tell with me by the amount and severity of temper outbursts. My specialty was smashing lamps and drop-kicking wastebaskets. When I smash something, I feel terrible about it. It is unlike the semi-relief that I get from hitting golf balls. Treatment should be commensurate with the severity of the disorder. I am not an MD, so I can't recommend drugs, but I think that, if the person is young enough, that is, has not had the disorder for a long period of time, then drugs should be a last resort or at least used in conjunction with other methods of treatment with the idea of getting off the drugs later.

If you are in a relationship with an anxious person, you are dealing with a complex disorder. Anxiety is accompanied in my case by low self-esteem and a tendency to depression or at least mood swings. It is going to be a roller coaster of a relationship for you. I have avoided relationships with some people because I did not want to hurt them. They were too nice and vulnerable. I have had a friendship with one person for thirty-nine years that is like that. I know that I could have had a love relationship with her, but I was afraid that my behavior would have driven her nuts. Perhaps I should have given her the chance to make up her own mind about the matter. Sometimes I feel I did nothing because I wanted for there to be one perfect person out there.

If you do choose to stay in a relationship with an anxious person, you have to be tough yet compassionate and help him or her to get help. If this does not sound like you, think about moving on. If the relationship is destructive, definitely move on. You are not going to help the anxious person by beating your head against the wall and self-destructing. Anxiety does not preclude the anxious person from being a nice, warm, and loving person, even though you can hear the bomb ticking inside. I understand my problem and would comprehend why someone would not want to be with me all the time. You can still be friends and help the person out.

It is too bad that there aren't support groups for "Friends of Anxietists," like there are for people who have friends, relatives, or spouses with Alzheimer's. It would be an effective method to help people with the disorder. Perhaps I'll start one. (I have recently heard about Al-Anon, which may be such a group, but I don't have any direct experience with them).

# APPENDIX 4—
# How I Judge the Effectiveness of a Method

The scale will be one to five with five being the highest

**Five**

- A method that involves physical action and an underlying philosophy
- A method that carries over longer than the period you are using it
- A method that has overall benefits that you cannot measure
- A method that involves control of breathing
- A method that is repetitive

Examples: Tai Chi and yoga

**Four**

- A method that relies on mental or physical action alone (usually in combination) but where the underlying philosophy is not adhered to
- A method that carries over longer than the period you are using it
- A method that involves control of breathing
- A method that is repetitive

Examples: Meditation, hatha yoga, walking, and swimming

**Three**

- A method that involves physical activity with no underlying philosophy
- A method that involves control of breathing

Examples: High-rep, low-pound free weights, lap swimming, and self-hypnotism

**Two**

- Activities that give general benefit

Examples: Being in or on the water, drawing, and playing music

**One**

- An idea that you can incorporate immediately is the best
- An idea that you can think about and incorporate at some time in the future

Example: Trying not to get upset about anything that you don't have control over and self-help books

82919580R00171

Made in the USA
Columbia, SC
07 December 2017